Drawing on the lives, letters, diaries and testimonies of many writers, and on her own personal experience, the great American writer Tillie Olsen examines the needs and work of creation, and those circumstances that obstruct it – circumstances of sex, economic class, colour, the times and climate into which the writer is born. Focusing on the financial and cultural pressures which silenced writers such as Melville, Hardy, Woolf, Blake, Cather, Rimbaud, Gerald Manley Hopkins, she concentrates particularly on those who have lost most: women writers, black writers.

Silences is a brilliant patchwork of ideas, excerpts, anecdotes and analysis which together form a powerful testament to the struggle of all artists to defy the enemies of their promise.

Tillie Olsen was born in Nebraska in 1913 and has lived in San Francisco for most of her life. Her two works of fiction, *Tell Me A Riddle* (1962) and *Yonnondio: From The Thirties* (1974) are both published by Virago and represent the works of one of America's most honoured writers. Tillie Olsen has taught at Amherst College, at Stanford University, was Writer-in-Residence at Massachusetts Institute of Technology, Distinguished Visiting Professor at the University of Massachusetts in Boston, and a Fellow of the Radcliffe Institute. She has received both a Ford Foundation and National Endowment for the Arts grants, a Guggenheim Fellowship, and an Award for Distinguished Contribution to American Literature from the American Academy and the National Institute of Arts and Letters. *Silences* is her first work of non-fiction. Tillie Olsen continues to write and lives in Santa Cruz in California.

Silences

BOOKS BY TILLIE OLSEN

YONNONDIO:
From the Thirties

TELL ME A RIDDLE

Silences
Tillie Olsen

Virago

Published by VIRAGO Limited 1980
5 Wardour Street, London W1V 3HE

Portions of this work were first published in slightly
different form as: "Silences" in *Harper's Magazine* (1965)
and *Ms.* Magazine (1978); "Women Who Are Writers in Our Century"
in *College English* (1972); and the Afterword to *Life in the Iron Mills*
by Rebecca Harding Davis, Feminist Press Reprint Series, #1, 1972

Copyright © 1965, 1972, 1978 by Tillie Olsen

ISBN Hardback Edition 0 86068 157 2
ISBN Paperback Edition 0 86068 158 0

Printed in Great Britain by
Lowe & Brydone Printers Limited, Thetford, Norfolk

ACKNOWLEDGMENTS

From THE LETTERS OF GERARD MANLEY HOPKINS TO ROBERT BRIDGES
edited by Claude Colleer Abbott: Published by Oxford University Press (1935). Used by
permission.

From THE CORRESPONDENCE OF GERARD MANLEY HOPKINS AND RICH-
ARD WATSON DIXON: Published by Oxford University Press (1935).

From THE LIFE OF THOMAS HARDY by Florence Emily Hardy: Used by permission of the Macmillan Company of London and Basingstoke.

From DIARIES 1910–1913 by Franz Kafka: Reprinted by permission of Schocken Books, Inc. Copyright © 1948 by Schocken Books, Inc. Copyright renewed © 1975 by Schocken Books, Inc.

From DIARIES 1914–1923 by Franz Kafka: Reprinted by permission of Schocken Books, Inc. Copyright © 1949 by Schocken Books, Inc. Copyright renewed © 1976 by Schocken Books, Inc.

From WHAT THE WOMAN LIVED: SELECTED LETTERS OF LOUISE BOGAN 1920–1970 edited by Ruth Limmer: Copyright © 1973 by Ruth Limmer, Trustee, Estate of Louise Bogan. Reprinted by permission of Harcourt Brace Jovanovich, Inc.

From THE ART OF SYLVIA PLATH by Charles Newman: Used by permission of Indiana University Press.

"The Munich Mannequins," "Stings," and "The Babysitters," by Sylvia Plath: Excerpts from ARIEL by Sylvia Plath. Copyright © 1965 by Ted Hughes. Excerpts from CROSSING THE WATER by Sylvia Plath. Copyright © 1971 by Ted Hughes. By permission of Harper & Row, Publishers, Inc. Published by Faber and Faber, London. Used by permission of Olwyn Hughes.

From PILGRIMAGE by Dorothy Richardson: Used by permission of Alfred A. Knopf, Inc.

From LETTERS OF RAINER MARIA RILKE 1892–1919, translated by Jane Bannard Green and M. D. Herter Norton: Selections are reprinted with the permission of W. W. Norton & Company, Inc. Copyright 1945 by W. W. Norton & Company. Copyright renewed 1972 by M. D. Herter Norton.

From RAINER MARIA RILKE: THE YEARS IN SWITZERLAND by J. R. von Salis: Translated by N. K. Cruickshank. Copyright © 1964 by Hogarth Press Ltd; reprinted by permission of the University of California Press.

Excerpts from A WRITER'S DIARY and other writings of Virginia Woolf: Reprinted by permission of Harcourt Brace Jovanovich, Inc.; Copyright 1953, 1954 by Leonard Woolf. Used by permission of the Author's Literary Estate and The Hogarth Press.

"On Woman" by William Butler Yeats: Reprinted with permission of Macmillan Publishing Co., Inc. from COLLECTED POEMS by William Butler Yeats. Copyright 1919 by Macmillan Publishing Co., Inc., renewed 1947 by Bertha Georgie Yeats. Used by permission of M. B. Yeats, Miss Anne Yeats and the Macmillan Company of London and Basingstoke.

Other Acknowledgments

To every writer quoted or named herein: For much of the content, as well as comprehension, in this book.

For means and time: The Radcliffe Institute (where "Silences" came into being); The MacDowell Colony (where I worked on Rebecca Harding Davis); the John Simon Guggenheim Foundation, who made possible the first work on this book.

For help when asked: Ann Lipow, Pat Ray, for books. Marilynn Meeker and Rachel Klein for literate copy-editing. Hannah Green and Mary Anne Ferguson for reading the entire ms., and Laurie Olsen, who kept with it from its beginning. Florence Howe, who

(1971) did all she could to make *Life in the Iron Mills* and my Afterword a book actuality. Julie Jordan, Martha Parry, Sue Gardinier, Kathie Olsen, Julie Edwards, Karla Lutz, Jack Olsen, Sally Wick Begardy, Pat Koontz, Addy and Merle Brodsky. For help when asked. And other reasons.

For inviting me to speak in 1971, and thus bringing "One Out of Twelve" into being: The Women's Commission of the Modern Language Association.

For remaining, reminding: My mother and my father, Sara Vore Taylor, Genya Gorelick, Jack Eggan, Patricia Thompson, Constance Smith, Michelle Murray (whose as yet unpublished journals must not be lost into silence), Theodora Ward, Amy Schechter, Harold Rice, Avrum Olshansky. All earth and air for years, now. "Shine on me still."

To the unnamed here, whose work and beings are also sustenance; among them those whose life coursings have schooled me ineradicably in the shaping power and inequality of circumstance; beginning when I was a child at Kellom and Long Schools in Omaha and crossed the tracks to Central High School (my first College-of-Contrast).

For permission to reprint from THE SAVAGE GOD: A Study of Suicide by A. Alvarez, my thanks are due to Weidenfeld & Nicholson Ltd.

For permission to reprint from THE LIFE OF THOMAS HARDY by Florence Emily Hardy, my thanks are due to the Trustees of the Thomas Hardy Estate.

For permission to reprint from DIARIES 1910–1913 and DIARIES 1914–1923 by Franz Kafka, my thanks are due to Secker & Warburg Ltd

[This] is sent out to those into whose souls the iron has entered, and has entered deeply at some time of their lives.

—Thomas Hardy, of his
Jude the Obscure

For our silenced people, century after century their beings consumed in the hard, everyday essential work of maintaining human life. Their art, which still they made —as their other contributions—anonymous; refused respect, recognition; lost.

For those of us (few yet in number, for the way is punishing), their kin and descendants, who begin to emerge into more flowered and rewarded use of our selves in ways denied to them;—and by our achievement bearing witness to what was (and still is) being lost, silenced.

Literary history and the present are dark with silences: some the silences for years by our acknowledged great; some silences hidden; some the ceasing to publish after one work appears; some the never coming to book form at all.

These are not natural silences, that necessary time for renewal, lying fallow, gestation, in the natural cycle of creation. The silences I speak of here are unnatural; the unnatural thwarting of what struggles to come into being, but cannot. In the old, the obvious parallels: when the seed strikes stone; the soil will not sustain; the spring is false; the time is drought or blight or infestation; the frost comes premature.

This book is about such silences. It is concerned with the relationship of circumstances—including class, color, sex; the times, climate into which one is born—to the creation of literature.

It consists of two talks given nearly a decade apart—"Silences" (1962), "Women Who Are Writers in Our Century" (1971); an essay-afterword, "Rebecca Harding Davis," written in 1971 to accompany reprint of work by a forgotten nineteenth-century woman writer; and a long aftersection: "Silences—II," "The Writer-Woman—II," for essential deepenings and expansions.

This book is not an orthodoxly written work of academic scholarship. Do not approach it as such. Nor did it come into being through choosing a subject, then researching for it. The substance herein was long in accumulation, garnered over fifty years, near a lifetime; the thought came slow, hard-won; the talks and essay, the book itself, elicited.

A passion and a purpose inform its pages: love for my incomparable medium, literature; hatred for all that, societally rooted, unnecessarily lessens and denies it; slows, impairs, silences writers.

It is written to re-dedicate and encourage.

I intend to bring you strength, joy, courage, perspicacity, defiance.

—André Gide

CONTENTS

PART ONE — SILENCES

In Heaven a spirit doth dwell
  "Whose heart-strings are a lute";
None sing so wildly well
  As the angel Israfel. . . .
And the shadow of [his] perfect bliss
  Is the sunshine of ours. . . .

If I could dwell where Israfel
  Hath dwelt, and he where I,
He might not sing so wildly well
  A mortal melody,
While a bolder note than this might swell
  From my lyre within the sky.
                              —Edgar Allan Poe

Had Milton's been the lot of Caspar Hauser,
Milton would have been vacant as he.
                              —Herman Melville

If Goethe had been stolen away a child, and
reared in a robber band in the depths of a
German forest, do you think the world would
have had Faust *and* Iphigenie? *But he*
would have been Goethe still. At night, round
their watch-fire, he would have chanted wild
songs of rapine and murder, till the dark
faces about him were moved and trembled.
                              —Olive Schreiner

If Tolstoy had been born a woman . . .
                              —Virginia Woolf

If. . . .

SILENCES
IN LITERATURE

Originally an unwritten talk, spoken
from notes at the Radcliffe Institute in
1962 as part of a weekly colloquium of
members. Edited from the taped transcription, it appears here as published
in *Harper's Magazine,* October 1965.

(Several omitted lines have been restored; an occasional name or phrase
and a few footnotes have been added.)

SILENCES

Literary history and the present are dark with silences: some the silences for years by our acknowledged great; some silences hidden; some the ceasing to publish after one work appears; some the never coming to book form at all.

What is it that happens with the creator, to the creative process, in that time? What *are* creation's needs for full functioning? Without intention of or pretension to literary scholarship, I have had special need to learn all I could of this over the years, myself so nearly remaining mute and having to let writing die over and over again in me.

These are not *natural* silences—what Keats called *agonie ennuyeuse* (the tedious agony)—that necessary time for renewal, lying fallow, gestation, in the natural cycle of creation. The silences I speak of here are unnatural: the unnatural thwarting of what struggles to come into being, but cannot. In the old, the obvious parallels: when the seed strikes stone; the soil will not sustain; the spring is false; the time is drought or blight or infestation; the frost comes premature.

The great in achievement have known such silences—Thomas Hardy, Melville, Rimbaud, Gerard Manley Hopkins. They tell us little as to why or how the creative working atrophied and died in them—if ever it did.

"Less and less shrink the visions then vast in me," writes Thomas Hardy in his thirty-year ceasing from novels after the Victorian vileness to his *Jude the Obscure.* ("So ended his prose contributions to literature, his experiences having killed all his interest in this form"—the official explanation.) But the great poetry he wrote to the end of his life was not sufficient to hold, to develop the vast visions which for twenty-five years had had expression in novel after novel. People, situations, interrelationships, landscape—they cry for this larger life in poem after poem.

It was not visions shrinking with Hopkins, but a different torment. For seven years he kept his religious vow to refrain from writing poetry, but the poet's eye he could not shut, nor win "elected silence to beat upon [his] whorled ear." "I had long had haunting my ear the echo of a poem which now I realised on paper," he writes of the first poem permitted to end the seven years' silence. But poetry ("to hoard unheard; be heard, unheeded") could be only the least and last of his heavy priestly responsibilities. Nineteen poems were all he could produce in his last nine years—fullness to us, but torment pitched past grief to him, who felt himself "time's eunuch, never to beget."

Silence surrounds Rimbaud's silence. Was there torment of the unwritten; haunting of rhythm, of visions; anguish at dying powers, the seventeen years after he abandoned the unendurable literary world? We know only that the need to write continued into his first years of vagabondage; that he wrote:

> Had I not once a youth pleasant, heroic, fabulous enough to write on leaves of gold: too much luck. Through what crime, what error, have I earned my present weakness? You who maintain that some animals sob sorrowfully, that the dead have dreams, try to tell the story of my downfall and my slumber. I no longer know how to speak.*

That on his deathbed, he spoke again like a poet-visionary.

Melville's stages to his thirty-year prose silence are clearest. The presage is in his famous letter to Hawthorne, as he had to hurry *Moby Dick* to an end:

> I am so pulled hither and thither by circumstances. The calm, the coolness, the silent grass-growing mood in which a man ought always to compose,—that, I fear, can seldom be mine. Dollars

---

A Season in Hell.

damn me. . . . What I feel most moved to write, that is banned,—
it will not pay. Yet, altogether, write the *other* way I cannot. So the
product is a final hash . . .

Reiterated in *Pierre*, writing "that book whose unfathomable
cravings drink his blood . . . when at last the idea obtruded that
the wiser and profounder he should grow, the more and the more
he lessened his chances for bread."

To be possessed; to have to try final hash; to have one's work
met by "drear ignoring"; to be damned by dollars into a Customs
House job; to have only weary evenings and Sundays left for
writing—

> How bitterly did unreplying Pierre feel in his heart that to most of
> the great works of humanity, their authors had given not weeks and
> months, not years and years, but their wholly surrendered and
> dedicated lives.

Is it not understandable why Melville began to burn work, then
ceased to write it, "immolating [it] . . . sealing in a fate subdued"?
And turned to occasional poetry, manageable in a time sense, "to
nurse through night the ethereal spark." A thirty-year night. He
was nearly seventy before he could quit the customs dock and
again have full time for writing, start back to prose. "Age, dull
tranquilizer," and devastation of "arid years that filed before" to
work through. Three years of tryings before he felt capable of
beginning *Billy Budd* (the kernel waiting half a century); three
years more to his last days (he who had been so fluent), the slow,
painful, never satisfied writing and re-writing of it.*

Kin to these years-long silences are the *hidden* silences; work
aborted, deferred, denied—hidden by the work which does come
to fruition. Hopkins rightfully belongs here; almost certainly William Blake; Jane Austen, Olive Schreiner, Theodore Dreiser,

---

*"Entering my eighth decade [I come] into possession of unobstructed leisure
. . . just as, in the course of nature, my vigor sensibly declines. What little of it
is left, I husband for certain matters as yet incomplete and which indeed may
never be completed." *Billy Budd* never was completed; it was edited from drafts
found after Melville's death.

Willa Cather, Franz Kafka; Katherine Anne Porter, many other contemporary writers.

Censorship silences. Deletions, omissions, abandonment of the medium (as with Hardy); paralyzing of capacity (as Dreiser's ten-year stasis on *Jennie Gerhardt* after the storm against *Sister Carrie*). Publishers' censorship, refusing subject matter or treatment as "not suitable" or "no market for." Self-censorship. Religious, political censorship—sometimes spurring inventiveness—most often (read Dostoyevsky's letters) a wearing attrition.

The extreme of this: those writers physically silenced by governments. Isaac Babel, the years of imprisonment, what took place in him with what wanted to be written? Or in Oscar Wilde, who was not permitted even a pencil until the last months of his imprisonment?

Other silences. The truly memorable poem, story, or book, then the writer ceasing to be published.* Was one work all the writers had in them (life too thin for pressure of material, renewal) and the respect for literature too great to repeat themselves? Was it "the knife of the perfectionist attitude in art and life" at their throat? Were the conditions not present for establishing the habits of creativity (a young Colette who lacked a Willy to lock her in her room each day)? or—as instanced over and over—other claims, other responsibilities so writing could not be first? (The writer of a class, sex, color still marginal in literature, and whose coming to written voice at all against complex odds is exhausting achievement.) It is an eloquent commentary that this one-book silence has been true of most black writers; only eleven in the hundred years since 1850 have published novels more than twice.**

There is a prevalent silence I pass by quickly, the absence of creativity where it once had been; the ceasing to create literature, though the books may keep coming out year after year. That suicide of the creative process Hemingway describes so accurately in "The Snows of Kilimanjaro":

---

*As Jean Toomer *(Cane)*; Henry Roth *(Call It Sleep)*; Edith Summers Kelley *(Weeds)*.

**Robert Bone. *The Negro Novel in America,* 1958.

He had destroyed his talent himself—by not using it, by betrayals
of himself and what he believed in, by drinking so much that he
blunted the edge of his perceptions, by laziness, by sloth, by snob-
bery, by hook and by crook; selling vitality, trading it for security,
for comfort.

No, not Scott Fitzgerald. His not a death of creativity, not
silence, but what happens when (his words) there is "the sacrifice
of talent, in pieces, to preserve its essential value."

Almost unnoted are the foreground silences, *before* the achievement. (Remember when Emerson hailed Whitman's genius, he
guessed correctly: "which yet must have had a long *foreground* for
such a start.") George Eliot, Joseph Conrad, Isak Dinesen, Sherwood Anderson, Dorothy Richardson, Elizabeth Madox Roberts,
A.E. Coppard, Angus Wilson, Joyce Cary—all close to, or in their
forties before they became published writers; Lampedusa, Maria
Dermout *(The Ten Thousand Things),* Laura Ingalls Wilder, the
"children's writer," in their sixties.* Their capacities evident early
in the "being one on whom nothing is lost"; in other writers'
qualities. Not all struggling and anguished, like Anderson, the
foreground years; some needing the immobilization of long illness
or loss, or the sudden lifting of responsibility to make writing
necessary, make writing possible; others waiting circumstances
and encouragement (George Eliot, her Henry Lewes; Laura
Wilder, a writer-daughter's insistence that she transmute her
storytelling gift onto paper).

Very close to this last grouping are the silences where the
lives never came to writing. Among these, the mute inglorious
Miltons: those whose waking hours are all struggle for existence; the barely educated; the illiterate; women. Their silence
the silence of centuries as to how life was, is, for most of humanity. Traces of their making, of course, in folk song, lullaby,
tales, language itself, jokes, maxims, superstitions—but we
know nothing of the creators or how it was with them. In the
fantasy of Shakespeare born in deepest Africa (as at least one
Shakespeare must have been), was the ritual, the oral storytell-

---

*Some other foreground silences: Elizabeth (Mrs.) Gaskell, Kate Chopin, Cora
Sandel, Cyrus Colter, Hortense Calisher.

ing a fulfillment? Or was there restlessness, indefinable yearning, a sense of restriction? Was it as Virginia Woolf in *A Room
of One's Own* guesses—about women?

> Genius of a sort must have existed among them, as it existed
> among the working classes,* but certainly it never got itself
> onto paper. When, however, one reads of a woman possessed by
> the devils, of a wise woman selling herbs, or even a remarkable
> man who had a remarkable mother, then I think we are on the
> track of a lost novelist, a suppressed poet, or some Emily
> Brontë who dashed her brains out on the moor, crazed with the
> torture her gift had put her to.

Rebecca Harding Davis whose work sleeps in the forgotten
(herself as a woman of a century ago so close to remaining mute),
also guessed about the silent in that time of the twelve-hour-a-day,
six-day work week. She writes of the illiterate ironworker in *Life
in the Iron Mills* who sculptured great shapes in the slag: "his
fierce thirst for beauty, to know it, to create it, to *be* something
other than he is—a passion of pain"; Margret Howth in the textile
mill:

> There were things in the world, that like herself, were marred, did
> not understand, were hungry to know. . . . Her eyes quicker to see
> than ours, delicate or grand lines in the homeliest things. . . .
> Everything she saw or touched, nearer, more human than to you
> or me. These sights and sounds did not come to her common; she
> never got used to living as other people do.

She never got used to living as other people do. Was that one of
the ways it was?

So some of the silences, incomplete listing of the incomplete,
where the need and capacity to create were of a high order.

Now, what *is* the work of creation and the circumstances it
demands for full functioning—as told in the journals, letters,
notes, of the practitioners themselves: Henry James, Katherine
Mansfield, André Gide, Virginia Woolf; the letters of Flau-

---

*Half of the working classes *are* women.

bert, Rilke, Joseph Conrad; Thomas Wolfe's *Story of a Novel,*
Valéry's *Course in Poetics.* What do they explain of the silences?

"Constant toil is the law of art, as it is of life," says (and
demonstrated) Balzac:

> To pass from conception to execution, to produce, to bring the idea
> to birth, to raise the child laboriously from infancy, to put it nightly
> to sleep surfeited, to kiss it in the mornings with the hungry heart
> of a mother, to clean it, to clothe it fifty times over in new garments
> which it tears and casts away, and yet not revolt against the trials
> of this agitated life—this unwearying maternal love, this habit of
> creation—this is execution and its toils.

"Without duties, almost without external communication,"
Rilke specifies, "unconfined solitude which takes every day like a
life, a spaciousness which puts no limit to vision and in the midst
of which infinities surround."

Unconfined solitude as Joseph Conrad experienced it:

> For twenty months I wrestled with the Lord for my creation
> . . . mind and will and conscience engaged to the full, hour after
> hour, day after day . . . a lonely struggle in a great isolation from
> the world. I suppose I slept and ate the food put before me and
> talked connectedly on suitable occasions, but I was never aware of
> the even flow of daily life, made easy and noiseless for me by a
> silent, watchful, tireless affection.

So there is a homely underpinning for it all, the even flow of
daily life made easy and noiseless.

"The terrible law of the artist"—says Henry James—"the law
of fructification, of fertilization. The old, old lesson of the art of
meditation. To woo combinations and inspirations into being by
a depth and continuity of attention and meditation."

"That load, that weight, that gnawing conscience," writes
Thomas Mann—

> That sea which to drink up, that frightful task . . . The will, the
> discipline and self-control to shape a sentence or follow out a hard
> train of thought. From the first rhythmical urge of the inward

creative force towards the material, towards casting in shape and
form, from that to the thought, the image, the word, the line, what
a struggle, what Gethsemane.

Does it become very clear what Melville's Pierre so bitterly
remarked on, and what literary history bears out—why most of
the great works of humanity have come from lives (able to be)
wholly surrendered and dedicated? How else sustain the constant
toil, the frightful task, the terrible law, the continuity? Full self:
this means full time as and when needed for the work. (That time
for which Emily Dickinson withdrew from the world.)

But what if there is not that fullness of time, let alone totality
of self? What if the writers, as in some of these silences, must work
regularly at something besides their own work—as do nearly all
in the arts in the United States today.

I know the theory (kin to "starving in the garret makes great
art") that it is this very circumstance which feeds creativity. I
know, too, that for the beginning young, for some who have such
need, the job can be valuable access to life they would not otherwise know. A few (I think of the doctors, the incomparables:
Chekhov and William Carlos Williams) for special reasons sometimes manage both. But the actuality testifies: substantial creative
work demands time, and with rare exceptions only full-time workers have achieved it. Where the claims of creation cannot be
primary, the results are atrophy; unfinished work; minor effort
and accomplishment; silences. (Desperation which accounts for
the mountains of applications to the foundations for grants—
undivided time—in the strange bread-line system we have worked
out for our artists.)

Twenty years went by on the writing of *Ship of Fools,* while
Katherine Anne Porter, who needed only two, was "trying to get
to that table, to that typewriter, away from my jobs of teaching
and trooping this country and of keeping house." "Your subconscious needed that time to grow the layers of pearl," she was
told. Perhaps, perhaps, but I doubt it. Subterranean forces can
make you wait, but they are very finicky about the kind of waiting
it has to be. Before they will feed the creator back, they must be
fed, passionately fed, what needs to be worked on. "We hold up
our desire as one places a magnet over a composite dust from

which the particle of iron will suddenly jump up," says Paul Valéry. A receptive waiting, that means, not demands which prevent "an undistracted center of being." And when the response comes, availability to work must be immediate. If not used at once, all may vanish as a dream; worse, future creation be endangered —for only the removal and development of the material frees the forces for further work.

There is a life in which all this is documented: Franz Kafka's. For every one entry from his diaries here, there are fifty others that testify as unbearably to the driven stratagems for time, the work lost (to us), the damage to the creative powers (and the body) of having to deny, interrupt, postpone, put aside, let work die.

"I cannot devote myself completely to my writing," Kafka explains (in 1911). "I could not live by literature if only, to begin with, because of the slow maturing of my work and its special character." So he worked as an official in a state insurance agency, and wrote when he could.

> These two can never be reconciled. . . . If I have written something one evening, I am afire the next day in the office and can bring nothing to completion. Outwardly I fulfill my office duties satisfactorily, not my inner duties however, and every unfulfilled inner duty becomes a misfortune that never leaves. What strength it will necessarily drain me of.

1911
> No matter how little the time or how badly I write, I feel approaching the imminent possibility of great moments which could make me capable of anything. But my being does not have sufficient strength to hold this to the next writing time. During the day the visible world helps me; during the night it cuts me to pieces unhindered. . . . In the evening and in the morning, my consciousness of the creative abilities in me then I can encompass. I feel shaken to the core of my being. Calling forth such powers which are then not permitted to function.

. . . which are then not permitted to function . . .

1911

I finish nothing, because I have no time, and it presses so within me.

1912

When I begin to write after such a long interval, I draw the words as if out of the empty air. If I capture one, then I have just this one alone, and all the toil must begin anew.

1914

Yesterday for the first time in months, an indisputable ability to do good work. And yet wrote only the first page. Again I realize that everything written down bit by bit rather than all at once in the course of the larger part is inferior, and that the circumstances of my life condemn me to this inferiority.

1915

My constant attempt by sleeping before dinner to make it possible to continue working [writing] late into the night, senseless. Then at one o'clock can no longer fall asleep at all, the next day at work insupportable, and so I destroy myself.

1917

Distractedness, weak memory, stupidity. Days passed in futility, powers wasted away in waiting. . . . Always this one principal anguish—if I had gone away in 1911 in full possession of all my powers. Not eaten by the strain of keeping down living forces.

Eaten into tuberculosis. By the time he won through to himself and time for writing, his body could live no more. He was forty-one.

I think of Rilke who said, "If I have any responsibility, I mean and desire it to be responsibility for the deepest and innermost essence of the loved reality [writing] to which I am inseparably bound"; and who also said, "Anything alive that makes demands, arouses in me an infinite capacity to give it its due, the consequences of which completely use me up." These were true with Kafka, too, yet how different their lives. When Rilke wrote that about responsibility, he is explaining why he will not take a job to support his wife and baby, nor live with them (years later will not come to his daughter's wedding nor permit a two-hour honeymoon visit lest it break his solitude where he awaits poetry). The "infinite capacity" is his explanation as to why he cannot even bear to have a dog. Extreme—and justified. He protected his creative powers.

Kafka's, Rilke's "infinite capacity," and all else that has been said here of the needs of creation, illuminate women's silence of centuries. I will not repeat what is in Virginia Woolf's *A Room of One's Own,* but talk of this last century and a half in which women have begun to have voice in literature. (It has been less than that time in Eastern Europe, and not yet, in many parts of the world.)

In the last century, of the women whose achievements endure for us in one way or another,* nearly all never married (Jane Austen, Emily Brontë, Christina Rossetti, Emily Dickinson, Louisa May Alcott, Sarah Orne Jewett) or married late in their thirties (George Eliot, Elizabeth Barrett Browning, Charlotte Brontë, Olive Schreiner). I can think of only four (George Sand, Harriet Beecher Stowe, Helen Hunt Jackson, and Elizabeth Gaskell) who married and had children as young women.** All had servants.

In our century, until very recently, it has not been so different. Most did not marry (Selma Lagerlof, Willa Cather, Ellen Glasgow, Gertrude Stein, Gabriela Mistral, Elizabeth Madox Roberts, Charlotte Mew, Eudora Welty, Marianne Moore) or, if married, have been childless (Edith Wharton, Virginia Woolf, Katherine Mansfield, Dorothy Richardson, H.H. Richardson, Elizabeth Bowen, Isak Dinesen, Katherine Anne Porter, Lillian Hellman, Dorothy Parker). Colette had one child (when she was forty). If I include Sigrid Undset, Kay Boyle, Pearl Buck, Dorothy Canfield Fisher, that will make a small group who had more than one child. All had household help or other special circumstances.

Am I resaying the moldy theory that women have no need, some say no capacity, to create art, because they can "create" babies? And the additional proof is precisely that the few women who have created it are nearly all childless? No.

The power and the need to create, over and beyond reproduc-

---

*"One Out of Twelve" has a more extensive roll of women writers of achievement.

**I would now add a fifth—Kate Chopin—also a foreground silence.

tion, is native in both women and men. Where the gifted among women *(and men)* have remained mute, or have never attained full capacity, it is because of circumstances, inner or outer, which oppose the needs of creation.

Wholly surrendered and dedicated lives; time as needed for the work; totality of self. But women are traditionally trained to place others' needs first, to feel these needs as their own (the "infinite capacity"); their sphere, their satisfaction to be in making it possible for others to use their abilities. This is what Virginia Woolf meant when, already a writer of achievement, she wrote in her diary:

> Father's birthday. He would have been 96, 96, yes, today; and could have been 96, like other people one has known; but mercifully was not. His life would have entirely ended mine. What would have happened? No writing, no books;—inconceivable.

It took family deaths to free more than one woman writer into her own development.* Emily Dickinson freed herself, denying all the duties expected of a woman of her social position except the closest family ones, and she was fortunate to have a sister, and servants, to share those. How much is revealed of the differing circumstances and fate of their own as-great capacities, in the diaries (and lives) of those female bloodkin of great writers: Dorothy Wordsworth, Alice James, Aunt Mary Moody Emerson.

And where there is no servant or relation to assume the responsibilities of daily living? Listen to Katherine Mansfield in the early days of her relationship with John Middleton Murry, when they both dreamed of becoming great writers:**

---

*Among them: George Eliot, Helen Hunt Jackson, Mrs. Gaskell, Kate Chopin, Lady Gregory, Isak Dinesen. Ivy Compton-Burnett finds this the grim reason for the emergence of British women novelists after World War I: ". . . The men were dead, you see, and the women didn't marry so much because there was no one for them to marry, and so they had leisure, and, I think, in a good many cases they had money because their brothers were dead, and all that would tend to writing, wouldn't it, being single, and having some money, and having the time —having no men, you see."

**Already in that changed time when servants were not necessarily a part of the furnishings of almost anyone well educated enough to be making literature.

The house seems to take up so much time. . . . I mean when I have to clean up twice over or wash up extra unnecessary things, I get frightfully impatient and want to be working [writing]. So often this week you and Gordon have been talking while I washed dishes. Well someone's got to wash dishes and get food. Otherwise "there's nothing in the house but eggs to eat." And after you have gone I walk about with a mind full of ghosts of saucepans and primus stoves and "will there be enough to go around?" And you calling, whatever I am doing, writing, "Tig, isn't there going to be tea? It's five o'clock."

I loathe myself today. This woman who superintends you and rushes about slamming doors and slopping water and shouts "You might at least empty the pail and wash out the tea leaves." . . . O Jack, I wish that you would take me in your arms and kiss my hands and my face and every bit of me and say, "It's all right, you darling thing, I understand."

A long way from Conrad's favorable circumstances for creation: the flow of daily life made easy and noiseless.

And, if in addition to the infinite capacity, to the daily responsibilities, there are children?

Balzac, you remember, described creation in terms of motherhood. Yes, in intelligent passionate motherhood there are similarities, and in more than the toil and patience. The calling upon total capacities; the reliving and new using of the past; the comprehensions; the fascination, absorption, intensity. All almost certain death to creation—(so far).

Not because the capacities to create no longer exist, or the need (though for a while, as in any fullness of life, the need may be obscured), but because the circumstances for sustained creation have been almost impossible. The need cannot be first. It can have at best, only part self, part time. (Unless someone else does the nurturing. Read Dorothy Fisher's "Babushka Farnham" in *Fables for Parents.*) More than in any other human relationship, overwhelmingly more, motherhood means being instantly interruptable, responsive, responsible. Children need one *now* (and remember, in our society, the family must often try to be the center for love and health the outside world is not). The very fact that these are real needs, that one feels them as one's own (love, not duty); *that there is no one else responsible for these needs,* gives them primacy. It is distraction, not meditation, that becomes habitual; interruption, not continuity; spasmodic, not constant toil. The rest has been said here. Work interrupted, deferred, relinquished, makes blockage—at best, lesser accomplishment. Unused capacities atrophy, cease to be.

When H. H. Richardson, who wrote the Australian classic *Ultima Thule,* was asked why she—whose children, like all her people, were so profoundly written—did not herself have children, she answered: "There are enough women to do the child-bearing and childrearing. I know of none who can write my books." I remember thinking rebelliously, yes, and I know of none who can bear and rear my children either. But literary history is on her side. Almost no mothers—as almost no part-time, part-self persons—have created enduring literature . . . so far.

If I talk now quickly of my own silences—almost presumptuous after what has been told here—it is that the individual experience may add.

In the twenty years I bore and reared my children, usually had to work on a paid job as well, the simplest circumstances for creation did not exist. Nevertheless writing, the hope of it, was "the air I breathed, so long as I shall breathe at all." In that hope, there was conscious storing, snatched reading, beginnings of writing, and always "the secret rootlets of reconnaissance."

When the youngest of our four was in school, the beginnings struggled toward endings. This was a time, in Kafka's words, "like a squirrel in a cage: bliss of movement, desperation about constriction, craziness of endurance."

Bliss of movement. A full extended family life; the world of my job (transcriber in a dairy-equipment company); and the writing, which I was somehow able to carry around within me through work, through home. Time on the bus, even when I had to stand, was enough; the stolen moments at work, enough; the deep night hours for as long as I could stay awake, after the kids were in bed, after the household tasks were done, sometimes during. It is no accident that the first work I considered publishable began: "I stand here ironing, and what you asked me moves tormented back and forth with the iron."

In such snatches of time I wrote what I did in those years, but there came a time when this triple life was no longer possible. The fifteen hours of daily realities became too much distraction for the writing. I lost craziness of endurance. What might have been, I don't know: but I applied for, and was given, eight months' writing time. There was still full family life, all the household responsibilities, but I did not have to hold an eight-hour job. I had continuity, three full days, sometimes more—and it was in those months I made the mysterious turn and became a writing writer.

Then had to return to the world of work, someone else's work, nine hours, five days a week.

This was the time of festering and congestion. For a few months I was able to shield the writing with which I was so full, against the demands of jobs on which I had to be competent, through the joys and responsibilities and trials of family. For a few months. Always roused by the writing, always denied. "I could not go to write it down. It convulsed and died in me. I will pay."

My work died. What demanded to be written, did not. It seethed, bubbled, clamored, peopled me. At last moved into the hours meant for sleeping. I worked now full time on temporary jobs, a Kelly, a Western Agency girl (girl!), wandering from office to office, always hoping to manage two, three writing months ahead. Eventually there was time.

I had said: always roused by the writing, always denied. Now, like a woman made frigid, I had to learn response, to trust this possibility for fruition that had not been before. Any interruption dazed and silenced me. It took a long while of surrendering to what I was trying to write, of invoking Henry James's "passion, piety, patience," before I was able to re-establish work.

When again I had to leave the writing, I lost consciousness. A time of anesthesia. There was still an automatic noting that did not stop, but it was as if writing had never been. No fever, no congestion, no festering. I ceased being peopled, slept well and dreamlessly, took a "permanent" job. The few pieces that had been published seemed to have vanished like the not-yet-written. I wrote someone, unsent: "So long they fed each other—my life, the writing—; —the writing or hope of it, my life—; but now they begin to destroy." I knew, but did not feel the destruction.

A Ford grant in literature, awarded me on nomination by others, came almost too late. Time granted does not necessarily coincide with time that can be most fully used, as the congested time of fullness would have been. Still, it was two years.

Drowning is not so pitiful as the attempt to rise, says Emily Dickinson. I do not agree, but I know whereof she speaks. For a long time I was that emaciated survivor trembling on the beach, unable to rise and walk. Said differently, I could manage only the feeblest, shallowest growth on that devastated soil. Weeds, to be burned like weeds, or used as compost. When the habits of creation were at last rewon, one book went to the publisher, and I dared to begin my present work. It became my center, engraved on it: "Evil is whatever distracts." (By now had begun a cost to our family life, to my own participation in life as a human being.) I shall not tell the "rest, residue, and remainder" of what I was "leased, demised, and let unto" when once again I had to leave work at the flood to return to the Time-Master, to business-ese and legalese. This most harmful of all my silences has ended, but I am not yet recovered; may still be a one-book silence.

However that will be, we are in a time of more and more hidden and foreground silences, women *and* men. Denied full writing life, more may try to "nurse through night" (that part-time, part-self night) "the ethereal spark," but it seems to me there would almost have had to be "flame on flame" first; and time as needed, afterwards; and enough of the self, the capacities, undamaged for the rebeginnings on the frightful task. I would like to believe this for what has not yet been written into literature. But it cannot reconcile for what is lost by unnatural silences.

1962

ONE OUT OF TWELVE: WRITERS WHO ARE WOMEN IN OUR CENTURY

An unwritten talk, spoken from notes in 1971 at the Modern Language Association Forum on Women Writers in the Twentieth Century. In this reconstituted, edited form, it appeared in the "Women Writing, Women Teaching" issue of *College English,* October 1972.

Happily, some of what follows is by now, in varying degrees, familiar. It was only beginning to be so in 1971. The tone, markedly different from that of "Silences," is distinctly of that year of cumulative discovery.

The content was conditioned somewhat by its being addressed to college teachers of literature. A few quotations from "Silences," then unavoidable, herein repetitious, are kept intact.

It is the women's movement, part of the other movements of our time for a fully human life, that has brought this forum into being; kindling a renewed, in most instances a first-time, interest in the writings and writers of our sex.

Linked with the old, resurrected classics on women, this movement in three years has accumulated a vast new mass of testimony, of new comprehensions as to what it is to be female. Inequities, restrictions, penalties, denials, leechings have been painstakingly and painfully documented; damaging differences in circumstances and treatment from that of males attested to; and limitations, harms, a sense of wrong, voiced.

It is in the light and dark of this testimony that I examine my subject today: the lives and work of writers, women, in our century (though I speak primarily of those writing in the English language —and in prose).*

Compared to the countless centuries of the silence of women, compared to the century preceding ours—the first in which women wrote in any noticeable numbers—ours has been a favorable one.

The road was cut many years ago, as Virginia Woolf reminds us:

> by Fanny Burney, by Aphra Behn, by Harriet Martineau, by Jane Austen, by George Eliot, many famous women and many more unknown and forgotten. . . . Thus, when I came to write . . . writing was a reputable and harmless occupation.

Predecessors, ancestors, a body of literature, an acceptance of the right to write: each in themselves an advantage.

In this second century we have access to areas of work and of life experience previously denied; higher education; longer, stronger lives; for the first time in human history, freedom from compulsory childbearing; freer bodies and attitudes toward sexuality; a beginning of technological easing of household tasks; and—of the greatest importance to those like myself who come from generations of illiterate women—increas-

---

*This is the poorer for such limitation.

ing literacy, and higher degrees of it. *Each one of these a vast gain.* *

And the results?

Productivity: books of all manner and kind. My own crude sampling, having to be made without benefit of research assistants, secretary, studies (nobody's made them), or computer (to feed the entire *Books in Print* and *Contemporary Authors* into, for instance) indicates that at present four to five books are published by men to every one by a woman.**

Comparative earnings: no authoritative figures available.

Achievement: as gauged by what supposedly designates it: appearance in twentieth-century literature courses, required reading lists, textbooks, quality anthologies, the year's best, the decade's best, the fifty years' best, consideration by critics or in current reviews—*one woman writer for every twelve men* (8 percent women, 92 percent men). For a week or two, make your own survey whenever you pick up an anthology, course bibliography, quality magazine or quarterly, book review section, book of criticism.

What weights my figures so heavily toward the one-out-of-twelve ratio are twentieth-century literature course offerings, and writers decreed worthy of critical attention in books and articles. Otherwise my percentage figures would have come closer to one out of seven.

But it would not matter if the ratio had been one out of six or five. Any figure but one to one would insist on query: Why? What, not true for men but only *for women, makes this enormous difference? (Thus, class—economic circumstance—and color, those other traditional silencers of humanity, can be relevant only in the special ways that they affect the half of their numbers who are women.)*

Why are so many more women silenced than men? Why, when

---

*These are measured phrases, enormously compressed. Each asks an entire book or books, to indicate its enabling relationship to literature written by women in this century—including the very numbers of women enabled to write.

**Richard Altick in his "Sociology of Authorship" found the proportion of women writers to men writers in Britain a fairly constant one for the years 1800 to 1935: 20 percent. This was based on books published, not on recognized achievement.

*women do write (one out of four or five works published) is so little
of their writing known, taught, accorded recognition? What is the
nature of the critical judgments made throughout that (along with
the factors different in women's lives) steadily reduce the ratio from
one out of three in anthologies of student work, to one out of
seventeen in course offerings.*

*This talk, originally intended to center on the writing, the
achievement of women writers in our century, became instead these
queryings. Yet—in a way sadder, angrier, prouder—it still centers
on the writing, the achievement.* *

One woman writer of achievement for every twelve men writers
so ranked. Is this proof again—and in this so much more favorable
century—of women's innately inferior capacity for creative
achievement?

Only a few months ago (June 1971), during a Radcliffe spon-
sored panel on "Women's Liberation, Myth or Reality," Diana
Trilling, asking why it is that women

> have not made even a fraction of the intellectual, scientific or artis-
> tic-cultural contributions which men have made

came again to the traditional conclusion that

> it is not enough to blame women's place in culture or culture itself,
> because that leaves certain fundamental questions unanswered
> . . . necessarily raises the question of the biological aspects of the
> problem.

Biology: that difference.**   Evidently unknown to or dismissed by her and the others who share her conclusion, are
the centuries of prehistory during which biology did not deny
equal contribution; and *the other determining difference—not*

---

*Added to text, 1976.

**Biologically, too, the change for women now is enormous: life expectancy
(USA) seventy-eight years—as contrasted with forty-eight years in 1900. Near
forty-eight years of life before and after one is "a woman," that is: "capable of
conceiving and bearing young." (And childbearing more and more voluntary.)

biology—between male and female in the centuries after; the
differing past of women—that should be part of every human
consciousness, certainly every woman's consciousness (in the
way that the 400 years of bondage, colonialism, the slave passage, are to black humans).

Work first:

> Within our bodies we bore the race. Through us it was shaped, fed
> and clothed. . . . Labour more toilsome and unending than that of
> man was ours. . . . No work was too hard, no labour too strenuous
> to exclude us.*

True for most women in most of the world still.

Unclean; taboo. The Devil's Gateway. The three steps behind;
the girl babies drowned in the river; the baby strapped to the back.
Buried alive with the lord, burned alive on the funeral pyre,
burned as witch at the stake. Stoned to death for adultery. Beaten,
raped. Bartered. Bought and sold. Concubinage, prostitution,
white slavery. The hunt, the sexual prey, "I am a lost creature, O
the poor Clarissa." Purdah, the veil of Islam, domestic confinement. Illiterate. Denied vision. Excluded, excluded, excluded
from council, ritual, activity, learning, language, when there was
neither biological nor economic reason to be excluded.

Religion, when all believed. In sorrow shalt thou bring forth
children. May thy wife's womb never cease from bearing. Neither
was the man created for the woman but the woman for the man.
Let the woman learn in silence and in all subjection. Contrary to
biological birth fact: Adam's rib. The Jewish male morning
prayer: thank God I was not born a woman. Silence in holy places,
seated apart, or not permitted entrance at all; castration of boys
because women too profane to sing in church.

And for the comparative handful of women born into the privileged class; being, not doing; man does, woman is; to you the
world says work, to us it says seem. God is thy law, thou mine.
Isolated. Cabin'd, cribb'd, confin'd; the private sphere. Bound
feet: corseted, cosseted, bedecked; denied one's body. Powerless-

---

*Olive Schreiner. *Woman and Labour*

ness. Fear of rape, male strength. Fear of aging. Subject to. Fear of expressing capacities. Soft attractive graces; the mirror to magnify man. Marriage as property arrangement. The vices of slaves:* dissembling, flattering, manipulating, appeasing.

Bolstering. Vicarious living, infantilization, trivialization. Parasitism, individualism, madness. Shut up, you're only a girl. O Elizabeth, why couldn't you have been born a boy? For twentieth-century woman: roles, discontinuities, part-self, part-time; conflict; imposed "guilt"; "a man can give full energy to his profession, a woman cannot."

> How is it that women have not made a fraction of the intellectual, scientific, or artistic-cultural contributions that men have made?

Only in the context of this punitive difference in circumstance, in history, between the sexes; this past, hidden or evident, that (though objectively obsolete—yes, even the toil and the compulsory childbearing obsolete) *continues so terribly, so determiningly to live on, only in this context can the question be answered or my subject here today—the women writer in our century: one out of twelve—be understood.*

How much it takes to become a writer. Bent (far more common than we assume), circumstances, time, development of craft—but beyond that: how much conviction as to the importance of what one has to say, one's right to say it. And the will, the measureless store of belief in oneself to be able to come to, cleave to, find the form for one's own life comprehensions. Difficult for any male not born into a class that breeds such confidence. Almost impossible for a girl, a woman.

The leeching of belief, of will, the damaging of capacity begin so early. Sparse indeed is the literature on the way of denial to small girl children of the development of their endowment as born

*Elizabeth Barrett Browning's phrase; other phrases throughout from the Bible, John Milton, Richardson's *Clarissa*, Matthew Arnold, Elizabeth Cady Stanton, Virginia Woolf, Viola Klein, Mountain Wolf Woman.

human: active, vigorous bodies; exercise of the power to do, to make, to investigate, to invent, to conquer obstacles, to resist violations of the self; to think, create, choose; to attain community, confidence in self. Little has been written on the harms of instilling constant concern with appearance; the need to please, to support; the training in acceptance, deferring. Little has been added in our century to George Eliot's *The Mill on the Floss* on the effect of the differing treatment—"climate of expectation"—for boys and for girls.

But it is there if one knows how to read for it, and indelibly there in the resulting damage. One—out of twelve.

In the vulnerable girl years, unlike their sisters in the previous century, women writers go to college.* The kind of experience it may be for them is stunningly documented in Elaine Showalter's pioneering "Women and the Literary Curriculum."** Freshman texts in which women have little place, if at all; language itself, all achievement, anything to do with the human in male terms—*Man in Crises, The Individual and His World.* Three hundred thirteen male writers taught; seventeen women writers: That classic of adolescent rebellion, *A Portrait of the Artist as a Young Man;* and sagas (male) of the quest for identity (but then Erikson, the father of the concept, propounds that identity concerns girls only insofar as making themselves into attractive beings for the right kind of man).† Most, *not all,* of the predominantly male literature studied, written by men whose understandings are not universal, but restrictively male (as Mary Ellmann, Kate Millett, and Dolores

*True almost without exception among the writers who are women in *Twentieth Century Authors* and *Contemporary Authors.*

**College English,* May 1971. A year later (October 1972), *College English* published an extensive report, "Freshman Textbooks," by Jean Mullens. In the 112 most used texts, she found 92.47 percent (5,795) of the selections were by men; 7.53 percent (472) by women (One Out of Twelve). Mullens deepened Showalter's insights as to the subtly undermining effect on freshman students of the texts' contents and language, as well as the minuscule proportion of women writers.

†In keeping with his 1950s–60s thesis of a distinctly female "biological, evolutionary need to fulfil self through serving others."

Schmidt have pointed out); in our time more and more surface, hostile, one-dimensional in portraying women.

In a writer's young years, susceptibility to the vision and style of the great is extreme. Add the aspiration-denying implication, consciously felt or not (although reinforced daily by one's professors and reading) that (as Virginia Woolf noted years ago) women writers, women's experience, and literature written by women are by definition minor. (Mailer will not grant even the minor: "the one thing a writer has to have is balls.") No wonder that Showalter observes:

> Women [students] are estranged from their own experience and unable to perceive its shape and authenticity, in part because they do not see it mirrored and given resonance in literature. . . . They are expected to identify with masculine experience, which is presented as the human one, and have no faith in the validity of their own perceptions and experiences, rarely seeing them confirmed in literature, or accepted in criticism . . . [They] notoriously lack the happy confidence, the exuberant sense of the value of their individual observations which enables young men to risk making fools of themselves for the sake of an idea.

Harms difficult to work through. Nevertheless, some young women (others are already lost) maintain their ardent intention to write—fed indeed by the very glories of some of this literature that puts them down.

But other invisible worms are finding out the bed of crimson joy.* Self-doubt; seriousness, also questioned by the hours agonizing over appearance; concentration shredded into attracting, being attractive; the absorbing real need and love for working with words felt as hypocritical self-delusion ("I'm not truly dedi-

---

*

> O Rose thou art sick./The invisible worm,
> That flies in the night/In the howling storm:
>
> Has found out thy bed/Of crimson joy:
> And his dark secret love/Does thy life destroy.
>   —William Blake

cated"), for what seems (and is) esteemed is being attractive to men. High aim, and accomplishment muteness toward it, discounted by the prevalent attitude that, as girls will probably marry (attitudes not applied to boys who will probably marry), writing is no more than an attainment of a dowry to be spent later according the needs and circumstances within the true vocation: husband and family. The growing acceptance that going on will threaten other needs, to love and be loved; ("a woman has to sacrifice all claims to femininity and family to be a writer").*

And the agony—peculiarly mid-century, escaped by their sisters of pre-Freudian, pre-Jungian times—that "creation and femininity are incompatible."** Anaïs Nin's words.

> The aggressive act of creation; the guilt for creating. I did not want to rival man; to steal man's creation, his thunder. I must protect them, not outshine them.†

The acceptance—against one's experienced reality—of the sexist notion that the act of creation is not as inherently natural to a woman as to a man, but rooted instead in unnatural aggression, rivalry, envy, or thwarted sexuality.

And in all the usual college teaching—the English, history, psychology, sociology courses—little to help that young woman understand the source or nature of this inexplicable draining self-doubt, loss of aspiration, of confidence.

It is all there in the extreme in Plath's *Bell Jar*—that (inadequate)‡ portrait of the artist as young woman (significantly, one of the few that we have)—from the precarious sense of vocation to the paralyzing conviction that (in a sense different from what she wrote years later)

---

*Plath. A letter when a graduate student.

**The Diary of Anaïs Nin, Vol. III, 1939–1944.

†A statement that would have baffled Austen, the Brontës, Mrs. Gaskell, Eliot, Stowe, Alcott, etc. The strictures were felt by them in other ways.

‡Inadequate, for the writer-being ("muteness is sickness for me") is not portrayed. By contrast, how present she is in Plath's own *Letters Home*.

Perfection is terrible. It cannot have children.
It tamps the womb.

And indeed, in our century as in the last, until very recently
almost all distinguished achievement has come from childless
women: Willa Cather, Ellen Glasgow, Gertrude Stein, Edith
Wharton, Virginia Woolf, Elizabeth Bowen, Katherine Mansfield,
Isak Dinesen, Katherine Anne Porter, Dorothy Richardson,
Henry Handel Richardson, Susan Glaspell, Dorothy Parker, Lil-
lian Hellman, Eudora Welty, Djuna Barnes, Anaïs Nin, Ivy
Compton-Burnett, Zora Neale Hurston, Elizabeth Madox Rob-
erts, Christina Stead, Carson McCullers, Flannery O'Connor,
Jean Stafford, May Sarton, Josephine Herbst, Jessamyn West,
Janet Frame, Lillian Smith, Iris Murdoch, Joyce Carol Oates,
Hannah Green, Lorraine Hansberry.

Most never questioned, or at least accepted (a few sanctified)
this different condition for achievement, not imposed on men
writers. Few asked the fundamental human equality question
regarding it that Elizabeth Mann Borghese, Thomas Mann's
daughter, asked when she was eighteen and sent to a psychiatrist for help in getting over an unhappy love affair (revealing
also a working ambition to become a great musician although
"women cannot be great musicians"). "You must choose between your art and fulfillment as a woman," the analyst told
her, "between music and family life." "Why?" she asked.
"Why must I choose? No one said to Toscanini or to Bach or
my father that they must choose between their art and personal, family life; fulfillment as a man. . . . Injustice everywhere." Not where it is free choice. But where it is forced because of the circumstances for the sex into which one is born
—a choice men of the same class do not have to make in
order to do their work—that is not choice, that is a coercive
working of sexist oppression.*

---

*"Them lady poets must not marry, pal," is how John Berryman, poet (himself
oft married) expressed it. The old patriarchal injunction: "Woman, this is man's
realm. If you insist on invading it, unsex yourself—and expect the road to be
made difficult." Furthermore, this very unmarriedness and childlessness has been
used to discredit women as unfulfilled, inadequate, somehow abnormal.

What possible difference, you may ask, does it make to literature whether or not a woman writer remains childless—free choice or not—especially in view of the marvels these childless women have created.

Might there not have been other marvels as well, or other dimensions to these marvels? Might there not have been present profound aspects and understandings of human life as yet largely absent in literature?

More and more women writers in our century, primarily in the last two decades, are assuming as their right fullness of work *and* family life.* Their emergence is evidence of changing circumstances making possible for them what (with rarest exception) was not possible in the generations of women before. I hope and I fear for what will result. I hope (and believe) that complex new richness will come into literature; I fear because almost certainly their work will be impeded, lessened, partial. For the fundamental situation remains unchanged. Unlike men writers who marry, most will not have the societal equivalent of a wife—nor (in a society hostile to growing life) anyone but themselves to mother their children. Even those who can afford help, good schools, summer camps, may *(may)* suffer what seventy years ago W.E.B. Du Bois

---

*Among those with children: Harriette Arnow, Mary Lavin, Mary McCarthy, Tess Slesinger, Eleanor Clark, Nancy Hale, Storm Jameson, Janet Lewis, Jean Rhys, Kay Boyle, Ann Petry, Dawn Powell, Meridel LeSueur, Evelyn Eaton, Dorothy Canfield Fisher, Pearl Buck, Josephine Johnson, Caroline Gordon, Shirley Jackson; and a sampling in the unparalleled last two decades: Doris Lessing, Nadine Gordimer, Margaret Laurence, Grace Paley, Hortense Calisher, Edna O'Brien, Sylvia Ashton-Warner, Pauli Murray, Françoise Mallet-Joris, Cynthia Ozick, Joanne Greenberg, Joan Didion, Penelope Mortimer, Alison Lurie, Hope Hale Davis, Doris Betts, Muriel Spark, Adele Wiseman, Lael Wertenbaker, Shirley Ann Grau, Maxine Kumin, Margaret Walker, Gina Barriault, Mary Gray Hughes, Maureen Howard, Norma Rosen, Lore Segal, Alice Walker, Nancy Willard, Charlotte Painter, Sallie Bingham. (I would now add Clarice Lispector, Ruth Prawer Jhabvala, June Arnold, Ursula Le Guin, Diane Johnson, Alice Munro, Helen Yglesias, Susan Cahill, Rosellen Brown, Alta, and Susan Griffin.) Some wrote before children, some only in the middle or later years. Not many have directly used the material open to them out of motherhood as central source for their work.

called "The Damnation of Women": "that only at the sacrifice of the chance to do their best work can women bear and rear children."*

> Substantial creative achievement demands time . . . and with rare exceptions only full-time workers have created it.**

I am quoting myself from "Silences," a talk nine years ago. In motherhood, as it is structured,

> circumstances for sustained creation are almost impossible. Not because the capacities to create no longer exist, or the need (though for a while as in any fullness of life the need may be obscured), but . . . the need cannot be first. It can have at best only part self, part time . . . Motherhood means being instantly interruptible, responsive, responsible. Children need one *now* (and remember, in our society, the family must often try to be the center for love and health the outside world is not). The very fact that these are needs of love, not duty, that one feels them as one's self; *that there is no one else to be responsible for these needs,* gives them primacy. It is distraction, not meditation, that becomes habitual; interruption, not continuity; spasmodic, not constant, toil. Work interrupted, deferred, postponed makes blockage—at best, lesser accomplishment. Unused capacities atrophy, cease to be.

There are other vulnerabilities to loss, diminishment. Most women writers (being women) have had bred into them the "infinite capacity"; what Virginia Woolf named (after the heroine of

---

Darkwater: Voices from Within the Veil.

**This does not mean that these full-time writers were hermetic or denied themselves social or personal life (think of James, Turgenev, Tolstoy, Balzac, Joyce, Gide, Colette, Yeats, Woolf, etc. etc.); nor did they, except perhaps at the flood, put in as many hours daily as those doing more usual kinds of work. Three to six hours daily have been the norm ("the quiet, patient, generous mornings will bring it"). Zola and Trollope are famous last-century examples of the four hours; the *Paris Review* interviews disclose many contemporary ones.

Full-timeness consists not in the actual number of hours at one's desk, but in that writing is one's major profession, practiced habitually, in freed, protected, undistracted time as needed, when it is needed.

a famous Victorian poem) *The Angel in the House,* who "must charm . . . sympathize . . . flatter . . . conciliate . . . be extremely sensitive to the needs and moods and wishes of others before her own . . . excel in the difficult arts of family life . . ."

> It was she who used to come between me and my paper . . . who bothered me and wasted my time and so tormented me that at last I killed her . . . or she would have plucked out my heart as a writer.*

There is another angel, so lowly as to be invisible, although without her no art, or any human endeavor, could be carried on for even one day—the essential angel, with whom Virginia Woolf (and most women writers, still in the privileged class) did not have to contend—the angel who must assume the physical responsibilities for daily living, for the maintenance of life.

Almost always in one form or another (usually in the wife, two-angel form) she has dwelt in the house of men. She it was who made it possible for Joseph Conrad to "wrestle with the Lord for his creation":

> Mind and will and conscience engaged to the full, hour after hour, day after day . . . never aware of the even flow of daily life made easy and noiseless for me by a silent, watchful, tireless affection.

The angel who was "essential" to Rilke's "great task":

> like a sister who would run the house like a friendly climate, there or not there as one wished . . . and would ask for nothing except just to be there working and warding at the frontiers of the invisible.

Men (even part-time writers who must carry on work other than writing**) have had and have this inestimable advantage toward productivity. I cannot help but notice how curiously absent both of these angels, these watchers and warders at the frontiers of the

---

Professions for Women.

**As must many women writers.

invisible, are from the actual contents of most men's books, except perhaps on the dedication page:

To my wife, without whom . . .

I digress, and yet I do not; the disregard for the essential angel, the large absence of any sense of her in literature or elsewhere, has not only cost literature great contributions from those so occupied or partially occupied, but by failing to help create an arousing awareness (as literature has done in other realms) has contributed to the agonizingly slow elimination of this technologically and socially obsolete, human-wasting drudgery: Virginia Woolf's dream of a long since possible "economical, powerful and efficient future when houses will be cleaned by a puff of hot wind."

Sometimes the essential angel is present in women's books,* though still most "heroines are in white dresses that never need washing" (Rebecca Harding Davis's phrase of a hundred years ago). Some poets admit her as occasional domestic image; a few preen her as femininity; Sylvia Plath could escape her only by suicide:

> . . . flying . . .
> Over the engine that killed her——
> The mausoleum, the wax house.

For the first time in literary history, a woman poet of stature, accustomed through years to the habits of creation, began to live the life of most of her sex: the honey drudgers: the winged un-miraculous two-angel, whirled mother-maintenance life, that most women, not privileged, know. A situation without help or husband and with twenty-four hours' responsibility for two small human lives whom she adored and at their most fascinating and demanding. The world was blood-hot and personal. Creation's needs at its height. She had to get up at

---

*Among them: Harriette Arnow, Willa Cather, Dorothy Canfield Fisher, H.H. Richardson (of *Ultima Thule*), Ruth Suckow, Elizabeth Madox Roberts, Sarah Wright, Agnes Smedley; Emily Dickinson, pre-eminently; Sylvia Plath, sometimes Christina Stead, Doris Lessing. (I would now add Edith Summers Kelley *(Weeds* and *The Devil's Hand),* the Marge Piercy of *Small Changes,* and my own fiction.)

> four in the morning, that still blue almost eternal hour before the
> baby's cry

to write at all.* After the long expending day, tending, caring,
cleaning, enjoying, laundering, feeding, marketing, delighting,
outing; being

> a very efficient tool or weapon, used and in demand from mo-
> ment to moment. . . . Nights [were] no good [for writing]. I'm
> so flat by then that all I can cope with is music and brandy and
> water.

The smog of cooking, the smog of hell floated in her head. The
smile of the icebox annihilated. There was a stink of fat and baby
crap; viciousness in the kitchen! And the blood jet poetry (for
which there was never time and self except in that still blue hour
before the baby's cry) there was no stopping it:**

> It is not a question in these last weeks of the conflict in a woman's
> life between the claims of the feminine and the agonized work of
> art

Elizabeth Hardwick, a woman, can say of Sylvia Plath's suicide,

> Every artist is either a man or woman, and the struggle is pretty
> much the same for both.

A comment as insensible of the two-angel realities ("so lowly as
to be invisible") as are the oblivious masculine assumptions, either
that the suicide was because of Daddy's death twenty-three years
before, revived and compounded by her husband's desertion; or
else a real-life *Story of O* (that elegant pornography) sacramental
culmination of being used up by ecstasy (poetry in place of sex this
time):

---

*In the long tradition of early rising, an hour here and there, or late-night
mother-writers from Mrs. Trollope to Harriette Arnow to this very twenty-four
hours—necessarily fitting in writing time in accordance with maintenance of life,
and children's, needs.

**Phrases, lines, throughout from Plath's *Ariel,* letters, BBC broadcasts.

the pride of an utter and ultimate surrender, like the pride of O,
naked and chained in her owl mask as she asks Sir Stephen for
death. . . .*

If in such an examined extremity, the profound realities of
woman's situation are ignored, how much less likely are they—
particularly the subtler ones—to be seen, comprehended, taken
into account, as they affect lesser-known women writers in more
usual circumstances.

In younger years, confidence and vision leeched, aspiration reduced. In adult years, sporadic effort and unfinished work;
women made "mediocre caretakers of their talent": that is, writing is not first. The angel in the house situation; probably also
the essential angel, maintenance-of-life necessity; increasingly in
our century, work on a paid job as well; and for more and more
women writers, the whirled expending motherhood years. Is it
so difficult to account for the many occasional-fine-story or one-
book writers; the distinguished but limited production of others
(Janet Lewis, Ann Petry, for example); the years and years in
getting one book done (thirty years for Margaret Walker's *Jubi-
lee,* twenty for Marguerite Young's *Miss Macintosh My Darling*);
the slowly increasing numbers of women who not until their
forties, fifties, sixties, publish for the first time (Dorothy Richardson, Hortense Calisher, Theodora Kroeber, Linda Hoyer—
John Updike's mother); the women who start with children's,
girls' books (Maxine Kumin), some like Cid Ricketts Sumner
(*Tammy*) seldom or never getting to adult fiction that would
encompass their wisdom for adults; and most of all, the unsatisfactory quality of book after book that evidence the marks of
part-time, part-self authorship, and to whose authors Sarah Orne
Jewett's words to the part-time, part-self young Willa Cather
still apply, seventy years after:

> If you don't keep and mature your force and above all have
> time and quiet to perfect your work, you will be writing things
> not much better than you did five years ago. . . . Otherwise,

---

*Richard Howard, in *The Art of Sylvia Plath,* edited by Charles Newman.

what might be strength is only crudeness, and what might be insight is only observation. You will write about life, but never life itself.*

Yes, the loss in quality, the minor work, the hidden silences, are there in woman after woman writer in our century.** We will never have the body of work that we were capable of producing. Blight, said Blake, never does good to a tree:

And if a blight kill not a tree but it still bear fruit, let none say that the fruit was in consequence of the blight.

As for myself, who did not publish a book until I was fifty, who raised children without household help or the help of the "technological sublime" (the atom bomb was in manufacture before the first automatic washing machine); who worked outside the house on everyday jobs as well (as nearly half of all women do now, though a woman with a paid job, except as a maid or prostitute, is still rarest of any in literature); who could not kill the essential angel (there was no one else to do her work); would not—if I could—have killed the caring part of the Woolf angel; as distant from the world of literature most of my life as literature is distant (in content too) from my world:

The years when I should have been writing, my hands and being were at other (inescapable) tasks. Now, lightened as they are, when I must do those tasks into which most of my life went, like the old mother, grandmother in my *Tell Me a Riddle* who could not make herself touch a baby, I pay a psychic cost: "the sweat beads, the long shudder begins." The habits of a lifetime when everything else had to come before writing are

---

Letters of Sarah Orne Jewett, edited by Annie Fields.

**Compared to men writers of like distinction and years of life, few women writers have had lives of unbroken productivity, or leave behind a "body of work." Early beginnings, then silence; or clogged late ones (foreground silences); long periods between books (hidden silences); characterize most of us. A Colette, Wharton, Glasgow, Millay, Lessing, Oates, are the exceptions.

not easily broken, even when circumstances now often make it possible for writing to be first; habits of years—response to others, distractibility, responsibility for daily matters—stay with you, mark you, become you. The cost of "discontinuity" (that pattern still imposed on women) is such a weight of things unsaid, an accumulation of material so great, that everything starts up something else in me; what should take weeks. takes me sometimes months to write; what should take months, takes years.

I speak of myself to bring here the sense of those others to whom this is in the process of happening (unnecessarily happening, for it need not, must not continue to be) and to remind us of those (I so nearly was one) who never come to writing at all.

We must not speak of women writers in our century (as we cannot speak of women in any area of recognized human achievement) without speaking also of the invisible, the as-innately-capable: the born to the wrong circumstances—diminished, excluded, foundered, silenced.

We who write are survivors, *"only's."** One-out-of-twelve.

---

*For myself, "survivor" contains its other meaning: one who must bear witness for those who foundered; try to tell how and why it was that they, also worthy of life, did *not* survive. And pass on ways of surviving; and tell our chancy luck, our special circumstances.

"Only's" is an expression out of the 1950s Civil Rights time: the young Ralph Abernathy reporting to his Birmingham Church congregation on his trip up north for support:

> I go to Seattle and they tell me, "Brother, you got to meet so and so, why he's the only Negro Federal Circuit Judge in the Northwest"; I go to Chicago and they tell me, "Brother, you've got to meet so and so, why he's the only full black professor of Sociology there is"; I go to Albany and they tell me, "Brother, you *got* to meet so and so, why he's the only black senator in the state legislature . . ." [long dramatic pause] . . . WE DON'T WANT NO ONLY'S.

Only's are used to rebuke ("to be models"); to imply the unrealistic, "see, it can be done, all you need is capacity and will." Accepting a situation of "only's" means: "let inequality of circumstance continue to prevail."

I must go very fast now, telescope and omit (there has already been so much telescoping and omitting), move to work, professional circumstances.

Devaluation: Still in our century, women's books of great worth suffer the death of being unknown, or at best a peculiar eclipsing, far outnumbering the similar fate of the few such books by men. I think of the writers Kate Chopin, Mary Austin, Dorothy Richardson, Henry Handel Richardson *(Ultima Thule),* Susan Glaspell *(Jury of Her Peers),* Elizabeth Madox Roberts *(Time of Man),* Janet Lewis, Ann Petry, Harriette Arnow *(The Dollmaker),* Agnes Smedley *(Daughter of Earth),* Christina Stead, Kay Boyle, Jean Rhys—every one of them absorbing, and some with the stamp of enduring.* Considering their acknowledged stature, how comparatively unread, untaught, are Edith Wharton, Ellen Glasgow, Elizabeth Bowen, Dorothy Parker, Gertrude Stein, Katherine Mansfield—even Virginia Woolf, Willa Cather, and Katherine Anne Porter.**

Critical attitudes: Two centuries later, still what Cynthia Ozick calls "the *perpetual* dancing dog phenomena,"† the injurious reacting to a book, not for its quality or content, but on the basis of its having been written by a woman—with consequent misreading, mistreatment.‡

One addition to the "she writes like a man" "with masculine power" kind of "praise." Power is seldom recognized as the power it is at all, if the subject matter is considered woman's:

---

*1976: At least some of these writers are now coming out of eclipse. But Glaspell, Mary Austin, Roberts, and H.H. Richardson are still out of print. So is most of Christina Stead.

**Eclipsing, devaluation, neglect, are the result of critical judgments, a predominantly male domain. The most damaging, and still prevalent, critical attitude remains "that women's experience, and literature written by women are, by definition, minor." Indeed, for a sizable percentage of male writers, critics, academics, writer-women are eliminated from consideration (consciousness) altogether. (See the one-out-of-twelve compilations beginning on page 186.)

†"Women and Creativity," *Motive,* April 1969.

‡Savor Mary Ellmann's inimitable *Thinking About Women.*

it is minor, moving, evocative, instinctive, delicate. "As delicate as a surgeon's scalpel," says Katherine Anne Porter of such a falsifying description for Katherine Mansfield's art. Instinctive?

> I judge her work to have been to a great degree a matter of intelligent use of her faculties, a conscious practice of a hard won craftsmanship, a triumph of discipline. . . .*

*Climate in literary circles for those who move in them:*** Writers know the importance of being taken seriously, with respect for one's vision and integrity; of comradeship with other writers; of being dealt with as a writer on the basis of one's work and not for other reasons; and how chancy is recognition and getting published. There is no time to speak of this today; but nearly all writers who are women are at a disadvantage here.

Restriction: For all our freer life in this century, our significantly greater access to work, education, travel, varied experience, there is still limitation of circumstances for scope, subject, social context, the kind of comprehensions which come only in situations beyond the private. (What Charlotte Brontë felt so keenly 125 years ago as a denial of "facilities for observation . . . a knowledge of the world" which gives other writers "Thackeray, Dickens . . . an importance, variety, depth greatly beyond what I can offer.")† "Trespass vision" cannot substitute.

Constriction: not always recognized as constriction. The age-old coercion of women toward one dimension continues to be "terribly, determiningly" present. Women writers are still suspect as unnatural if they concern themselves with aspects of their experience, interests, being, beyond the traditionally defined women's sphere. Hortense Calisher is troubled that women writers

---

*"The Art of Katherine Mansfield," *The Collected Essays of Katherine Anne Porter.*

**See Carolyn Kizer's "Pro Femina" in her *Knock Upon Silence.*

†Letter to her publisher, W. S. Williams, 1849.

straining toward a world sensibility, or one equivalent to the
roaming consciences of the men . . . or dispens[ing] with whatever was clearly female in their sensibility or experience . . . flee
from the image society projects on [them].*

But conscience and world sensibility are as natural to
women as to men; men have been freer to develop and exercise
them, that is all. Indeed, one of the most characteristic strains
in literature written by women (however dropped out of sight,
or derided) *is* conscience, concern with wrongs to human beings in their time—from the first novel in our language by a
woman, Aphra Behn's *Oroonoko,* that first by anyone against
slavery, through Harriet Martineau, Elizabeth Gaskell, George
Sand, Harriet Beecher Stowe, Elizabeth Barrett Browning,
Rebecca Harding Davis, Helen Hunt Jackson, Olive Schreiner,
Ethel Voynich, Charlotte Perkins Gilman—to our own century's Gabriela Mistral, Virginia Woolf (the essays), Nelly
Sachs, Anna Seghers, Rachel Carson, Lillian Hellman, Lor-
raine Hansberry, Theodora Kroeber *(Ishi),* Agnes Smedley,
Harriette Arnow, Doris Lessing, Nadine Gordimer, Sylvia
Ashton-Warner.

In contradiction to the compass of her own distinguished
fiction, Calisher defines the "basic female experience from pu-
berty on through childbed" as women's natural subject:

> For myself the feminism that comes straight from the belly,
> from the bed, and from childbed. A sensibility trusting itself for
> what it is, as the *other* half of basic life.

Constriction to the stereotypic biological-woman (breeder, sex-
partner) sphere. Not only leaving out (what men writers usually
leave out), ongoing motherhood, the maintenance-of-life, and
other angel in the house so determiningly the experience of most

---

*"No Important Woman Writer . . . ," *Mademoiselle,* February 1970. These
excerpts and my exceptions to them are not wholly fair to this superb essay,
which I read originally and quoted from in a copy with an important page
(unnoticed) missing. My abashed apologies to Calisher.

women once they get out of bed and up from childbed, but other common female realities as well.*

And it leaves out the rest of women's biological endowment as born human (including the creative capacity out of which women and men write). *It was the denial of this endowment to live the whole of human life,* the confinement of woman to a sphere, that brought the Women's Rights movement into being in the last century—feminism born of humanism (and that prevented our Calishers from writing throughout centuries).

The acceptance of these age-old constrictive definitions of woman at a time when they are less true than ever to the realities of most women's lives—and need not be true at all—remains a complex problem for women writing in our time. (Mary Wollstonecraft defined it as "the consciousness of being always female which degrades our sex.")

So Anaïs Nin: accepting the constriction to a "feminine sensibility that would not threaten man." Dwelling in the private, the inner; endless vibrations of mood; writing what was muted, exquisite, sensuous, subterranean. That is, in her fiction. In her *Diaries* (along with the narcissistic), the public, the social; power of characterization, penetrating observation, hard intellect, range of experience and relationship; different beauties. Qualities and complexities not present in her fiction—to its impoverishment.

The Bold New Women, to use another example (this from the title of a recent anthology), are the old stereotypic women, depicting themselves within the confines of the sexual-creature, biological-woman literary ghetto; mistaking themselves as new because the sex is explicit as in current male genre; the style and conception of female sexuality, out of Lawrence or Miller. "Whole areas of me are made by the kind of experience women haven't had

---

*Among them: ways in which innate human drives and capacities (intellect; art; organization; invention; sense of justice; love of beauty, life; courage; resilience, resistance; need for community) denied development and scope, nevertheless struggle to express themselves and function; what goes on in jobs; penalties for aging; the profound experience of children—and the agonizing having to raise them in a world not yet fit for human life; what it is to live as a single woman; having to raise children alone; going on; causes besides the accepted psychiatric ones, of breakdown in women. The list goes on and on.

before," reminds Doris Lessing. "Liberty is the right not to lie," says Camus.

These pressures toward censorship, self-censorship; toward accepting, abiding by entrenched attitudes, thus falsifying one's own reality, range, vision, truth, voice, are extreme for women writers (indeed have much to do with the fear, the sense of powerlessness that pervades certain of our books, the "above all, amuse" tone of others). Not to be able to come to one's truth or not to use it in one's writing, even in telling the truth having to "tell it slant," robs one of drive, of conviction; limits potential stature; results in loss to literature and the comprehensions we seek in it.*

My time is up.

You who teach, read writers who are women. There is a whole literature to be re-estimated, revalued. Some works will prove to be, like the lives of their human authors, mortal—speaking only to their time. Others now forgotten, obscured, ignored, will live again for us.

Read, listen to, living women writers; our new as well as our established, often neglected ones. Not to have audience is a kind of death.

Read the compass of women writers in our infinite variety. Not only those who tell us of ourselves as "the other half," but also those who write of the other human dimensions, realms.

Teach women's lives through the lives of the women who wrote the books, as well as through the books themselves; and through autobiography, biography, journals, letters. Because most literature concerns itself with the lives of the few, know and teach the few books closer to the lives of the many. It should not be that Harriette Arnow's *The Dollmaker,* Elizabeth Madox Robert's *Time of Man,* Grace Paley's *Little Disturbances,* are out of paperback print; that a Zora Neale Hurston is reprinted for the first time; that Agnes Smedley's classic *Daughter of Earth,* ** has been

---

*Compounding the difficulty is that experiences and comprehensions not previously admitted into literature—especially when at variance with the canon—are exceedingly hard to come to, validate, establish as legitimate material for literature—let alone, shape into art.

**In 1976 these books are all back in print.

out of print, unread, unknown, for forty years—a book of the greatest meaning, too, for those many students who are the first generation of their families to come into college.

Be critical. Women have the right to say: this is surface, this falsifies reality, this degrades.

Help create writers, perhaps among them yourselves. There is so much unwritten that needs to be written. There are others besides the silenced eleven-out-of-twelve who could bring into literature what is not there now. That first generation of their families to come into college, who come from my world which (in Camus's words) gives "emotion without measure," are a special hope. It does not matter if in its beginning what emerges is not great, or even (as ordinarily defined) "good" writing.

> Whether that is literature, or whether that is not literature, I will not presume to say,

wrote Virginia Woolf in her preface to *Life As We Have Known It, Memoirs of the Working Women's Guild,*

> but that it explains much and tells much, that is certain.

The greatness of literature is not only in the great writers, the good writers; it is also in that which explains much and tells much* (the soil, too, of great literature).

---

*Lessing's description of the novel (in her afterword to Schreiner's *Story of an African Farm*) pertains to this writing which "explains much and tells much": "com[ing] out of a part of the human consciousness which is trying to understand itself, to come into the light. Not on the level where poetry works, or music, or mathematics, the high arts; no, but on the rawest and most workaday level, like earthworms making new soil where things can grow." But there are other forms of expression which can do this, and more: the journal, letters, memoirs, personal utterances—for they come more natural for most, closer to possibility of use, of shaping—and, *in one's own words,* become source, add to the authentic store of human life, human experience. The inestimable value of this, its emergence as a form of literature, is only beginning to be acknowledged. As yet, there is no place in literature analogous to the honored one accorded "folk" and "primitive" expression in art and in music.

Soil or blossom, the hope and intention is that before the end of our second writing century, we will begin to have writers who are women in numbers equal to our innate capacity—at least twelve, for every one writer-woman of recognized achievement now.*

---

*And for every twelve enabled to come to recognized achievement, remember: there would still remain countless others still lessened or silenced—as long as the other age-old silencers of humanity, class and/or color, prevail.

1971, 1972

REBECCA HARDING DAVIS

Her Life and Times

Written as an afterword for the Feminist Press 1972 reprint of the 1861 *Life in the Iron Mills; or, The Korl Woman* by Rebecca Harding Davis (*Atlantic Monthly,* April 1861).

A few notes have been added to the original ones.

You are about to give the life of your reading to a forgotten American classic, Rebecca Harding's Life in the Iron Mills, *reprinted here after 111 years from the April 1861* Atlantic Monthly.

Without precedent or predecessor, it recorded what no one else had recorded; alone in its epoch and for decades to come, saw the significance, the presage, in scorned or unseen native materials—and wrought them into art.

Written in secret and in isolation by a thirty-year-old unmarried woman who lived far from literary circles of any kind, it won instant fame—to sleep in ever deepening neglect to our time.

Remember, as you begin to read of the sullen, clinging industrial smoke, the air thick, clammy with the breath of crowded human beings: this was written when almost everywhere the air was pure; and these lives, hitherto unknown, invisible (though already the lives of millions), are brought here for the first time into literature. *

(So was *Life in the Iron Mills* prefaced in its 1972 republication.)

---

*Excerpts from *Life in the Iron Mills* begin on p. 265. The complete text is available in the Feminist Press reprint.

Until *Life in the Iron Mills* appeared in that April 1861 *Atlantic,* there had been no Blakean dark Satanic mills in American literature; outside of slavery, no working people whose lives were "tragedy . . . a reality of soul starvation . . . living death." There had been no Hugh Wolfes, consumptive puddler in a steel mill, or Debs, hunchbacked cotton mill girl, deformed by work since early childhood at the looms; no slums, kennel-like dwellings, incessant labor, alcoholism; no "is that all of their lives? nothing beneath? all?"; no implicit: *"Wrong, all wrong."*

Nowhere in fiction was industrialization, the significant development that would transform the nation, a concern—nor its consuming of the lives of numberless human beings. No one in literature had opposed the prevalent "American right to rise . . . A man may make himself anything he chooses" with Rebecca Harding's living question: "What are rights without means?"

No one had delineated a Kirby, twelve hundred "hands" in his mill, who would say:

> If I had the making of men, these men who do the lowest part of the world's work should be machines,—nothing more,—hands. It would be kindness. . . . What are taste, reason, to creatures who must live such lives?

—nor had any writers concerned themselves with the shape that taste, reason, might have to take "in such lives."

In the creature, Hugh Wolfe, is "a fierce thirst for beauty,—to know it, to create it; to *be*—something . . . other than he is." Off hours he sculptures crude, powerful shapes out of the pig-iron waste; (dissatisfied, hacks them to pieces afterward). One is a giant korl woman. "She be hungry," he tries to explain to Kirby and his party of sightseers who are "of the mysterious class . . . of another order of being." "Not hungry for meat . . . [For] summat to make her live . . . like you. . . . Whiskey ull do it, in a way."

"Boy, you have it in you to be a great sculptor," Wolfe is told. "Make yourself what you will. It is your right." When the question of means arises, the admirer shortly explains that exercise of rights depends upon money. And adds: "Why should one be raised, when myriads are left?"

Wolfe, the sense of his capacities kindled, sees his life as it "might—but never can, be," (What are rights without means?) "never."

Deborah steals to free him from the mill. "Free. To work, to live, to love. His right." He is caught; judged "by man's law that seizes on one isolated act, not . . . God's justice that weigh[s] the entire life"; sentenced to nineteen years. "Half a lifetime! . . . A hard sentence—all the law allows; but it was for 'xample's sake. These mill hands are gettin' onbearable."

"It was only right," Wolfe thinks, "he had done wrong. But was there right or wrong for such as he? What was right?"

Rather than suffer the lingering death of the penitentiary (he knew "how it went with men there"), with "a dull old bit of tin, not fit to cut korl with," sharpened on the prison bars, he takes his life.

Near the beginning of *Life in the Iron Mills,* the narrator had said:

> There is a secret down here . . . in this nightmare fog. . . . From the very extremity of its darkness, . . . the most solemn prophecy which the world has known of the Hope to come.

The secret is the great capacities hidden in humanity, latent, denied—yet struggling for expression.

The book ends with one of the oldest of human symbols, the promise of dawn.*

---

*These prefatory remarks have been especially written for this reprint of the 1971 "Afterword," which follows.

Life in the Iron Mills was not written out of compassion or condescending pity. Rebecca Harding wrote it in absolute identification with "thwarted, wasted lives . . . mighty hungers . . . unawakened power"; circumstances that denied use of capacities; imperfect, self-tutored art that could have only odd moments for its doing—as if these were her own. And they were—however differently embodied in the life of a daughter of the privileged class.

It was in front of the Harding house that the long train of mules dragged their masses of pig iron and the slow stream of human life of the story crept past, night and morning, year after year, to work their twelve- to fourteen-hour shift, the six or seven days a week. The little girl who observed them grew into womanhood, into (near) spinsterhood, still at the window in that house, and the black industrial smoke was her daily breath.

The town was Wheeling, on the Ohio, in the border slave state of what was then Virginia. When the Harding family moved there in 1836 (Rebecca was five), it was one of only a handful of steel towns in the nation. All her growing years, the slave South, the free North; the industrial future, the agrarian present, the wilderness that was once all the past—were uniquely commingled here. In the streets, farmers were as familiar a sight as Irish and Cornish steelworkers, slaves, free blacks, commercial travelers, bargemen, draymen, Indians, and rawboned mountain people in to work at the mills.

Over the country's single north-south National Road, snaking mostly through wilderness to this halting point, came huge vans with cotton bales for Northern mills, returning with manufactures for the South; stagecoaches carrying passengers to and from the river boats that connected St. Louis and New Orleans with the East; and Conestoga wagons with emigrants, or immigrants still in European dress, heading west. And over all—through the night and morning river mists, through the constant changes of light— was a sense of vast unpeopled distance from the hills that curved fold on fold far as eye could see.

"These sights and sounds did not come common to her." The slow-moving thoughtful Rebecca absorbed them into herself with the quiet intensity that marked all her confrontation with life, and with an unshared sense of wonder, of mystery.

She was the eldest of five children. Her father, Richard W. Harding, a successful businessman, later City Treasurer, hated "vulgar American life" and its world of business, secluding himself evenings for what he did love: reading Elizabethan literature, mostly Shakespeare. "He was English and homesick," Rebecca wrote of him years later. "We were not intimate with him as with our mother." The household revolved around him. Her mother, Rachel Leet Wilson Harding ("the most accurate historian I ever knew, with enough knowledge to outfit a dozen modern college-educated women"), was kept busy with an ever increasing family and running the large household noiselessly.

It was a house that had servants, perhaps slaves, for necessary tasks. Public schools did not yet exist. Rebecca's mother did the early teaching, and later there were occasional tutors, usually brought in for her brothers. Rebecca rambled; she read. The books (Maria Edgeworth, Bunyan, Scott) were of a remote world of pilgrims, knights and ladies, magic, crusaders. But once, in her soot-specked cherry tree hideout, in a new collection of *Moral Tales* (it was years before she discovered the anonymous author was Hawthorne), she found three unsigned stories about an ordinary American town, everyday sights and sounds, the rambles of a little girl like herself.* She read and reread them so often that "I know almost every line of them by heart, even now." In them her own secret feelings, so opposite to those of her complex, austere father, were verified: that "the commonplace folk and things which I saw every day had mystery and charm ... belonged to the magic world [of books] as much as knights and pilgrims."

When she was fourteen (an age when most Wheeling girls had already been working in the mills or as domestic slaveys for years), Rebecca was sent—not too far away—to live with her mother's sister in Washington, Pennsylvania, to attend the three-year Female Seminary there and be "finished."

---

*The tales were: "Rill from the Town Pump," "Little Annie's Rambles," and "Sunday at Home." Some time after publication Hawthorne wrote to Longfellow: "I feel that I have nothing but thin air to connect from. Sometimes through a peephole I have caught a glimpse of the real world. . . . These three stories please me most."

"Of all cursed places under the sun, where the hungriest soul can hardly pick up a few grains of knowledge," Olive Schreiner writes of that century, "a girls' boarding-school is the worst. . . . They finish everything but imbecility and weakness, and that they cultivate. They are nicely adapted machines for experimenting on the question, 'Into how little space can a human soul be crushed?' "*

Probably the indictment is too severe in this instance, but certainly it was not an atmosphere conducive to learning, development, attainment. The ardent "hunger to know" (later ascribed to Hugh Wolfe and other of her fictional people) was already deep in Rebecca. She was eager for companions, for stimulus, exploration, range, substance.

Little of substance beyond religion and "soft attractive graces" was offered the young ladies. "Enough math to do accounts, enough astronomy to point out constellations, a little music and drawing, and French, history, literature at discretion" is how Rebecca describes it.

Nor did she find satisfactory companionship. For all her classmates' shocked delight at her irreverent wit, Rebecca's very seriousness of purpose and "hunger to know" set her apart.

Still it was a larger world than home. It was a college town, site of (the all male, of course) Washington College. There were more books, more current literature available. Speakers came through regularly on the college circuit, and sometimes Seminary girls were permitted to attend. There was a bracing sense of currents

---

*The Story of an African Farm, 1883.

In Eminent Women of the Age (1869), Elizabeth Cady Stanton says of the far superior seminary she attended: "If there is any one thing on earth from which I pray God to save my daughters, it is a girls' seminary. The two years which I spent in one were the dreariest years of my whole life." And in the same book, in regard to the seminary schooling of a contemporary, sculptor Harriet Hosmer, writes: "Public sentiment . . . as to the education of girls prevails . . ." that they should be

"Ground down enough
To flatten and bake into a wholesome crust
For household uses and proprieties."

and concerns of the time, and the stimulation of hearing famous figures such as Horace Greeley.

And there was Francis LeMoyne, the town physician, radical reformer, agnostic, abolitionist (their vice-presidential candidate in 1840). "He should have lived in a . . . great arena. . . . He had the power for any work." Unquestionably, the most challenging experience of those years was her acquaintance with him.*

This "uncouth mass of flesh," "mad against Destiny . . . unconquerable ills," "smothered rights and triumphant wrongs," "inflamed with the needs and sufferings of . . . countless lives" brought to Rebecca a troubling sense of "a gulf of pain and wrong . . . the under-life of America," and deepened her childhood feeling of something of great mystery and portent in this "vulgar" everyday American life.

Fourteen years later, in her first novel, *Margret Howth,* she was still trying to come to terms with the meaning of LeMoyne's radical life and beliefs, so diametrically opposed to the precepts and assumptions of her own upbringing.

She graduated as valedictorian, still hungry to know. The "larger life" away from home was over. It was 1848. She was seventeen. Even had she wanted to go on with education, there was but one college in the entire country that would admit a female, the scandalous, unthinkable (abolitionist) Oberlin. The massed social structure prescribed one sphere, one vocation for a woman of her class: domestic—marriage, or serving as daughter, sister, aunt where needed. Only in case of extreme economic necessity did a girl or woman of her class live away from home, with but one "respectable" occupation open to her—teaching (at a third of a man's pay).

That summer, a few hundred miles north at Seneca Falls, the first women's rights convention in the world was being held. Their Declaration spoke of the situation of women as:

---

*Rebecca writes of him directly in *Bits of Gossip,* a volume of reminiscences (1904). The LeMoyne family home in Washington, Pennsylvania, is now a historical museum, centering mostly on Dr. LeMoyne.

The succeeding quotations are from *Margret Howth.*

a history of repeated injuries and usurpations on the part of man toward woman. . . . He has monopolized nearly all profitable employments, and from those she is permitted to follow, she receives but a scanty remuneration. He closes against her all avenues to wealth and distinction which he considers most honorable to himself. . . . He has denied her the facilities for obtaining a thorough education, all colleges being closed against her. . . . He has endeavored, in every way that he could, to destroy her confidence in her own powers, to lessen her self-respect, and make her willing to lead a dependent and abject life.

It is doubtful that Rebecca read the Declaration. Even if she had, it is doubtful that the seventeen-year-old girl would have seen in it a description of her circumstances. To her they were personal, singular; something awry, unnatural *in her* to harbor needs, interests, longings for which there seemed no place or way or precedent.

She was a dark, vigorous, sturdily built girl, with a full, handsome face that decades later was to become the most admired, sketched, photographed face of its generation in the person of her famous son Richard. In her own time, when what was prized in female features was delicacy, her appearance was probably considered unfortunate—for a girl. Her manner was direct, "unvarnished," quiet.

The Wheeling to which she returned, and in which she was to be immured for the next thirteen years, was not Boston, nor Amherst, nor Concord—nor even Washington, Pennsylvania, with college circuit lectures, traveling theater, a Francis Le-Moyne. It was a yeasty, booming industrial town of nearly 13,000 people, but with no intellectual or literary circles of any kind. The fever for gold, just beginning in California, had long dominated here; the heavy industrial smoke, manifesting its own kind of gold dust, pervaded more than the atmosphere.

The social life open to Rebecca in her own class was with young men intent on making the most of the possibilities for "getting on," and with young women whose concern—natural under the circumstances of but one sanctioned vocation—was with getting asked into the most advantageous possible marriage. All social activities were calculated toward these ends. Rebecca did not involve herself in the expected social round.

Whatever the reasons were—subtle family ones,* the lonely pull of obviously unshared interests—among them must have been Rebecca's refusal to remain in situations of emptiness, of falsity, of injuries to her sense of selfhood** where there was choice. She stayed almost exclusively within the family circle.

As the eldest daughter in a large household, even one with servants, there was much help to be given her mother in the commonplace, necessary tasks of caring for family needs, younger children; keeping the atmosphere pleasant, especially for her father. The bonds of love were strong—she writes of "the protection and peace of home"—but they were not bonds of mutuality. She had to keep her longings, questionings, insurrections, secret.

She could not even freely discuss literature. She had come home excited over living native writers. "We were in the first flush of our triumph in the beginnings of a national literature . . . these new men—Holmes and Lowell and Hawthorne—were our own, the indigenous growth of the soil." To her father, all literature had ended with Shakespeare; the United States was incapable of culture. No other viewpoint was expressible.

Nor was there any of LeMoyne's concern with "the unhelped pain of life." All through the fifties—that earthquake decade of antislavery, bleeding Kansas, women's rights, the fugitive slave law, Dred Scott, John Brown, the struggle for a ten-hour workday—her family and its circle stayed removed, indifferent, when not hostile. Except through reading, Rebecca was shut in their narrowness. She tells of one family, "radicals, believers in divorce and women's rights, refusing to eat sugar or use cotton" (products of slavery), furthermore visited by John Brown. Naturally they were "social outcasts." Rebecca did not question the taboo.

---

*Her father may have preferred to keep her home, as fathers of the time—including some fathers of famous literary women—often did. Think of Elizabeth Barrett (Browning), Emily Dickinson, Charlotte Brontë, Mary Ann Evans (George Eliot).

**"I know that if women wish to escape the stigma of husband-seeking, they must act and look like marble or clay-cold-expressionless, bloodless—for every appearance of feeling of joy-sorrow-friendliness, antipathy, admiration-disgust are alike construed by the world into an attempt to hook in a husband." —Charlotte Brontë, as a young woman of about Rebecca's age to her friend Ellen Nussey.

Thirteen years are to go by before the seventeen-year-old girl-valedictorian emerges as the thirty-year-old author of *Life in the Iron Mills*. Shrouded years. The outward, known facts are so few, it is to the writings one must turn to piece together what those thirteen years must have been.

In Rebecca's first published fiction, there is a gallery of girls before marriage, devoted to their families, especially their usually difficult fathers. They are "hungry to make some use of themselves, . . . undergoing fierce struggles to tame and bind to some unfitting work, the power within."* They responsibly carry out household tasks "though heart and brain need more than this." Unlike those dear to them, they are "hurt" by

> the filth, injustice, bafflings in the world . . . she [Dode] never glossed them over as "necessity," or shirked them as we do: she cried hot, weak tears, . . . over the wrongs of the slaves about her, her old father's ignorance, her own cramped life . . . these passion-fits were the only events of her life.

Throughout her work, there is another recurrent figure: proud, vulnerable young women, subjected to indignities and rejection because their appearance and being do not fit the prevailing standards of female beauty or behavior. Young men say to them patronizingly: "You are built for use, but not for show." They are made to feel shame for their energy and strength, which "they cannot remember to dissemble into fragility that appeals." They are penalized because they cannot "blush and flutter and plume themselves when a man comes near." They are "freaks" for their "rare sincerity" or "seriousness."

If they attract, they at the same time repel:

> He took her short, thick hand in his delicate fingers, but dropped it again quickly. The fiery spirit in his veins rose to meet the heat in hers . . . but he really could not bear to see a young girl with a paw shaped like a man's.

When they love, it is in an agony of intensity—love most often unspoken, or despised; or if mutual, having to be denied.

---

*Quotations in this and the next five paragraphs are from *David Gaunt, Margret Howth, Earthen Pitchers, John Andross,* and *A Law Unto Herself.*

There are older women, realizing that theirs is to be the social obloquy of the unchosen, the unmarried, "loathing themselves as one whom God had thought unworthy of every woman's right— to love and be loved, . . . their strength drying up within them, jeered at, utterly alone." "We laugh at their trial," Rebecca goes on to say. "I think the quick fagots at the stake were fitter subjects for laughter." Like the younger women, they school themselves to maintain dignity, integrity; they armor, imprison themselves in "the great power of reticence."

There is nothing sexless about them. They suffer physically as well as socially. Their "hopeless thirst is freshly bitter." Margret Howth "kindles at the look or touch" of the man she unrequitedly loves "as if her veins were filled with subtile flame."

With Rebecca's younger women, they comprise the most openly physical women in the fiction of the time. Here is a bride-to-be, dressing up as the month of June, "the moist warm month," for a costume party:

> Some tranced summer's day might have drowsed down into such a human form . . . on the thick grass-crusted meadows. There was the full contour of the limbs hid under warm green folds, the white flesh that glowed when you touched it as if some smothered heat lay beneath, the snaring eyes, the sleeping face, the amber hair uncoiled in a languid quiet, while yellow jasmine deepened its hue into molten sunshine, and a great tiger-lily laid its sultry head on her breast.

And always there is the vein of "unused powers, thwarted energies, starved hopes"; the hunger for a life more abundant than in women's sanctioned sphere—one in the full human context of Hugh Wolfe's definition: "A true life is one of full development of faculties."

Clues? Autobiography? Of a sort. There is enough correspondence to outward fact, and if all was not experienced directly, it went deep enough to be carefully and caringly recorded.

But of what is most singular in those thirteen years—the development of that girl in her cramped life, fiercely struggling to tame and bind to some unfitting work the power within; of what made it a cramped life; of how she faced down the harm and maimings of her personal situation, the self-scorn, the thwartings; and— fitted in between tasks and family needs, in secret and in isolation, without literary friendship and its encouragement—developed an ear, a discipline, made of herself a writer; *against the prevalent, found her own subject:* of this there is scarcely a word.

The "hunger to know" and for "summat to make her live" must have gone on, unsatisfied. Like Emily Dickinson, in withdrawing from the social round she created some measure of time for herself beyond the inescapable family pulls and responsibilities; and she was of those rare fortunate who had "a room of one's own." When her brother Wilson went to Washington College—where, unlike the Female Seminary, the courses had to have substance and range —she set herself to studying the books and subjects she had not had, giving herself his lessons. Then that too was over. She writes somewhere of "the curse of an education one cannot use."

She continued to read avidly. But books, for all their companionship, could only have intensified the sense of constriction, of waste, of the unattainable. Like the young Harriet Beecher (not yet Stowe) at the same age and in somewhat similar circumstances: "thought, intense emotional thought" became a "disease."*

Almost the first sentence in *Life in the Iron Mills* is: "I open the window, and looking out . . ." She must have opened her window and looked out at the life beyond her a great deal in those years. (Something of this must have fed the sense of unattainable longing, the intensity of sight, sound, emotion, the impulse to art that she conveys near the end of *Life in the Iron Mills* where Hugh presses his face to the rusty prison bars and looks out.)

Year after year, Rebecca saw changes: the factories and mills spreading over more and more of the landscape, thieving the farms; the coming of the first railroad, the Baltimore & Ohio; coal mine smoke beginning to stain the once pure mists over the Appalachians; the Ohio River darkening with wastes; the throngs and traffic in the streets, thickening; and always, night and morning, the workers on their way to or from the mills.

And she walked. Not the carefree rambles of childhood, for she was encumbered now by the steel-ribbed corsets and dragging

---

*"All that is enthusiastic, all that is impassioned in admiration of nature, of writing, of character, or in the motions of affection, I have felt with vehement and absorbing intensity—felt till my mind is exhausted and seems to be sinking into deadness. Half of my time I am glad to remain in a listless vacancy, to busy myself with tasks, since thought is pain and emotion is pain."

skirts of her sex and class,* the restrictions as to where she might go and how she must behave. She walked in stupor, in vacancy, in self-scorn; walking off a "passion-fit" or seeking release from the walls of family; in joy of motion, the one active exercise of a lady's body permissible, or "in an ecstasy of awareness . . . in the peopled maze of the streets." Walking was her travel, her adventure, her transaction with the world—living substance for her idling intellect and imagination. It is significant that much of *Life in the Iron Mills* and *Margret Howth* takes place during walks.

At some point she began secretly, seriously, to write. Whatever the roots, all might have fallen away into silence as with nearly all women before her, but the times were nurturing. Writing was being demonstrated as the one profession it was possible to carry on within the sphere, the one male domain in which there was beginning to be undeniable, even conspicuous, success by women. The upswelling Women's Rights movement had created an atmosphere, a challenge, an interest.

Eighteen hundred and fifty, the year Rebecca was nineteen, began the decade called by literary historians "the feminine fifties."** Two years before, *Jane Eyre* had appeared, with its

---

*"The present regime to which custom dooms the sex: steel-ribbed corsets with hoops, heavy skirts, trains, high heels, panniers, chignons and dozens of hairpins sticking in our scalps; cooped up in the house year after year with no exhilarating exercise, no hopes, aims nor ambitions."—Lucy Stone in a debate at Oberlin.

Such clothing was a mark of class distinction. Contrast it with the "half clothed" cotton mill girls at the beginning of *Iron Mills,* or indeed, the dress of most women of that time: farm, slave, and working class.

** . . . which it was not.

Though Hawthorne complained in a letter to his publisher of "the damned mob of female scribblers," the field was dominated by men: editors, publishers, and staff were men; the overwhelming number of novels, stories, articles, were still being written by men. The comparatively few women writers were conspicuous because they were a new phenomenon, for the first time in any numbers successful, recognized. And the Women's Rights movement had focused attention on women. The 1850s was the decade of Whitman, Thoreau, Melville, Hawthorne, Dana, Emerson, Lowell, Holmes, Whittier, though not all had popular fame.

Fred Pattee, the literary historian who affixed the label "feminine fifties," writes that he did so because ten words characterized the decade: "Fervid, fevered, furious, fatuous, fertile, feeling, florid, furbelowed, fighting, funny"— and the "single adjective that would combine them all" is "feminine."

unprecedented heroine who was plain and earned her own living and was rebelliously conscious of unused powers, restrictions because of her sex. Harriet Beecher Stowe's *Uncle Tom's Cabin,* which reached and affected more readers the world over than any work of fiction before (or since), came out in 1852. Grace Greenwood and Fanny Fern (Sara Willis Parton), joined later by the devastating Gail Hamilton, were earning splendid and well-publicized incomes with their writing. Parton's *Ruth Hall* (1855) stunned readers, including an admiring Hawthorne, with its account of the struggles of a woman genius against poverty and prejudice. For the first time, year after year, there were successful novels by women. Contrary to received opinion, in its first high tide this "feminine" writing was predominantly serious—about something—not romantic fluff or sentimental slush.

The ardor, "the fierce thirst for beauty, to know it, to create it, to be something other than [she] was," turned in this direction. At first, Rebecca says, she "rashly" tried her hand at "idylls delicately tinted . . . heroines in white dresses that never need washing . . . deep-dyed villains, full-blooded saints . . . dark conspiracies, women rare and radiant in Italian bowers." "I never was there," she says. "I am willing to do my best, but I live in the commonplace."

She *chose* to live in the commonplace, this commonplace that was nowhere in books. Her changing changing Wheeling, the huge mills, the new men of power: owners, managers, whom she observed obliquely in her father's house; the despised, ignored life she saw from her windows, mingled among in the streets; "filth, injustice, bafflings," "vulgar American life." All those years of seeming vacancy and waste, they had drawn her more and more with LeMoyne's sense of great portent, great meaning, hid within them.

Now in this dazzling possibility of expression, use, she came to this as subject. Without realizing it, she had the advantage of the writer's deepest questions: what is happening here, what does this mean? Of the "massed, vile, slimy lives" she asked, "Is that all of their lives? nothing beneath? all?"*

---

*The "Is that all of their lives?" may well have been partially roused by the determined struggles of working people—all through the 1850s—for a ten-hour workday. These must have been strongly visible in Wheeling.

But this "commonplace" was outside the permitted sphere. She was house-bound, class-bound, sex-bound; there was no way of natural, direct (participatory) access to the worlds of work and power for her.

It is almost impossible for us at a later, freer time, to conceive the difficulties of accumulating the dense accretion of significant details out of which *Life in the Iron Mills* springs so terribly to life* (details that could no more come out of books than do Wolfe or, for that matter, Clarke, Kirby, May, Mitchell).

Perhaps only once was Rebecca able to take Deborah's night walk to the "city of fires." She would not have been permitted to go unescorted, or to linger, or to initiate or participate too actively in any conversation. In homes such as the Hardings', labor relations, politics, gritty subjects, were not discussed around the ladies socially. How did she come then by the observation, the knowledge, of the incomparable rainy night mill scene with its seizing descriptions and its unequaled encompassing of various class attitudes? How, too, did she come to know the fetid kennel-like room where the Wolfes lived, with its slimy moss-covered earth floor; and the dress, the differing talk and *beings* of its potato eaters?

She must have had to use "trespass vision," eavesdrop, ponder everything, dwell within it with all the resources of intellect *and imagination;* literally make of herself (in Henry James's famous phrase) "one on whom nothing is lost." Each walk, each encounter, had to be freighted with significance, each opportunity for knowing seized. More, with demeaning, painful, excited stratagem, she must have had to *create* opportunities for knowledge; and for a knowing relationship with those outside the bounds of her class.

And in the process, the noting of reality was transformed into comprehension, Vision.

In *Margret Howth,* she writes of Lo (Lois), a black peddler girl, crippled in a cotton mill accident:

---

*"... the starry leap from the springboard of exact observation."

. . . this creature, that Nature had thrown impatiently aside as a
failure, so marred, imperfect . . . came strangely near to her [Mar-
gret], claimed recognition by some subtle instinct . . . some strange
sympathy drew her to this poor wretch, dwarfed, alone in the
world,—some tie of equality.

Some tie of equality, of kinship. The subtle recognition that
these were not of a lower order, but human beings like herself,
capable of—with the right to—but denied circumstances for full
development. As Hugh saw himself, she saw them. *As they might
be.*

Her father had maintained that tragedy could have only to
do with the noble, the high born. But she recognized that this
misuse of human beings by industry *was* tragedy, "terrible
tragedy, a reality of soul (and body) starvation, of living
death." And "from the very extremity of its darkness, the
most solemn prophecy which the world has known of the
Hope to come." *As they might be.*

"I want to make it a real thing for you. . . . You, busy in making
straight paths for your feet on the hills."

It may have taken her years to embody her vision. "Hewing
and hacking," like Hugh, "working at one figure for months
and, when it was finished, breaking it to pieces in a fit of disappointment." Writing, discarding, trying again. Often the
effort and the transport must have seemed a kind of insanity, a
vain delusion. There was nothing or no one outside herself to
verify or justify it. Only the Vision, and the need to make it a
real thing.

When at last it was done, she did not know what to call it:
a story? a parable? an article? It was not like any of these.
Furthermore, the only magazine she could think of that might
possibly publish something so different was also the most un-
likely: the *Atlantic Monthly,* the most prestigious, influential
magazine of the day. Revered by readers and writers alike, the
great of the time, Emerson, Thoreau, Lowell, Stowe, Holmes,
Whittier, appeared regularly in it. But it also published odd
things, new things; had indicated it would welcome material
dealing with "real life"; and had shown friendliness to

women—rights and writers.*   Rebecca sent the piece there.

A letter came back in January 1861. She carried it around "half a day without opening it, being so sure it would be a refusal." Instead it was a laudatory acceptance, signed for the editorial board by the publisher himself, James T. Fields. Fifty dollars— a huge sum then—was enclosed in payment, the first paid earnings of all her thirty years.

They had but a single suggestion for change: the name of the "story" was not "taking" enough. In that case, Rebecca wrote back, the *article* could be called "The Korl Woman" or "Beyond"; but she still preferred "Life in the Iron Mills." And that her name not be revealed as author. No hint of the tumult of joy she must have felt at their acceptance, the sense of vindication of years of solitary effort. The great power of reticence managed two sentences: "Your letter is kind, and gave me much pleasure," and "I thank you for your encouragement."

They wrote back, again lauding the story. They wanted more work; they wanted exclusive rights to everything she wrote; they offered $100 at once toward anything she might write in the future.

"I see that the novelty of the scene of the story has made you overestimate me; another most probably would disappoint you." As for the advance, no. "If I were writing with a hundred dollar bill before me, the article would be broad and deep just $100 and no more—dollarish all over."

She did not say that in a fever of work, wrought up by the confirming recognition and by the possibility of further publication, she was writing (or perhaps had gone back to writing) some-

---

*"The supremacy of the *Atlantic* was unquestioned. To have published . . . in it . . . was to be known among writers all over the country. It was a force . . . setting the critical standard and spreading suggestions."

To Emily Dickinson it was "a temple." To appear in it was a true accolade, and guaranteed a wide and distinguished audience. It was the first to use the expression "realism." One of its editors, Thomas Wentworth Higginson, a great and influential male champion of women's rights, actively promoted the development and publication of women writers. An *Atlantic* article of his—"Women and the Alphabet"—was credited with resulting directly in the founding of Smith College and the opening of the University of Michigan to women.

thing else—a longer, more ambitious piece that would give her greater scope. Hugh Wolfe's cry (her cry), "Wrong, it's all wrong," was again to be authenticated; the portent and vision of *Life in the Iron Mills* made more manifest; the tie of equality made flesh and blood. There was still the troubling, radical figure of Francis LeMoyne to write of, he who thirteen years ago had given her her first awareness of the gulf of pain and wrong outside herself, who had insisted that work for change was the only worthy way to live. The dialogues between LeMoyne and her father had gone on in her head all these years; she would translate them into fiction. And there were the "new men" of power to be more fully delineated; and love, female sacrifice, the embittering scorn, unknowingness of society toward women not married, all to be written.

The three-hundred-page novel, *A Story of Today* (afterward called *Margret Howth*), was near completion when *Life in the Iron Mills* appeared.

To the readers of that April 1891 *Atlantic, Life in the Iron Mills* came as absolute News, with the shock of unprepared-for revelation.

(To repeat:) in the consciousness of literary America, there had been no dark satanic mills;* outside of slavery, no myriads of

---

*Yet by 1860, one of every seven Americans were mine and mill "hands," who lived and worked in circumstances like Deb and Hugh.

There had been a white Satanic mill, the paper factory in Herman Melville's "Tantalus of Maids," sequel to "Paradise of Bachelors" (*Harper's,* 1855). It left no impress, perhaps because it was written as sexual analogy. As for furnace fires, they burned but three times before in American literature: in that small hillside lime kiln where Hawthorne's Ethan Brand incinerated himself for his Unpardonable Sin—(the separation of the intellect from the heart); in the "try works" on the "red hell" of the "Pequod" in Melville's *Moby Dick;* and in occasional descriptive lines in Whitman's "Crossing Brooklyn Ferry," "A Song for Occupations," and "A Song of Joys":

> The fires from the foundry chimneys burning
>   high and glaringly into the night,
> Casting their flicker of black contrasted
>   with wild red and yellow light over the
>   tops of houses, and down into the clefts
>   of streets.

No satanic mills. The human being is omitted. Contrast the critiques of the machine, of industry, of materialism in that period, with that in *Life in the Iron*

human beings whose lives were "terrible tragedy . . . a reality of soul starvation, of living death." When industry was considered at all, it was as an invasion of pastoral harmony, a threat of materialism to the *spirit*. If working people (again, outside of slavery) existed—and nowhere were they material for serious attention, let alone central subject—they were "clean-haired Yankee mill girls," "mind[s] among the spindles," or Whitman's

> workwomen and workmen of these States having your own divine
> and strong life . . .

"Life lies about us dumb," Emerson had written. "How few materials are yet used by our arts. The mass of creatures and of qualities are still hid and expectant." This reality, hitherto "dumb . . . secret . . . in this nightmare fog," verified him beyond expectation with its crowding of implications, troublings, its new themes and types, images, sounds. smells, dictions.

Life in the Iron Mills was an instant sensation; it was recognized as a literary landmark. A wide and distinguished audience, shaken by its power and original vision, spoke of it as a work of genius.

Far off in her native Wheeling, little of this acclaim reached Rebecca. Forwarded letters began to arrive, but her first real indication of the impact her work was having came with a note from Hawthorne, Hawthorne himself, the author of those three anonymous tales she had memorized as a child. He was in Washington, would be going on to Harpers Ferry, and might he come on from there to meet her?

"Well, I suppose Esther felt a little in that way when the king's scepter touched her," Rebecca wrote.

Hawthorne never came. The Civil War had broken out; the railroad was cut.

Much else was severed. Virginia seceded. Wheeling became the center of pro-Union loyalties, soon the capital of self-proclaimed free New (later West) Virginia. Martial law was declared; the local theater turned into a jail; an island in the river, visible from

---

Mills and *Margret Howth*. Instead of "things are in the saddle and ride mankind," Rebecca Harding alone concerned herself with the wrong of how those making the things were being ridden.

Rebecca's window, a prison camp. The house directly across the street from the Hardings' was commandeered for General Rosecrans's Union Army Western Department headquarters.

Rebecca's brother Dick, along with several other young men of the Harding circle, made plans to join the Secessionists. They were talked out of it only at the last minute by the mayor: "It would ruin their families . . . he spoke particularly of Pa," Rebecca wrote a cousin.

And in the midst of this, in mid-May, Fields sent back *A Story of Today:* "It assembles the gloom too depressingly."

Rebecca's letter reveals how shaken she was. She begged Fields to tell her "if that was the only objection, the one you assign?" She "thanked him for candor and kindness." She asked: "If you do not think I could alter the story, shall I try again, or do you care to have me as a contributor?"

He wrote back at once, assuring her that the *Atlantic* wanted very much to keep her—and suggesting that she dispel some of the gloom, then resubmit the book. Fearful lest he lose his great discovery, he asked his young wife, Annie, to write also—a letter of such strong intelligent admiration, it was the start of Rebecca's closest and most supporting literary friendship, though in this beginning, not necessarily in the right direction. "I will try to meet Mr. Fields' wishes of being more cheerful," Rebecca agreed, "though humor had need to be as high as God's sunshine to glow cheerily on Virginia soil just now."

What made her agree? Isolated, had she so little confidence in her own judgment? Was the terror of the oblivion from which she was just emerging so great, the need for the verification publication gives so compelling? Was she (a woman in that day) so afraid of jeopardizing the one way seemingly open to independence, occupation, public esteem, self-worth?

At just this time, one of Rebecca's literary admirers, L. Clarke Davis, already a regular correspondent, wrote asking her to contribute to a new Philadelphia magazine, *Peterson's,* for which he was a reader. It would be a different kind of writing—entertainment not literature.

Perhaps *Life in the Iron Mills had* been a fluke, "the novelty of the scene," and not the achievement she had tried to make it, had believed it to be. Perhaps the merit of *A Story of Today* was self-delusion too, as was her being worthy of a place in the exalted *Atlantic* company. She promised to write for *Peterson's*.

For six weeks Rebecca struggled with the revision of *A Story of Today*. Without the original manuscript, there is no way of knowing what the gloom was that she dispelled, and how much was marred and lost thereby; how much of the imperfect working out of character, the marks of haste and of patching, are in the original, how much the result of shaken judgment in a revision having to be made, furthermore, under "the shadow of death," "from the border of the battlefield."

In the beginning, she defends the very concerns of the book:

> The shadow of death has fallen on us. . . . Do not call us traitors . . . who choose to be cool and silent through the fever of the hour, —who choose to search in common things for auguries . . . hint that there are yet other characters besides that of Patriot in which a man may appear creditably. . . .
>
> I want you to go down into this common every-day drudgery . . . and consider if there might not be in it also a great warfare. . . . It has its slain. Men and women, lean-jawed, crippled in the slow, silent battle, are in your alleys.

Margret Howth has gone into a textile mill as a bookkeeper to "support a helpless father and mother. It was a common story."* Holmes, the man she loves and who loves her, has broken off their secret engagement.

> He had turned his back on love and kindly happiness and warmth, on all that was weak and useless in the world. . . . All men around him were doing the same,—thrusting and jostling and struggling up, up. It was the American motto, Go ahead; mothers taught it to their children; the whole system was a scale of glittering prizes. He at least saw the higher meaning of the truth.

---

*She is one of Rebecca's precedents, the first "working girl" heroine in American fiction, and shown in her working habitat. Even the occupation is ahead of its time. Women bookkeepers were exceptional; keeping books was primarily a man's occupation then.

He is "one of the new men who will mould the age."

Knowles (not too successfully modeled after Doctor LeMoyne), Margret's employer and the mill owner, is in the process of selling his mill. "His veins thick with the blood of a despised race"—he is part Indian—"a disciple of Garrison, you know," he plans to use the money to organize in "the great city, with its stifling gambling hells, its negro-pens, its foul cellars," and to make available a communal "new Arcadia." It is for this work he seeks Margret's help.

"You will fail, Knowles," predicts Margret's blind father (long-time adversary to Knowles, as Rebecca's father was to LeMoyne):

> ". . . any plan, Phalanstery or Community, call it what you please, founded on self-government, is based on . . . the tawdriest of shams. . . . There never was a thinner-crusted Devil's egg in the world than democracy. . . .
>
> "Any despotism is better than that of newly enfranchised serfs. . . . Your own phantom, your Republic, your experiment to prove that all men are born free and equal—what is it to-day?"

"Don't sneer at Knowles," the author says:

> Your own clear, tolerant brain, that reflects all men and creeds alike, like colorless water, drawing the truth from all, is very different, doubtless, from this narrow, solitary soul, who thought the world waited for him to fight down . . . evil. . . . An intolerant fanatic, of course. But the truth he did know was so terribly real to him. . . . And then, fanatics must make history for conservative men to learn from, I suppose.

From Knowles, and from the black peddler Lo with whom she feels the tie of identity, Margret glimpses and feels the "unhelped pain of life." During an early morning walk with Lo, memorable for the descriptive immediacy of the changing mists, the transition from the countryside's beauty into the city slums where Margret works, Lo, in the closeness of shared response, tells Margret of how her childhood in the mill deformed her:

> It was a good while I was there: from seven year old till sixteen. 'T seemed longer t' me 'n 't was. 'T seemed as if I'd been there allus,

—jes' forever, yoh know . . . like as I was part o' th' engines, somehow. Th' air used to be thick in my mouth, black wi' smoke 'n' wool 'n' smells.

In them years I got dazed in my head, I think. 'T was th' air 'n' th' work. . . . 'T got so that th' noise o' th' looms went on in my head night 'n' day,—allus thud, thud. 'N' hot days, when th' hands was chaffin' 'n' singin', th' black wheels 'n' rollers was alive, starin' down at me, 'n' th' shadders o' th' looms was like snakes creepin', —creepin' anear all th' time.

As Margret and Knowles later walk the city, he looks

about him as into a seething caldron in which . . . the blood of uncounted races was fused . . . where creeds, philosophies, centuries old, grappled hand to hand in their death-struggle,—where innumerable aims and beliefs and powers of intellect, smothered rights and triumphant wrongs, warred together, struggling for victory.

Vulgar American life? He thought it a life more potent, more tragic in its history and prophecy, than any that has gone before.

They go to a hovel, a temporary one-room refuge he has established,

swarming with human life. Women, idle trampers, whiskey-bloated, filthy, lay half-asleep, or smoking, on the floor. . . . Half-naked children crawled about in rags. . . . In the corner slept a heap of half-clothed blacks. Going on the underground railroad to Canada.

"Did I call it a bit of hell? [Knowles rages.] It's only a glimpse of the under-life of America,—God help us!—where all men are born free and equal . . .

"And you," he said, savagely, "you sit by the road-side, with help in your hands, and Christ in your heart, and call your life lost, quarrel with your God, because that mass of selfishness has left you. . . . Look at these women. What is *their* loss, do you think? Go back, will you, and drone out your life whimpering over your lost dream, and go to Shakespeare for tragedy when you want it? Tragedy! Come here,—let me hear what you call this."

Lo, much mourned, dies from burns after a fire set in the mills by her father, who has been hounded as an ex-convict. Knowles, an old man now, has no money left to finance his dreams.

The tacked-on happy ending is grotesquely evident, a contrived reformation, out of it true love triumphing: the success-is-all Holmes converts to plainer, older virtues; Margret, obeying "the law of her woman's nature" marries him and gives up working for social change. There is even an oil well opportunely gushing up in the back yard to keep them from poverty.

It is an awkward book, sometimes embarrassingly bad. Nevertheless, it is also a rewarding, fascinatingly native book of substance and power. It accomplishes much of what Rebecca set out to do in that first ardent fever of work after the *Atlantic*'s acceptance. Essential reading for any literary or social historian concerned with the period, *Margret Howth: A Story of Today* justifies re-evaluation, perhaps resurrection.

Fields had the revision back at the end of July and accepted it at once. Rebecca hastily concocted the promised mystery novel for *Peterson's*. Then she stopped writing.

She could no longer "search in common things for auguries." That "poor everyday warfare for bread" could not hold attention with the bloody, physical war all around. Wheeling was under threat of immediate attack from Lee's surrounding armies and in "a state of panic not to be described."

She had schooled herself to observe and read behaviors; now the behaviors were more than she could absorb. "Malignant personal hatreds wearing patriotic masks . . . a slavery of intolerance; hands wet with a brother's blood for Right"; fears, corruptions, political jobbery. The behavior of women—that she thought she understood:

> They had taken the war into their whole strength, like their sisters, North and South: as women greedily do anything that promises to be an outlet for what power of brain, heart, or animal fervor they have, over what is needed for wifehood or maternity.

If there were, as there must also have been, evidences of true conviction, nobility, they were obscured for her by the other behaviors, and by her inability to come to a whole-selfed stand on the war.

Southern bred, nearly all her blood ties were Secessionist in sympathy, when not in action. Her other bonds and allegiances were Northern. She believed uncompromisingly that slavery, the greatest of wrongs, must be ended. But the federal government was making it clear that the war was not to end slavery, it was to end secession from the Union. Secession to her was a state's right, "though I never would, never could, live in a slave confederacy." Neither should slaves: the enslaved had an absolute right to their freedom. Yet how would they—who had never been permitted freedom—know how to use it? Deep in her was the Southern guilt-fear; freed slaves might take revenge, justified retribution. Then the innocent would suffer as well, wrong again come out of right. Round and round ·vithin her, the doubt and fear and contradiction, while all about her was destruction and bloodletting, with slavery seemingly no closer to being ended.

Margret Howth: A Story of Today began appearing serially, the lead piece in the October 1861 *Atlantic*. Whether it was this evidence of herself as a writer that helped, or not, Rebecca returned to writing—the most chilling and perfectly executed of her stories, "John Lamar."

Set in the West Virginia hills in icy November, where Secesh Bushwhacker atrocities have been followed by Union Snakehunter reprisals, John Lamar, a Georgian slaveowner, is being held captive by Union forces under the command of his closest friend since childhood, Captain Dorr. Lamar is planning escape, an escape completely dependent on his barefoot body slave, Ben, to whom the North secretly means freedom. ("At two, Ben, remember. We will be free to-night, old boy." It is typical of Lamar's obliviousness that he says "we" without irony.) Ben listens to the two friend-enemies talk. Dorr begins:

> "This slave question must be kept out of the war. It puts a false face on it." . . .
>
> "There is Ben. What, in God's name, will you do with him? Keep him a slave, and chatter about self-government? Pah! The country is paying in blood for the lie, to-day. . . ."
>
> . . . As for Ben, crouching there, if they talked of him like a clod, heedless [of his presence] . . . we all do the same, you know. . . .
>
> ". . . Let the white Georgian come out of his sloth, and the black will rise with him. . . . When we have our Lowell, our New York . . . when we stand where New England does, Ben's son will be ready for his freedom."

Ben concludes that North *or* South, the "kind" intention is the same: to keep him (and his) always in slavery. An hour before the planned escape, half frozen, "crushing down and out the old parasite affection for his master . . . [his] muddy blood heating, firing with the same heroic dream that bade Tell and Garibaldi lift up their hands to God, and cry aloud that they were men and free," Ben kills the sleeping Lamar, then turns south, not north —he has "a past of cruelty and oppression, . . . a lost life, to avenge." The "canting abolitionist" Union soldier who had earlier called Ben "man and brother," and at a camp prayer meeting, while Ben listened, had preached the Lord's vengeance to the Babylon South—"As she hath done unto my people, be it done unto her"—is left to stand sentry over the dead man. "Humble, uncertain," the words he has said earlier reiterate themselves: "The day of the Lord is nigh; it is at hand; and who can abide it?" *And who can abide it?**

For months, invitations had been coming from the North, some from fabled names. The Fieldses, who had invited her from the beginning, stepped up the frequency of their urgings. Now Rebecca was desperate to go.

It was not only the need to get away from the war. The old sense of constriction, of longing for more than her life was, had roused up, intensified by the constant presence of death. She wanted to be, for a while, with people to whom literature was life; she wanted responding flesh and blood confirmation of her reality as a thinking, writing being. Nothing in Wheeling, outside of herself, confirmed it. No one regarded her as the nation's most significant new writer. She was still just Harding's spinster daughter, devoted, quiet, queer in her unshared interests. Within her family,

---

*In this remarkable story, a century ahead of its time in its understanding of racism and the right of the enslaved to freedom, the white southern guilt-fear— the fear that the oppressed when free will behave as oppressively as they were treated—breaks out at the end. What had been understood earlier as "the same heroic dream" as William Tell's and Garibaldi's to be "men and free," becomes an animal lust for revenge, to be master—and for the young sister of Lamar. As to the actuality, years later in *Bits of Gossip* Rebecca makes a special point that "during the Civil War, the women and children of the South were wholly under the protection of their slaves, and I have never heard of a single instance in which they abused a trust."

life went on as before—her writing fitted in, their needs prior. Proud as they probably were of the recognition given her, her very subject matter may have precluded any discussion of it.

When her father became ill, a breakdown—"strain of the war" —it was taken for granted (most of all by herself) that she would put her writing aside, as if it were china painting, to devote herself to him. No one expected of her brothers that they should do the same.

Across the street, to take over the Western Department, came General Frémont, the "Pathfinder." For a few hours now and then, when she could leave her father, she had occasional heady draughts, from Frémont, from his remarkable wife Jessie Benton, of what friends of range, culture, response, might mean to her. But the Frémonts were not to be in Wheeling long.

Famed as a wilderness explorer, the man who had won the popular, if not the electoral, vote for the presidency in 1856, Frémont was being maneuvered out of the command. "The incarnation of the chivalric and noble side of Abolitionism"; "simple, high-bred, courteous; always at a white heat of purpose" (Rebecca's words) he was suspect. The fall before (1861) when in command of the Missouri Territory, he had ordered the slaves therein freed, the first and only such order of emancipation. The action was annulled by Lincoln.

Months before she had promised Annie Fields a photograph of herself. Now she had one taken, and a copy sent to her Philadelphia correspondent, Clarke Davis, as well. (She was coming to count on his letters more and more in this drouth time.) The eyes look directly out of an ardent, compelling face, a strong intelligent face; the hair, carefully arranged, severely parted, falls in luxurious black curls onto plump beautiful shoulders that the dress is cut low enough to disclose. Was it at this time she copied out from Margaret Fuller:

> With the intellect I always have, always shall overcome: but that is not the half of the work. The life, the life, O my God shall the life never be sweet? Nature vindicates her right, and I feel all Italy glowing beneath the Saxon crust.*

---

*Quotations from Margaret Fuller appear throughout Rebecca's writings.

Money was on her mind. For what? Family needs? The journey? The sweet freedom of being able—for the first time in her life, without dependence—to buy something without asking, or give money away or save it? She asked Fields for the advance of $100 refused earlier for the book publication of *Margret Howth.* He sent $200, and as the book was doing well (2,500 copies in three editions), another $200. She scribbled some stories for *Peterson's.* That fitted in with her shredded time, as serious writing could not (and any one of them paid more than all of *Margret Howth* had brought her).

It was April, one year after publication of *Life in the Iron Mills,* before she could write Annie that yes, she *would* come North, "as soon as her father's health permitted." But still she could not go —the "minor trouble of an escort." No unmarried lady, not even a well-known author with earnings of her own to finance a journey, was free to travel by herself. "O Annie," she wrote her Boston friend, "how good it must be to be a man when you want to travel."

The power of reticence again. The bitterness with which Rebecca felt this restriction is revealed by her obsessed fascination with Ellen, "a girl of the laboring classes," who wandered penniless and freely through state after state, looking for a soldier brother who had disappeared. In later years, Rebecca wrote Ellen's story not once, but twice, the second time as fiction. The first was "Ellen" in *Peterson's,* 1863; the second in the *Atlantic,* July 1865.

In the uninterrupted hours that came sometimes now, free too of the worst of the weight of concern about her father, Rebecca returned to serious writing: another Civil War story, *David Gaunt,* published in 1862 in the *Atlantic.* The sense of torn loyalties, intermixed right-wrong, "hands wet with a brother's blood for the Right," are in this too. A pacifist minister, after agonizing introspection—*must* murder be the way to justice, peace?—enlists in the war against slavery; is betrayed by his noble beliefs into killing his benefactor. A love theme (she Confederate, he Northern, of course) twines mawkishly through it all, and there is a distraught, watery, hasty quality to the writing.

The distraught quality was not only in the story. Her schoolteacher brother, Wilson, needing to go to Boston anyway, had agreed to take her with him in early June. Now that the trip was

definite, its terrors and temerities overcame her. In the long or-
deal-hours sitting by her father without the stay of her writing, it
had come to seem odd and dreamlike that she was an established
writer, let alone one thought fit to be invited into the most select
of companies. In her was something of Hugh Wolfe's outsider
feeling of "a mysterious class that shone down with glamour of
another order of being." She who was reticent, who had kept to
herself, would be on display, expected to respond. She who was
backwoods and self-taught and terribly conscious of the deficien-
cies of that; she who was lonely, opinionated, defiantly so if necessary (for that was the other side of her reticence, a tart outspoken-
ness), was going into the Temple of Athens, where perhaps she
had no right, was an interloper. Frightening.

It was in this condition that she arrived at the Fieldses'. She had
come to the right house. Annie Fields, that great "angel in the
house" of literature, was so excited by the prospect of having her
admired Rebecca there that her joy was infectious. "You never
knew, did you, Annie," Rebecca wrote later, "how downrightedly
scared and lonesome I felt that night, and how your greeting took
it all away." In the sun of this genuine love and delight in her
company, Rebecca bloomed.

All through her Boston visit, she had the exhilarating experience of being her best self, without self-consciousness. No one
seemed put off by directness, or participation, or interest, or seriousness. She was feted, dined, entertained, honored, *appreciated,*
by the Brahmins, the *Atlantic* circle, the Areopagites. They found
her intellectually impressive, witty, captivating; in one recorded
instance, shockingly full blooded and direct, for she observed that
women too, not only men, feel physical desire.

Oliver Wendell Holmes, "the Autocrat [of the Breakfast Table],
to whom the whole country was paying homage," was delighted
to discover their mutual love for inscriptions in burying yards
("the strange bits of human history to be found or guessed at in
them") and took a day off to show her his favorite gravestones in
Mount Auburn cemetery.*

At an evening reception, Rebecca went over to talk with

---

*The quotations in the account of Rebecca's New England visit, if not otherwise
footnoted, come from her *Bits of Gossip.*

. . . a tall, thin young woman standing alone in a corner. She was plainly dressed, and had that watchful, defiant air with which the woman whose youth is slipping away is apt to face the world which has offered no place to her.

She had wanted so much to meet her, she told Rebecca, that she had walked all the way home to Concord for her one decent dress. " 'I'm very poor' . . . she had once taken a place as a 'second girl' [maid]." It was Louisa May Alcott.*

Before I met her I had known many women and girls who were fighting with poverty and loneliness, wondering why God had sent them into a life where apparently there was no place for them . . . soon after [Louisa] wrote her "Hospital Sketches." Then she found her work and place in the world.

There were rich hours talking with Annie of books, of others, of themselves. Rebecca discovered that her friend, whose gifted, dedicated expenditure of self had already made the Fieldses' house a center of inspiration and hospitality for writers, herself hid a painfully shy need to write.**

Concord was a different experience. Some profound, un-recorded hurt which she never forgave occurred to Rebecca there. It never healed, indeed cankered with the years, and had

---

*"Saw Miss Rebecca Harding, author of *Margret Howth,* which has made a stir, and is very good. A handsome, fresh quiet woman, who says she never had any troubles, though she writes about woes. I told her I had had lots of troubles, so I write jolly tales; and we wondered why we each did so."—Louisa May Alcott's *Journal,* May 1862.

**Annie Fields's "angel in the house" contribution to American literature (and British-American literary relations) has never been assessed. For half a century, "writers as famous as Thackeray and Dickens, down to starving poets from the western prairies" came and stayed there; friendships were formed, cemented. She was Sarah Orne Jewett's closest friend. They invariably summered together, and it was she who introduced Willa Cather to Jewett. There is a memorable tribute to Annie Fields in Cather's *Not Under Forty,* and a book on her by Mark de Wolfe Howe, *Memories of a Hostess.* After Fields's death, Annie published two books of poems, *Under the Olive* and *The Singing Shepherd and Other Poems,* as well as *The Life and Letters of Harriet Beecher Stowe* and a book of reminiscences, *Authors and Friends.*

serious consequences to herself, her attitudes, her writing. The nature of it is implied in the way she writes more than forty years later of Bronson Alcott and of Emerson, in her guarded (and not necessarily reliable) reminiscences, *Bits of Gossip,* published in 1904:

> ... the first peculiarity which struck an outsider [was] ... that while they thought they were guiding the real world, they stood quite outside of it, and never would see it as it was. . . . Their views gave you the same sense of unreality, of having been taken, as Hawthorne said, at too long a range. . . . Something was lacking, some back-bone of fact. . . . To the eyes of an observer belonging to the commonplace world, they . . . walked and talked . . . always apart from humanity.

She stayed with the Hawthornes at Wayside, Hawthorne who permitted almost no visitors now. "Here comes the Sage of Concord," Hawthorne told her at breakfast early her very first morning. "He [Alcott] is anxious to know what kind of human beings come up from the back hills in Virginia."

Emerson came shortly thereafter. Her tongue was "dry with awe" ("I went to Concord, a young woman from the backwoods, firm in the belief that Emerson was the first of living men"). It loosened, after listening the entire morning, along with Emerson and Hawthorne,* to Alcott's "orotund" sentences, his "paeans to the war . . . the armed angel which was wakening the nation to a lofty life unknown before."

> I had just come up from the border where I had seen the actual war; the filthy spewings of it; the political jobbery in Union and Confederate camps; the malignant personal hatreds wearing patriotic masks, and glutted by burning homes and outraged women, the chances in it, well improved on both sides, for brutish men to grow more brutish, and for honorable gentlemen to degenerate into

---

*"Mr. Emerson stood listening, his head sunk on his breast, with profound submissive attention, but Hawthorne sat astride of a chair, his arms folded on the back, his chin dropped on them, and his laughing, sagacious eyes watching us, full of mockery."

thieves and sots. War may be an armed angel with a mission, but she has the personal habits of the slums.

Rebecca found herself tartly, though tremblingly, saying substantially the above.

> This would-be seer who was talking of it, and the real seer who listened, knew no more of war as it was, than I had done [as a child] in my cherry-tree when I dreamed of bannered legions of crusaders debouching in the misty fields.

Alcott's orotund sentences went right on, till Hawthorne "rose lazily to his feet, and said quietly: 'We cannot see that thing at so long a range. Let us go to dinner,' and Mr. Alcott suddenly checked the droning flow of his prophecy and quickly led the way to the dining-room."

Her dislike for Alcott, "the vague, would-be prophet," is unconcealed and sometimes vitriolic. She found Emerson's deep respect for him "almost painful to see."

For all Emerson's flattering and receptive attention to her, his "exquisite courtesy," she felt he regarded her not as Rebecca Harding, writer, human being, but as some kind of specimen:

> He studied souls as a philologist does words, or an entomologist beetles. He approached each man with bent head and eager eyes. "What new thing shall I find here?" . . . He took from each man his drop of stored honey, and after that the man counted for no more to him than any other robbed bee.

Hawthorne, by contrast, was the Boston feeling all over again, vivified by the happiness and sense of privilege of being near the revered writer who meant so much to her.

There was one awkward evening though. Elizabeth Peabody, Hawthorne's sister-in-law, seized the presence of the celebrated, mysterious author of *Life in the Iron Mills* as an occasion for a surprise party. "They've been here [back from Europe] two years," she told Rebecca, as townspeople filtered in, "and nobody has met Mr. Hawthorne. People talk. It's ridiculous! There's no reason why Sophia should not go into society. So I just made an excuse of your visit to bring them in."

Hawthorne's wife rescued him; he was permitted to escape. Rebecca understood, approved—but "I have not yet quite forgiven [Miss Elizabeth] the misery of that moment."

The next morning Hawthorne took Rebecca for a long walk; made a special point of showing her the Old Manse where he had lived when he first married; and then, perhaps at her request, they wandered through Sleepy Hollow cemetery. He was in high spirits. "Yes," he said, surveying the surroundings, the hills and river below, "we New Englanders begin to enjoy ourselves—when we are dead."

They sat a long while in the deep grass and quiet beauty, the sense of communion strong between them. It was that bad time in Hawthorne's life Van Wyck Brooks describes so affectingly:

> He had wasted away . . . and, hard as he tried to write, pulling down the blinds and locking his door, he could not bring his mind into focus. The novel became two novels, and the two became four. . . . [All] drifted in confusion through his mind, their outlines melting into one another. Even his theme eluded him . . . until he could scarcely bear to touch his blurred and meaningless manuscripts.*

What kinship did he feel with this young writer beside him, for whom he had broken his seclusion? He had written greatly of the unpardonable sin, of irremediable evil within. She had written—in one instance close to greatly—of another kind of unpardonable sin, of an evil she believed was socially remediable. He was near the close of his work.** Her literary life was at the beginning. Or so it seemed.

> As we walked back, the mists gathered and the day darkened overhead. Hawthorne . . . grew suddenly silent, and before we reached home the cloud had settled down again upon him, and his steps lagged heavily.
>
> I left Concord that evening and never saw him again. He said good-by, hesitated shyly, and then, holding out his hand, said:—"I

The Flowering of New England.

**Hawthorne died in May 1864, within two years of their meeting.

am sorry you are going away. It seems as if we had known you
always."

With that accolade, she turned toward home.

There was a stop in New York, where she stayed with the
Frémonts. One Sunday she sat in an immense audience as an
invited guest at Plymouth Church, where the most unusual of the
tributes to her was paid. Henry Ward Beecher, that "huge, lumbering man," foremost preacher of his day, had sat next to her at
a dinner party, had listened to her tell of and sing certain old
forgotten backwoods hymns. That morning, in her honor, the
congregation sang, one by one, all of those hymns. "I shall never
forget that morning."

In Philadelphia, the personal (and secret) reason for the journey
from home waited: L. Clarke Davis. Their correspondence, begun
with his admiration for *Life in the Iron Mills* a year before, continuing with the request that she become a contributor to *Peterson's,* had deepened into intimacy—on his side, into courtship. He
was attracted by what would have made most men shun her: her
very achievement, seriousness, power; her directness and sardonic
eye for sham; the evidence of a rich secret life.

He, like her, was schooled in protective reticence. Freed in
letters from the self-consciousness of outside selves, social situations, the dialogue of bodies, they had come to know each other
in a way that their actual presence might have precluded. Now
they wanted the presence.

They were delighted by what they found. He liked her reticence
with others. He liked her unvarnished, outspoken, intense. He
liked her physically. It was reciprocal. By the time the week was
over, they had agreed to marry.

There is no record of when she told her family. For thirty-one
years (except for those unknowns out of whom she wrote Lo,
Hugh Wolfe, Holmes), they had been her emotional life. In the last
years she had come closer and closer to her solitary, austere father.
Bound to them as deeply as she was, she could not help but care
what their reaction would be.

At that time, a woman who had not married by the age of
thirty-one had long ago ceased to be thought of as marriageable.
There would be the flavor of something unnatural, vaguely shame-

ful about it happening now. To Rebecca's father, not yet completely recovered, the impending loss might be considered betrayal —so dependent had he become on her devotion and companionship. And both parents would naturally feel concern about the nature of the match.

Clarke Davis was four years younger than Rebecca, without established situation or income. He had to work on various additional jobs (editing legal periodicals, reading for *Peterson's*) to support himself while he clerked in a law office, preparing for the bar. How then could he responsibly marry? Furthermore, he was a declared abolitionist, and radical.

The family secreted the knowledge among themselves. No public announcement of the betrothal was made. But Rebecca must have made her determination to marry Davis clear: it was understood that the marriage *would* eventually take place.

Home again, Rebecca sat down almost at once to write—not romance, not another Civil War story (though the war was as agonizing to her as ever)* —but, out of the "wrong, all wrong" caring center from which *Life in the Iron Mills* came, an almost unendurable account of the misuse, the refusal of development to a blind slave child, "an infant Mozart," a musical genius. "Blind Tom" appeared in the *Atlantic* in November 1862.

Was there a Blind Tom? A "coal-black" child "of the lowest negro type, from which only field-hands can be made," who never received instruction, yet played consummate counterpoint on the piano to music heard for the first time as he played; could reproduce perfectly from memory any music heard once—"intricate symphonies, Beethoven, Mendelssohn—intact in brilliancy and symmetry"; who, left to himself, composed "unknown, wild . . . harmonies which he had learned from no man. . . . one inarticulate, unanswered question of pain in all."

Was he paraded before audiences ("a more fruitful source of revenue than tobacco-fields"), subjected to exhausting tests, exhibited at the White House ("Being a slave . . . never was taken into

---

*"O Annie," she wrote on returning, "the inexpressible loathing I have for it [the war]. If you could only see the other side enough to see the wrong, the tyranny on both. I could tell you things I know that would make your heart sick."

a Free State; for the same reason his master refused advantageous offers from European managers.")? And

> ... that feature of the concerts which was the most painful ... the moments when his master was talking [to the audience], and Tom was left to himself,—when a weary despair seemed to settle on the distorted face and the stubby little black fingers, wandering over the keys, spoke for Tom's own caged soul within ... all the pain and pathos of the world [in it].

Was it so? Or is this fiction, the kind of fiction that is truth for the tearing possibility in it?*

"You cannot help Tom, either," she ends, addressing the North directly, revealing her consciousness of more than parlors during her stay there:

> He was in Richmond in May. But (do you hate the moral to a story?) in your own kitchen, in your own back-alley, there are spirits as beautiful, caged in forms as bestial, that you *could* set free, if you pleased ... they are more to be pitied than Tom,—for they are dumb.

Whatever transport there was in the writing of it, the small payment the *Atlantic* made was shock into a different reality. She set herself to concoct a serial, *The Second Life,* for *Peterson's,* and wrote to Fields, appealing to him to make such writing unnecessary. Even anonymously, she told him, she did not want to write the thrillers, Gothics, mysteries, plot romances suitable for *Peterson's.* She wanted to write only her best, for discriminating *Atlantic* audiences. But *Peterson's* was now paying $300 and more a story, $1,000 and more for serials. *Atlantic* had paid $200 for the six-part *Margret Howth,* $400 for the book publication of it.

---

*1976—Yes, there was a Blind Tom. It was probably in 1858 that Rebecca heard him. Mary Austin in *Earth Horizon* records an early childhood memory of hearing him (or a similarly named, gifted, Blind Tom) play. Martha Collins suggests that possibly Blind D'Arnaud in Willa Cather's *My Antonia* is also based on him.

As times are, I am not justified in refusing the higher prices
. . . I thought that I could say to you as a friend . . . that I
hope Mr. Ticknor and you will give as much for future articles
as you can legitimately afford.

She did not explain that "as times are" had to do with the
economic necessities of a forthcoming marriage: hers. It was not
until January, half a year after the betrothal, that the Fieldses were
told in a letter to Annie, her closest (and only) woman friend:

It isn't easy for me to tell you this I don't know why. But you who
are so happy in your married life will know how to ask for a blessing
on mine. I *want* to tell you . . . of someone else, but it is harder than
even to talk about myself. When you know him you won't think
much of *me,* in comparison. . . . Our marriage was to have been
the first of the winter, but I had to defer it [because of family illness]
until March the 5th, and . . . it will be strictly private. . . . Will you
please . . . not to speak of this to anyone? No one here knows it
except ourselves. . . . I never told you what my name would be—
Davis. But I never *had* such trouble to write a letter before. O
Annie, my summer days are coming now.

My summer days are coming now.
All that had been impressed on her from babyhood impelled her
to the believing of it. "Love and marriage—a woman's fulfillment." "When you loved, you fulfilled the law of your woman's
nature." You were no longer of those whom "God had thought
unworthy of every woman's right, to love and be loved."
My summer days are coming now.
All that was passionate and loving and had had to be denied in
her nature, never doubted it. "Nature vindicates her right, and I
feel all Italy glowing beneath the Saxon crust."* "The *natural*
need to love and be loved." Nature, God, Right; Need, Law,
Fulfillment.
And yet, and yet:
Rebecca, writer, thirty-two, had known another kind of summer days, fulfilling another need and law of her nature, vindicat-

---

*Margaret Fuller.

ing another kind of natural right. Where was *their* place to be?

In "Paul Blecker,"* a mawkish story begun about the time of her letter to Annie, there is a girl (not otherwise like Rebecca), wanting marriage, children, *and* to use her "dumb power" in men's world of achievement. She "is perpetually self-analyzing—in a hysteric clinging, embracing the chimera of the Women's Rights prophets with her brain, and thrusting it aside with her heart." But heart and brain are not separates. To attain the health of happiness, they must find harmony—not be split in a war within the being that must contain them both. Chimera is a monster only in myth; in actuality, it is a whole organism containing both female and male.

A part—or the whole? War or harmony? Myth or reality? The needs and laws of nature? What would happen now?

Rebecca Harding, thirty-two, and Clarke Davis, twenty-eight, were married on March 5, 1863, in Wheeling. Only her family was present. No honeymoon. They went directly to Philadelphia, to the home of Clarke's sister Carrie, where for the next fourteen months they were to live. It was a house crowded with children; meals and housekeeping had to be shared; Carrie was often ill, and always (it was her house) present.

Even more than Clarke, Rebecca came to marriage with strongly established patterns of living, including the practice of solitude. Now neither had even the physical space of a room of one's own. The most intimate and tasking of relationships had to seek a tenable way to live in the midst of the clamor of everyday unavoidable relationship with others—necessitating (Rebecca, as a woman, would feel it most) constant consciousness and consideration for them.

In Wheeling, years of close living had bought the safety of unspoken understanding; knowledge of limits, one's own and oth-

---

Atlantic Monthly, May, June, and July 1863. The comment is made in the story that contrary to expressed attitudes, although supposedly "women are angels," they are invariably treated as if they were idiots, but "in these rough & tumble days, we'd better give 'em their places as flesh and blood, with exactly the same wants and passions as men."

ers'; what to accept, resist, avoid; what one spoke of, what was best
kept silent. Here it was all to be learned.

Rebecca's first venture out was to the Philadelphia public library—at last she lived somewhere where there was a circulating
library, and a great one. She used her status as a leading *Atlantic*
writer to secure reserved desk space, as well as a card.

Annie Fields came down for a flying one-day visit. Concealing
any dismay she may have felt at the newlyweds' circumstances,
she set about arranging a series of visits and invitations from
distinguished Philadelphians. She knew in Rebecca "the longing
for music, art, the companionship of thinkers, scholars." Lucretia
Mott, the great, long-time abolitionist and women's rights leader,
came to call. Rebecca loved her: "a little, vivid, delicate creature,
alive with magnetic power . . . no man had a more vigorous brain
or ready eloquence."* But she evaded further relationship with
other Philadelphians, the "ponderous matrons whose turrets of
white hair atop symbolize a sort of social Gibraltar." Even those
with whom Annie had hoped she and Clarke would find mutuality
were dismissed by Rebecca (the shadow of Concord?) as "philan-
thropists, litterateurs, people with missions."

The avoidance may have been partly self-protective. They had
no home in which to entertain reciprocally; the position of husband to a famous wife was not easy for an as yet unestablished
man; Clarke's likings for people had to be considered; and there
was the problem of Rebecca's time and energies, seemingly less
and less hers than ever.

Letters from Wheeling kept telling her how frail and lonesome her father was. Clarke, increasingly obsessed with the

---

*The full description of Lucretia Mott in *Bits of Gossip,* is recommended as of
special interest for biographers, students, and historians.

Lucretia Mott [is] one of the most remarkable women that this country has
ever produced. . . . Even in extreme old age she was one of the most beautiful
women I have ever seen . . . a little, vivid, delicate creature, alive with magnetic
power . . . that charming face with its wonderful luminous eyes . . . is as real
to me at this moment as ever. . . . When you were with [her], you were apt
to think of her as the mother and housekeeper, rather than as the leader of
a party. . . . Her fingers never were quiet. Until the day of her death she kept
up the homely, domestic habits of her youth."

(mis)conduct of the war, seemed to speak of nothing else; passionately involved himself in organizing abolitionist meetings against Lincoln's expediency. Rebecca reminded him that it was God who had the war in His hand, and not Clarke—to little effect. She wrote the story of "Ellen" who wandered freely, but it was not *Atlantic* quality. She had to send it to *Peterson's*. Carrie was ill, recovered, was ill again. There were always children, and things that needed doing, and then redoing. Clarke and she never seemed to be alone when he was home—and the walls were so thin. *"If any individual live too much in relations, so that [s]he becomes a stranger to the resources of his [her] own nature; [s]he falls, after a while, into a distraction, or imbecility which can only be cured by a time of isolation which gives the renovating fountains time to rise up."** Carrie and the children were always about. The library hours and location were not really convenient. Clarke kept smoking all those cigars though she tried to help him cut down by offering him ice cream, and then had to eat half herself. Carrie was sick. It looked as if Clarke would enlist, or let himself be drafted. It was five months and she was not writing at all. Her father was worse. There were always children and a lot of things that needed doing and redoing.

Then, in late July, she did the only thing. She fell into a distraction or imbecility, an "undefined illness" (brain fever and nervous prostration are hinted at) that in our day we call a breakdown. Immediately she had freedom from household tasks, isolation, care, indulgence, removal; release to herself.

Although she probably did not know it yet, she was also pregnant.

Late in September, she could write a note to Annie. Without specifying why she had needed treatment, she told her abruptly that allopathy and homeopathy had been useless, and now "finally desperately" she had "gone back to [her] old Western habit [her girlhood habit] of walking" walking walking to exhaustion. Philadelphia streets, not Wheeling's. Now she was better: "I'm so glad, for I didn't know how to be sick."

---

*Margaret Fuller. *Women in the Nineteenth Century*.

The "better" was premature. Late in October, there is another letter:

> My dear *dear* Annie: I wanted to write before only to say I love you. God knows how dear and tender all love has grown to me now, but at first I was not able and now the doctor forbids the least reading or writing for fear of bringing back the trouble in my head. Ma is with me. Clarke has been waiting every day to have some good news to send you, to write. Sometimes I wish the time would be longer. I don't know—these days have been so like the valley of the shadow of death that I grow afraid of the end. . . . I wish you would pray for us.
>
> I must tell you one happy thing. If I get well we are going directly to live by ourselves—it is all clear now. *You* know all that means to me.

Her mother brought her to Wheeling to convalesce. She wrote she was thinking of composing a Christmas story, forgetting that it was far too late for any publication. Sometime in November she went back to Philadelphia:

> It was such a happy homecoming, but I was still weak enough to feel my heart beat and the tears come at a little petting, and they did pet me. . . . How dear you are to me, Annie. I never felt before how hard it was to justify my right to love as since I was sick. . . . Sometimes I have a horror, Annie, that it will all disappear like a dream, that I will become suddenly indifferent to you all—I am foolish to speak in this way, but I cannot help it.

She returned for Christmas to her family in Wheeling, sending Annie a mysterious note the night before going:

> I have had much to think of and to feel—for others, not myself. I could tell you a story which I cannot write, sadder and stranger than any fiction, which has made the days and nights very feverish for a long time. Someday I will tell you but maybe now, I ought not to have even said this much.
>
> There's a happy ending coming at last, I hope.

The first hint to Annie of the coming baby.

"It was not a very merry Christmas. Father is not dangerously ill," she wrote Annie, "but enough to make him nervous and even morbid in his desire to have me with him." The good-bys were agonizing, the more so for the constraint.

After Rebecca came home, rearrangements in their living situation were made. She had some space and time. All January, February, March,* the six-seven-eight-month pregnant Rebecca wrote and rewrote a story which the July 1864 *Atlantic* featured as its lead piece. It deserved that honor, and perhaps a more permanent one.

"The Wife's Story" is about a "terror and temptation which had beset" a married life from the beginning, and is now taking "a definite shape and hold." The wife had married fifteen months before into a ready-made family (five children and a ward) whose habits and temperaments are alien to her. Economic disaster has come to them; they face "the coarse struggle . . . for bread and butter."

The temptation is a life in art; the terror is in considering it, for it might mean having to give up human love, hurting and abandoning those who need her. She yields to the temptation—to discover that the talent is mediocre, self-delusion; the world in which it has to function, commercial and degrading; and the end result is shame; death to her loved husband; the fate of a social outcast for herself.

But wait: it is all in the fantasies of a brain-fever dream; she never yielded. The wife wakes from the nightmare illness "thirsty for love, and to love," and safe: babe at her breast, husband at her side, loved ones surrounding her. An example, furthermore, for the young ward:

> . . . mother, here, will tell you a woman has no better work in life than the one she has taken up: to make herself a visible Providence to her husband and child.

---

*Clarke was ill in March, and Rebecca wrote Annie of herself: "And then I was just enough ailing in mind to be nervous and irritable, a stupid desire to be quiet and forgotten. Do you never feel as if every faculty has been rasped and handled unbearably and must rest?"

Happy conclusion, and satisfyingly reassuring to the prevalent attitudes of her readers. But there is anguish in the story. It is there in the torment of Hetty's situation, which Rebecca makes so actual. It is there in the extremity of Hetty's punishment had she acted—self-deluded fool, death-causer, outcast. And it is implicit in the choice of endings: even 108 years ago, there were a handful of women with family who had demonstrated that in exceptional instances, for a few, a third ending might be possible.

Aside from any light or dark that it casts on factors in Rebecca's breakdown, "The Wife's Story" is important (and fascinating) for the detailing of this anguish, the working of woman's "conflict" in the insoluble situation of commitment to the real needs of other human beings and the real need to carry on one's other serious work as well. The literature of this anguish is sparse.* "The Wife's Story" is the first, and still among the most revealing:

> I was so hungry for affection that night! I would have clung to a dog that had been kind to me. . . . The motherless boy, holding himself up by my knees, was more sturdy than I that night and self-reliant: never could have known, in his most helpless baby-days, the need with which I, an adult woman, craved a cheering word, and a little petting.

This immediately after she has acceded for the first time to the "temptation" of thinking of a life in art. Each succeeding concern with it is followed by a similar craving for love, for tenderness; an intensified sensitivity to her husband's admirable qualities; or a rousing of physical desire at the touch or look of him. And this in turn is followed by resentment of what she makes herself scorn as "weak fever of the flesh"; or by a devaluation of her husband and their relationship; or by a redwelling on her work, and her circumstances that deny it.

In a long passage, Hetty tries to "judge" the years of her married life:

---

*Among others, and still unequaled, the 1877 classic by Elizabeth Stuart Phelps, *The Story of Avis* (partially reprinted in *American Voices, American Women,* 1974); Dorothy Canfield Fisher's "Babushka Farnham," in *Fables for Parents* (1937); Mary Gray Hughes's "The Thousand Springs," in her collection so entitled (1970); and Cora Sandel's *Alberta.*

. . . other [previous] years of my life thrust them aside persistently, as foreign, alien to me. Those others were to me Home,—the thoughts that had held me nearest the divine life. . . . "The only object in life is to grow," [it was] Margaret Fuller's motto. . . . There had been a time when I had dreamed of attaining Margaret's stature; and as I thought of that, some old subtile flame stirred in me with a keen delight. New to me, almost; for, since my baby was born, my soul as well as my body had been weak and nauseated. . . . I had intended my child should be reared in New England: what I had lacked in gifts and opportunities he should possess. . . . But the child was a girl,* a weazen-faced little mortal, crying night and day like any other animal. It was an animal wearing out in me the strength needed by-and-by for its mental training. I sent it to a nurse in the country. . . . For days after that he [the father] looked paler, and his face had a quiet, settled look, as if he had tested the world and was done with it. . . . I do not remember that after this he ever called me Hetty. But he was cheerful as ever with the boys.

"Some latent, unconscious jar of thought" brings her back to a time when she saw Rosa Bonheur's famous painting, *Horse Fair:*

I remembered how some one had quoted her as saying, "Any woman can be a wife or mother, but this is my work alone."

I, too, had my gift: but one . . . again the quick shiver of ecstasy ran through me;—it was my power, my wand with which to touch the world . . . was I to give it unused back to God? I could sing: not that only; I could compose music,—the highest soul-utterance. . . . I *had* been called, then,—set apart to a mission . . . and I had thrust it all aside—for what? A mess of weakest pottage,—a little love, silly rides behind Tinker, petting and paltering such as other women's souls grew imbecile without. It was the consciousness of this that had grown slowly on me in the year just gone; I had put my husband from me day by day because of it. . . . I could look now at my husband, and see the naked truth about us both. Two middle-aged people with inharmonious intellects: tastes and habits jarring at every step, clenched together only by faith in a vague whim or

---

*The self-belittlement, the wound to a woman, in having to feel that a male child is preferable, more to be valued than a female child, is written of for the first time here. It was realistic recognition of objective fact: "man's world"; (". . . what I had lacked in gifts and opportunities, he should possess").

fever of the blood called love. Better apart: we were too old for
fevers. If I remained with Doctor Manning, my *role* was outlined
plain to the end: years of cooking, stitching, scraping together of
cents: it was the fate of thousands of married women without
means. . . . Better apart.

As I thought that, he laid Teddy [the small boy] down, and came
towards me,—the usual uncertain, anxious half-smile on his face
with which he regarded me. . . .

. . . He . . . put his hard hand gently on my shoulder. It made
me turn faint, with some weakness that must have come down to
me from my infant days. . . . I caught the sleeve of his dressing-gown
in my fingers, and began smoothing it. It was the first thing I had
ever made for him. I remembered how proud I was the evening he
put it on.

"I was sure the life meant so much more to you than food or
raiment," her husband says to her.

"What do you mean by the life? Have I found it here, Daniel?"
"No, Hester?"

"I want work fit for me," I said, almost fiercely. "God made me
for a good, high purpose."

"I know," cheerfully. "We'll find it, dear: no man's work is kept
back from him. We'll find it together."

But under the cheerfulness there was a sad quiet, as of one
who has lost something forever, and tries to hide the loss from
himself.

In her intensified sensitivity, his pain overwhelms her. She caresses
him:

"Why, why, child!"
"Call me Hetty, Daniel, I'd like to think that name belonged to
me yet."

She gets up, brings him his slippers, kneels to put them on:

Another of the old foolish tricks gone long ago. There was a look
on his face which had not been there this many a day. He had such
a credulous heart, so easy to waken into happiness. I took his wrist
in my bony hands, to raise myself; the muscles were like steel, the

cording veins throbbing with health; there was an indescribable rest in the touch.

"Daniel," I said, looking him full in the face, "I'd like to have no mission in God's world. I'd like to give up my soul, and forget everything but you."

"Yes," she says later. "It's a fever . . . In the blood."

Each hardening of determination comes out of situations of drudgery ("Was [it] for this in reality God had made me?") or out of reinvolvement with her music,

> the work of my life. . . . I got it [the score of an opera] out now by stealth, at night, putting my pen to it here and there, with the controlled fever with which a man might lay his hand on a dear dead face, if he knew the touch would bring it back to life. Was there any waking that dead life of mine?

Her final decision—to accept an offer for her opera to be produced, and to sing in it herself—is made as she sits mending the weekly heap of the boys' half-washed, leather-stained socks after a long exhausting day of making-do:

> *The actual dignity and beauty of [this family] life, God's truth itself, may have grown dim to me, behind a faint body and tired fingers; but let the hard-worked woman who is without that sin throw the first stone at me.*

Each hardening is followed by acts of love; renewal of responsibility; magnified sensitivity to others' feelings; and terrible longing not to have the conflict:

> To nestle down into this man's heart and life. To make his last years that warm Indian-summer day! I could do it! I! What utter rest there were in that!
>
> Yet was this power within me to rot and waste?

The movement of the story is that of *David Gaunt:* the back and forth embracing of the chimera with her brain, and the thrusting it aside with her heart—until the resolution.

The happy ending is what Rebecca, big with child, must

have believed those last few months, sitting beside a bleak stove thinking of "the great talking fires at home." She wrote to Annie:

> The air is warmer and the sunshine clearer. We read and walk and I sew a little. . . . The time has been full of a deep breath of content and waiting.
>   All good things lie in the future.

Richard Harding Davis was born on April 18, 1864. He was named after Rebecca's father, whose death three weeks before had been kept secret from her until her mother could come and tell her. The telling coincided with the onset of labor. For a month she was very ill, kept to her bed. When Annie wanted to come and visit, Rebecca asked her not to until she was stronger and the baby had had "a chance to grow fat and better pleased with the new world he has found. Just now he is the smallest tiredest little thing, and homely too, only with big dark eyes."

Clarke found a cheap rooming house in Point Pleasant near the sea for the summer, and in fall they moved at last from Carrie's into a place by themselves—a rented yardless Philadelphia row house, "not a scrap of growing green anywhere in sight," one of several hundred others exactly like it for streets around. They christened it "Centre of the Universe," a name to be attached to wherever they lived.

In December she took her baby to Wheeling, where Clarke—building a law practice, immersed in political activities, editing, and working at the post office part time—wrote her: "Dearest Pet, will you help your old Boy a little" with some writing?

Dearest Pet helped her "old Boy" and herself a lot in those next months. Five *Atlantic* stories and *Haunted Manor House,* a book-length mystery for *Peterson's:* writing very fast and from the surface, nothing she really cared about, not stopping to rewrite or revise. She wanted help in the house and a yard and vista and to live by the sea that in the one summer she had come so dearly to love.

She got help with the baby and another summer by the sea. She was pregnant again, and after a while the writing raveled off. It was just as well; in that seaside time she was dreaming up a new book. It would be a major work. She would write it carefully, take her time, not as with those potboilers she had spun off.

Charles Belmont was born in January 1866. It was nearly a year more before Rebecca got to her book. In a cooped-up winter and spring, the babies, then Clarke, were sick. She wrote about Holmes again, his disillusionment with Rapp's Harmonist commune (an actual commune) in Pennsylvania. That was a lead piece in the *Atlantic* too (in May 1866), her last. The money managed Point Pleasant for a third vivifying summer, and in the fall, with the noises of new neighbors from the adjoining houses in her ears (Clarke had moved them to another row house without telling her) and her toddlers in healthy voice, Rebecca started her planned major novel.

Her intention was to "publish it in book form, after giving it care and time," but as usual there were money problems. An offer from a new magazine, *Galaxy,* to serialize it was too tempting: she earned $3,600 for the serial rights alone.

From the beginning, the situation was nightmarish. Often there were only exhausted tag-ends of herself in tag-ends of time left over after the house, Clarke, the babies, for a book that demanded all her powers, all her concentration. Sometimes she had to send off great chunks, unread, unworked, to meet the inexorable monthly deadline.

Editorial problems developed. *Galaxy* was changing its format, wanted the installments cut. "It was only at your request that I gave it to Galaxy to publish serially," Rebecca protested in a tone different from the shaken Rebecca to Fields six years before. "You must allow me the feeling which the humblest workman has for his work. . . . Whether it mutilates the story or not [seems] a secondary consideration to you."

But primary to her. To no avail. Her situation as contracted-for employee was made clear. They cut, and sometimes she cut. Yet the pages poured on and on—868 printed pages.

Waiting for the Verdict, finished in 1868, was intended to pose what Rebecca considered the basic question of the time: how was the nation going to redress the wrong of slavery? Were the freed slaves to have work, education, respect, freedom?* The blacks, the nation, the future, were waiting for the verdict.

Her black characters would show the full human spectrum, the "as they might be"; her white characters would show the reasons for hope—and for hopelessness. The best and worst of the South would be juxtaposed with what was best and worst in the North.

The Civil War is still going on. Nathan (Nat), a slave, makes his hazardous escape to freedom, involving many black and white lives with his own, learning all the way, and instructing others by example and words.

He puts the horrors of insurrection into perspective:

> De white people in de Souf, dey want der own guver'ment, an' dey fights for it wid artillery an' Parrott guns, an' kills tousands, an' dey calls it war; an' Nat Turner, he want his freedom, an' he fights wid knives an' pikes, an' sech wepons as he gets, an' kills fifty odd, an dey calls it murder.

Unprepossessing outwardly and in his own esteem, with surface slave manners, Nat is a mover, deep observer, prophet, resourceful hero, whose dedication to freedom and opportunity for his people is unshakable.

A Randolph of Virginia falls in love with Rosslyn, a Northern girl, for qualities the Southern belles do not possess. She converts him to her Northern practices of "democracy and energy and practicality and opening fields of work . . . where help is needed." He accepts her background: abolitionist, working class—"the

---

*Anny, Nat's wife, is speaking to Rosslyn, a white woman:

"De debt de whites owes us is to give us a chance to show what stuff's in us. . . . De next five years is de trial day for us. . . . Your chile has every chance open to him; but dar's few schools in de country beside dem kept by de Quakers dat will admit a cullored boy or girl. Dey calls us lazy an' idle, but wher's de mechanics' shop or factory open for Tom to learn a trade? What perfession is free to him? His hands is tied. His father giv' his blood free for de country." Proudly: "He has a right to ask de chance for his son dat neber was gib to himself!"

"The negroes will be given a vote," confidently.

"I don't see what real use to dem dat is yet," gravely. "It's edication my people needs, and ways for work. It's de fever time wid 'em now in de Souf; dey's made for de chance to learn. Ole men an' young stretch out dere hands for de books. It won't last if dey're balked now. . . ."

class which you place on a par with your slaves"—accepts even the secret of her birth: she is illegitimate.

His cousin, Margaret, also a Randolph though raised in the North,* is wooed and won by a brooding, immensely cultured, eminent Philadelphia surgeon, Dr. Broderip, who has cured her father. The doctor too has a birth secret—he is part black. Strongly affected by Nat—who turns out to be his half brother, not seen since early childhood—and through Nat by a new sense of the black situation, Dr. Broderip tells his fiancée *his* birth secret.

"The negro blood is abhorrent" to her. She lets the truth about him be known. He is excluded from his hospital, spurned by his patients, and ostracized by "polite society." "The knowledge and skill acquired in all those patient years lay dead weight in his hands to-day." Margaret's Northern father, however, not only keeps his door open to the doctor, but organizes patients to fight for Broderip's right to continue practicing.

Nat slowly and successfully convinces Broderip that his place is helping to organize and lead a regiment of freed slaves:

> ". . . dey don't know who to trust. Dey hears dat de Yankees 'll sell dem down inter Cuba, an' as fur dere ole marsters—well, dey knows dem. . . . Dey'd fight like debbils under a man ob dere own cullor. . . . Dey calls M's Linkum Moses. Moses warn't a white man, an' a stranger," deliberately. "He wur a chile ob de slave woman, an' he went an' stole all de learnin' ob his masters, an' den come back an' took his people cross de riber inter freedom. *His own people,* suh."

Broderip is killed in action. There are numerous other characters and situations: battle, escape, plantation, army, hospital, street scenes; life-going-on-as-usual social scenes; bigotry, apathy, humanity, degrees of hypocrisy; action, suspense, talk, talk, talk—intense debate, "warring creeds," dissensions; confusion, contra-

---

*Margaret says to a house slave who asks her what freedom does for blacks up North:

"It does nothing for them" carelessly, remembering to whom she was speaking. . . . "They are like Mose. He does light work here; he shaves beards, or whitewashes walls, or steals; he does the same in Philadelphia. He is thick-lipped and thriftless and affectionate, go where he will; only in the South they hunt him with dogs, and in the North they calculate how many years of competition with the white race it will need to sweep him and his like off of the face of the earth."

dictions, terror. There are surprising depths in the development of the main characters, most in Nat, Rosslyn, and the unprecedented, complex Dr. Broderip, torn between his whiteness and his blackness. There is also stereotype, slush, excess, caricature, melodrama, and occasional racism on Rebecca's part.

Waiting for the Verdict never became a great book. More than anyone else, Rebecca knew that she had failed. She had conceived, intended to write, a great novel. She had failed to write it: had not given (had) the self and time (or the knowledge always) to write it. "A great hope fell, you heard no noise, the ruin was within." She never attempted such an ambitious book again.

She also knew that *Waiting for the Verdict* was a book of far more substance and compass than any other fiction being written —and praised—at the time; and that it alone recorded, tried to make sense of, the seething currents of the Civil War period. Partly because of the unselected unwieldiness, the first-draft character of some of the pages, partly because of disturbing truths and portents in the book, understandings far ahead of the time, almost no one recognized this.*

---

*This remains true to this date. In Daniel Aaron's *The Unwritten War, American Writers and the Civil War* (1973), considered to be the authoritative volume on the subject (it was commissioned by the Civil War Bicentennial Commission), his major thesis is that the war remained largely unwritten. With a few notable exceptions, writers, "the antennae of the race," "had revealed little of the meaning or causes of the War; nor discerned its moral and historical implications, nor written the complexities, the seamy and unheroic side." Rebecca Harding Davis is not included among his few notable exceptions—nor does her fiction figure anywhere.

Aaron mentions "the sterility of the American literary imagination" as a possible explanation for writers avoiding the war as subject, does not examine the idea, but instead ascribes the phenomenon to "emotional resistance [because race cannot be dealt with] blurring literary insight" and to "spiritual censorship," primarily "the fastidiousness of lady readers. . . . The 'real war' [was] too indelicate for female ears."

As Rebecca Harding Davis ("a lady writer" furthermore), almost alone, and singularly in her time wrote directly of meaning, causes, moral and historical implications, the seamy and unheroic, the complex question of race ("disturbing truths and portents . . . understandings far ahead of her time") it seems the gravest of omissions to have ignored discussion of her work as Aaron does. One paragraph of her *Bits of Gossip* account of Emerson, Alcott, and Hawthorne is included.

"Sentimental propaganda for the negro dictates *Waiting for the Verdict,*" is how one reviewer dismissed it. The kindest remark *The Nation* made in a lengthy three-column review on November 21, 1867, was that,

> As it stands, it preserves a certain American flavor. The author has evidently seen something corresponding to a portion of what she describes, and she has disengaged herself to a much greater degree than many of the female story-tellers of our native country from heterogeneous reminiscences of English novels.

Then it went on to say:

> Mrs. Davis has written a number of short stories, chiefly of country life in Virginia and Pennsylvania, all distinguished by a certain severe and uncultured strength, but all disfigured by an injudicious straining after realistic effects which leave nature and reality at an infinite distance behind and beside them. The author has made herself the poet of poor people—laborers, farmers, mechanics, and factory hands. She has attempted to reproduce in dramatic form their manners and habits and woes and wants. The intention has always been good, but the execution has, to our mind, always been monstrous. . . . She drenches the whole field beforehand with a flood of lachrymose sentimentalism, and riots in the murky vapors which rise. . . . It is enough to make one forswear for ever all decent reflection and honest compassion, and take refuge in cynical jollity and elegant pococurantism.

Pococurantism. I looked it up. It means caring little, being indifferent, nonchalant.

> . . . nothing is left but a crowd of ghastly, frowning, grinning automatons. The reader, exhausted by the constant strain upon his moral sensibilities, cries aloud for the good, graceful old nullities of the "fashionable novel."*

---

*Harriet Beecher Stowe wrote to her later: "*The Nation* has no sympathy with any deep & high moral movement—no pity for human infirmity. It is a sneering respectable middle-aged sceptic who says I take my two glasses & my cigar daily . . . dont mind them & dont hope for a sympathetic word from them *ever.*"

It was about this time that Rebecca began her practice of ignoring reviews. Primarily though, this was part of her rapid process of devaluing herself as a writer aspiring to art.

Never mind. She was at a time when she could say (indeed *had* to say, for it was true): "That is not all there is to life." The almost total immersion that comes to a woman in a culture where full responsibility for home and growing new lives are hers, had engulfed Rebecca. The immediacy of Clarke, the house, two little ones at their most demanding, absorbing, alluring, "each day a new discovery in the unfolding miracle of human life," left little over for other intensities. She began keeping a diary—a wife and mother diary, not a writer's diary—wishing she

> could put in words the happy sense of home and love that is under and over all, the thousand little ways in which my Darling shows how strong and tender is his love, Harding's funny antics, the look of Charley's earnest blue eyes.

She went on writing, of course, contracting for a serial (after having said she never would again) for *Lippincott's*. No ambitious compass this time: this was going to be manageable, though still about something. The monthly deadlines once more proved "a tax on one's endurance. And the horror of being sick, or the children being sick," or of any of the other pulls and claims on her time.

The *Nation* reviewer, on October 22, 1868, approved of this book, *Dallas Galbraith:*

> In the conception and arrangement of her story, . . . [the author] displays no inconsiderable energy and skill. She has evidently done her best to make it interesting, and to give her reader, in vulgar parlance, his money's worth. . . .
> Mrs. Davis, in her way, is an artist.

Mrs. Davis having intended to be, and for a while having practiced being, an artist, had no such illusions. Mrs. Davis, in her way, had become a professional workhorse in the field of letters for income, doing the best she could. Her writing had bought an end to the old economic terrors, and to drudgery; it had bought servant help and summers by the sea, and made keeping on writing possible.

It had also bought the need to keep writing—for money. She was writing articles and comments on the times now, as well as fiction. She added children's stories—highly moral—for *Youth's Companion.* She joined the staff of the New York *Tribune* as contributing editor and began a long stream of articles and editorials. Clarke became an editor too—for the Philadelphia *Inquirer*—and forgot about a law practice.

Home almost always, Rebecca longed more and more for sky, vista, sea, another view than brick. She was "making fresh attacks on Papa to move out of town," she wrote Annie, "but Papa reads his paper and won't hear."

With Rebecca's earnings, Papa in 1870 bought their permanent home. In Philadelphia. Another row house flanked for blocks around by identical twins—but impressive three-story brick ones this time, with yards.

If Rebecca looked out her window anymore, for the rest of her life (except for the sea summers) it was to be to this sliver of sky and those brick houses endlessly repeating themselves. No river, no hills, no slow stream of human life moving by on its way to and from work in the mills. Her commonplace, her "Centre of the Universe," was suburban domestic now. She records a typical day:

> The boys' bed is close by ours and at daylight they are awake. Charley generally asserting that he is "chivering cold" until he is taken into my arms. Then dear old Hardy puts his head up on the pillow and we whisper a while till the light in the transom shows that Annie [the maid] is ready to dress. Then I get up and we have breakfast. Clarke rises at 9 or 10. After he has his breakfast he reads the *Inquirer,* smokes his pipe, and goes [to work]. . . . When he comes home he has a supper of raw oysters with me and a cup of tea and then to bed.

Up two or three hours before Clarke was, and until 10 or 11 at night when he came home, Rebecca was running the house, seeing to the things that had to be done or doing them herself; mothering, teaching, when necessary nursing the boys; evading the neighbors ("Love thy neighbor? . . . The well to do, fat person across the way? I hate my kind when they come within meddling distance") —and getting her writing done.

That first year in the new house, she revised some articles written in the high-tide time of "happy sense of home and love," wrote a few more, and published *Pro Aris et Focis* (For Altar and Hearth), a small book all for domesticity, motherhood—and against women's rights.*

What were these "voices . . . high, shrill and occasionally discordant" going on so about women's rights? Yes, "shrill" was the recurrent adjective even then.

Equality? Women should no more feel inferior because they are not fit for men's work than men feel inferior because they are not fit for women's work.

Professions for women? "Some of that surplus female population who have no chance of rest** in a husband's house and many of whom unhappily have no provision for the actual wants of life" should have public occupations open to them; but *not* potential wives and mothers. Was it more a woman's work "to dissect babies rather than to suckle them"? And woman's brain,

> being like the rest of her frame, of more delicate organization, is not capable of such sustained and continuous mental exertion as man's.†

Women vote? Most were properly far too occupied with home responsibilities even to consider taking that on; the rest, the idle, vain, rich, were interested only in fashion and amusement. Besides, husbands did not *want* their wives in the coarse political arena; and wives would not go against their husbands' wishes. Nor should. The Bible was clear on the matter: wives must obey their husbands. "If you do not wish to obey, do not marry."

Had Rebecca joined that succession of professional women

---

*1976: There is now some question as to whether she was its author.

**Yes, Rebecca, who did not do much resting in her husband's house, said "rest." In "The Wife's Story," she also uses the word "rest"—in a differing meaning: "To nestle down into this man's heart and life! To make his last years that warm Indian summer day! I could do it! I! What utter rest there were in that."

†Prevalent—and oft expressed—medical opinion of the period.

(they are still with us today) who discourse—profitably—to other women on the ordained rightness, naturalness, and glories of keeping to woman's sphere, while themselves exercising the privilege of wider realms and fuller use of self? No.

The glories, Rebecca believed; it was for her a time of genuine, deep family satisfactions. The ordain-edness, she also believed. It was a time of strict, literal interpretation of the Bible. That she wrote, worked at a "man's" occupation, did not occur to her as contradiction. She carried it on privately, at home, in a woman's way: that is, not as a man would, but fitted in, secondary to family; at the cost of none of her responsibilities to them. And she obeyed the Biblical injunctions: she kept to her place. It was Clarke's natural right, as husband, to make the decisions, including where they should live. She accepted unquestioningly that, whatever their respective capacities, it was Clarke—as a man—who should be enabled to do his best work, while her ordained situation as woman was to help him toward that end: to be responsible for house, children, the proper atmosphere for his concentration and relaxation—and manage her writing when and as best as she could. Men could have love, home, children, and work, without cost to the work. Not women.

She did not say "Wrong, all wrong." Violations of human potentiality which she refused to accept as natural, as ordained, in *Life in the Iron Mills,* she accepted as natural and ordained in the situation of women (including her own).

For all the insights throughout her writings on the narrowness, triviality, drudgery, hurts, restrictions in women's lives—yes, and evidences of capacity within those restrictions—she could not envision women "as they might be." Of their domestic, fourteen-hour-a-day, seven-day workweek, she did not ask Hetty's question, so terribly punished in "The Wife's Story": "Was [it] for this reality that God made me?" Nor did she apply to her own sex Hugh Wolfe's measure of "a true life," one of "full development of faculties."

When the high-tide time of family happiness out of which *Pro Aris et Focis* was written receded for Rebecca, she did not see its relationship to the situation of her sex. She knew only that something had gone terribly wrong with her life, her writing.

She was forty-one now. For eight years—often with exhilaration—she had been juggling cumulative responsibilities, selves, other beings. At last, the children old enough, she was beginning to have some space for time-self. Old aspirations began to rise. When, once more, she discovered she was pregnant.

The third child ("but the child was a girl"), Nora, was born in 1872.

The following year, Rebecca wrote another revealing "Wife's Story," but this time there is neither terror nor temptation in it: the gift is used—without punishment—for family needs; the anguish is explicit only on the last page.

She called it *Earthen Pitchers,* a seven-part serial in *Scribner's Monthly* (1873 and 1874) about the fate of two young women earning their living professionally at a time when professional women were an extreme rarity.

Jenny, "built for use but not for show," is a no-nonsense journalist, with no pretensions to art.

> Men who wanted to stand well with Jenny were wont to talk of the strength of her articles, quite as masculine as if they had been done by a man.

Audrey is a musician—violinist, singer, composer. She has been rigorously training herself since early childhood, eight to ten hours a day, for a life in music. Music "is all there is of me," she says. One of the men in love with her answers:

> "The best of you, I grant, but not all. . . . Half of your nature will be fallow. Besides, what do you know to teach by your art? What experience have you of life?"

On a night of auroral light and wild ocean storm, Audrey's whole-selved concentration on music is momentarily breached by a rousing of desire, a hunger for human love. Later, unable to sleep, she goes out again into the storm:

> . . . It seemed to her, she had grown to the age of sea and woods: they had received her into their company; she was one with them . . . she would have penetrated into the heart of this eternal world

if she could; its mysteries, its vastness, its infinite, inaccessible repose. . . . The longing, the hope, which belong to those who are akin with Nature, for which no man has ever found words, oppressed and choked her. "And I," she said, looking up and around her, as one who seeks a familiar face, "I too!"

She knows she must find a way to express this longing, this hope. "Strains of simple powerful harmony, unknown before," come to her. In what is a transcendent experience, she stays all night by the sea. Toward dawn, when "all things seemed waiting, glad, questioning, having accepted her as their own," kingbirds, sandpipers "fixing their eyes on her in recognition," she floats far out to deep water. It has "the solemnity of a baptism." She knows she has been "summoned by a heavenly call to do her work; forbidden to do any other."

But Kit, the man she loves, is blinded in a train accident. She marries after all:

> During those years, while he was both blind and helpless, . . . [she] supported the family by giving music lessons to all the children in the neighborhood. Her old uncle opposed her bitterly. . . .
>
> "Don't make a market of your birthright," he said, "hide it, bury it in a napkin if you will. You sold yourself, but don't sell that for your own selfish ends, or God will punish you."
>
> "My birthright is to love," said Audrey, and laid her hand on her husband's arm.

Both women are disillusioned in marriage but manage what happiness they can. Jenny's husband is a philanderer, dilettante, poseur, who takes all comforts and luxuries as his due. ("Jenny . . . knew all his maxims as she did her alphabet.") As for Audrey, "No wife could be more loving and cheerful with Kit. Yet, unconsciously, she gives you the impression that she has her own home and her own people elsewhere and will be gone to them presently."

The novel ends by the sea:

> The sun is heat to her now, and the sea, water.
>
> Presently, when evening begins to gather, and the sunset colors the sky and the pools in the marshes behind them blood-red, and the sea washes into their feet, dark and heavy, with subdued cries

and moans as though all the love and unappeased longing of the world had gone down into it, and sought to find speech in it, Audrey takes up the child, and begins to hush it on her breast, singing a little cradle song, a simple chant with which she was always crooning it to sleep. It is so hopeful, so joyful, so full of the unutterable brooding tenderness of mother's love, that Kit, who cares little for music, finds his heart swell and his eyes dim.

"Your uncle and that Goddard," he observes, "used to think you had a pretty talent for music Audrey. You were going to teach the whole world by your songs, I remember. But that little tune is all you ever made, eh? . . . And nobody ever heard it but Baby and me. However, it's very pretty, very pretty. And it was lucky your uncle taught you as thoroughly as he did. Your scales and notes helped us over a rough place. They served their purpose very well, though your voice is quite gone with teaching."

He strolls on up the beach.

When he was out of sight, a flock of kingbirds fly up from the hedges of bay bushes, and light near her, turning on her their bright black eyes with a curious look of inquiry. When was it they had looked at her so before?

For one brief moment the tossing waves, the sand dunes, the marshes put on their dear old familiar faces. Old meanings, old voices came close to her as ghosts in the sunlight. The blood rushed to her face, her blue eyes lighted. She buried her hands in the warm white sand. She held the long salt grass to her cheeks. She seemed to have come home to them again. "Child," they said to her, as the statues to Mignon, "where hast thou stayed so long?"

It seemed to her that she must answer them. She began to sing, she knew not what. But the tones were discordant, the voice was cracked. *Then she knew that whatever power she might have had was . . . wasted and gone.* She would never hear again the voice that once had called to her.

She rose then, and, taking up her child, went to the house, still looking in its face. Kit joined her, and was dully conscious that she had been troubled. "You're not vexed at what I said down there, eh?" he asked. "You're not really sorry, that you leave nothing to the world but that little song?"

"I leave my child," said Audrey; repeating after awhile, "I leave my child."

> Her husband, at least, was sure that she made no moan over that which might have been and was not. [Italics added.]

No happy ending. The wife had forsaken her heavenly call, taken up what was "no better work in life for a woman." She had literally made herself a visible Providence for her husband and child. The punishment came anyway. It was her birthright world of art out of which she was cast, whose faces were averted. The death was to the self that had had the power to achieve, the murder had been to her calling, the practice of art which was her life.

How much of the disillusion with marriage, the pain pulsing through the strong last chapter and distilled in its ambiguous last sentence, was also Rebecca's, writing in the tenth year of her marriage?

In the ten years she had lost her place in the literary world. She no longer published in the *Atlantic*. The letters from Annie were lapsing. She no longer believed in, acted upon, the possibility of high achievement for herself. It was the price for children, home, love.

Was part of the price, too, that there was no one to whom she could speak the dimensions, the pain, of her loss—not even Clarke *(perhaps not even herself)*?

Hints in *Earthen Pitchers* support the outward facts that this was so. From the beginning, Clarke had not respected her aspiration to art. His own approach was writing as journalistic commodity, not writing as literature. Nor after marriage had he concerned himself with circumstances for her best writing. For all his love, his initial recognition of her potential greatness as writer (her first attraction for him), he had settled easily into what Rebecca too accepted unquestioningly: the "ordained" man-wife pattern of *his* ambitions, activities, comforts, needs coming first.

Well, most adults, she observed in an editorial about this time, find themselves having to put their own needs, dreams, aspirations, aside when they take on responsibilities for growing lives. She did not specify female or male. She also made it clear that other satisfactions, fulfillments, came. Her husband, at least, whether dully conscious or not, would be sure that "she made no moan over that which might have been, and was not."

The power for art might be wasted and gone, but the power for work remained. The alive social intelligence kept listening to its society, though it might never hear again the voice that once had called. In 1874 she published *John Andross,* calling attention to the control of government by special interests, through bribery of legislators, gangsterism if necessary; and the corruption of character through subservience to wealth. It was the first novel of this kind.

The first year in the new house, she had written another first book of its kind—a defense of the rights of supposedly insane persons. Clarke had told her in his lawyer days of the malign practice whereby family members or enemies could, without notice, commit a sane person as insane to an institution, to be held there incommunicado ("buried alive") for life—simply on the basis of a statement by one cooperative doctor. Now her *Put Out of the Way* (published in *Peterson's* in 1871), along with editorials and articles by Clarke, resulted in getting the Pennsylvania lunacy laws changed.

The Philadelphia Centennial Exposition of 1876 came and went. "Though Clarke was one of the most active managers . . . I was only down there one evening," Rebecca wrote Annie. She was not present, then, when Susan B. Anthony, Elizabeth Cady Stanton, and other women "sat in" at the assembly celebrating that hundredth year of the Declaration of Independence and took over the platform to read their Women's Declaration of Rights.

Rebecca went almost nowhere now. Clarke went everywhere. He was a leading citizen, an increasingly influential man-about-town; his fishing companions included Grover Cleveland. Their social circle consisted of Clarke's friends, many of them theatrical people. The Drews, the Barrymores; when they were in town, Ellen Terry, Sir Henry Irving, Joseph Jefferson, Edwin Booth. Pre-matinee breakfasts at the Davises' became a custom. There is no record that Rebecca went on to the theater with Clarke afterward.

In 1878, the *The Nation* reviewed *A Law Unto Herself:*

Mrs. Rebecca Harding Davis writes stories which can hardly be called pleasant, and which frequently, as in "A Law Unto Herself," deal with most unpleasant persons, but there is an undercurrent of recognized aptitude and a capacity for calling a spade a spade which sets her writing in a category far removed from French morality . . . though she shows bad taste in various ways, or perhaps because of this, she succeeds in giving a truer impression of American conditions than any writer we know except Mr. Howells, while there is a vast difference between his delicately illuminated preparations of our social absurdities and Mrs. Davis's grim and powerful etchings. Somehow she contrives to get the American atmosphere, its vague excitement, its strife of effort, its varying possibilities. Add to this a certain intensity, a veiled indignation at prosperity, and doubt of the honesty of success, and we get qualities which make Mrs. Davis's books individual and interesting if not agreeable.

She did not feel very agreeable. The rasp of asperity characterized her more and more. She wrote the young Kate Fields in England: "Don't come home if you are happy there. You can have no idea of the stagnation of . . . all life here. The country is like a man whom somebody is holding by the throat."

In 1881, into this supposed stagnation, Helen Hunt Jackson published her documented denunciation of the genocidal treatment of the American Indian, *A Century of Dishonor* (a first of *its* kind). To the keen disappointment of its author, who regarded Rebecca as a still-active champion of the wronged ("I counted on you to bring out the facts as I wanted them brought out"), she did not review it.

There is a picture of Rebecca taken during this time. The hair is still severely parted in the middle, but now the luxuriant curls are stiff; the eyes, slits; the face clamped; the hands clamped together. She looks old, shrewd, grim, somehow formidable; not at all the ardent young woman who twenty years before had been a Hope in native letters and had had her picture taken before going up North to be welcomed as such.

Oliver Wendell Holmes had not forgotten that younger Rebecca. Richard, now eighteen, stopped by to visit him: "He talked a great deal about Mamma."

Mamma thought a great deal about Richard. "I leave my child," Audrey had said stubbornly at the end of *Earthen Pitchers,* "I leave my child." It was beginning to seem that Rebecca's child might become the fine writer she had not. She encouraged him, with advice still helpful for young writers:

> I don't say like Papa, stop writing. God forbid. I would almost as soon say stop breathing, for it is pretty much the same thing. But only to remember that you have not yet conquered your art. You are a journeyman, not a master workman, so if you don't succeed [now] it does not count. The future is what to look to. . . . I've had 30 years experience and I know how much [getting published] depends on the articles suiting the present needs of the magazine, and also on the mood of the editor when he reads it. Develop . . . your dramatic eye; your quick perception of character and of the way character shows itself in looks, tones, dress; . . . your keen sympathy with all kinds of people. Add to that your humour. Just in proportion to your feeling more deeply and noticing more keenly, [you will] acquire the faculty of expressing more delicately and powerfully. Not inspiration, practice. A lasting real success takes time and patient steady work.
>
> I had to stop my work to say all this, so goodbye dear old chum.

And mamma went back to her work in which, through habits of years, she seldom stopped to use her advice. Richard went on to become famous.*

Rebecca's first critical and popular success in years ("These *young* writers are crowding me to the wall," wrote Richard) came

---

*Though Richard Harding Davis's multitude of books do not have the intrinsic merit and interest of his mother's, he was one of the celebrated writers of his time, a man of action and letters whose example supposedly influenced Hemingway and John Reed.

His was the most famous face of his generation. Booth Tarkington wrote of him: "To the college boy of the 90's, he was the beau ideal. His stalwart good looks were as familiar to us as were those of our own football captain; we knew his face as we knew the face of the President of the United States, but we infinitely preferred Davis'."

Davis was the model for Charles Dana Gibson's man-about-town, appearing over and over in the famous Gibson Girl drawings. Later, during his roving correspondent days, he was often seen in press photographs with presidents, warring generals, revolutionary leaders, explorers.

He wrote Rebecca almost every day of her life, and took care of her the last few years.

in 1892 with *Silhouettes of American Life,* her first collection of stories.* A strain from *Earthen Pitchers* and from "The Wife's Story" sounds within it: the power for art wasted and gone—but this time there is doubt, had there ever been power?

> It was with her precisely as when her heart swelled with a song that ought to silence heaven itself—and she uttered a cracked piping falsetto; or as when years ago, she felt herself inspired with poetry, and had written miserable rhymes—vapid and pretentious.

And there is a significant story, "Anne," of an older woman, a woman in her sixties, who runs away from home. Though she is shrewdly successful in business, and her children patronizingly love her, somewhere else is her heart's country of books and music "and the companionship of thinkers." On the train she sits close enough to overhear a famous poet, a great painter of human suffering, a noted woman reformer, all traveling together. But they prove false, "mere hucksters," who "had made a trade of art and humanity . . . until they had lost the perceptions of their highest meanings."

The train is wrecked. She is brought back home, "petted like a baby":

> Yet sometimes in the midst of all this comfort and sunshine a chance note of music or the sound of the restless wind will bring an expression into her eyes which her children do not understand, as if some creature unknown to them looked out. . . .
>
> At such times [she] will say to herself, "Poor Anne!" as of somebody whom she once knew that is dead.
>
> *Is* she dead?

Probably to the end of her days, a creature unknown to those around her lived on in Rebecca, a secret creature still hungry to know; living (like Audrey) ecstatically in nature, in the sea, summers; living (like Anne) "with her own people, elsewhere" in the year-round red-brick house.

---

*All the stories previously quoted from, including *Life in the Iron Mills,* remain uncollected.

Seldom does she appear in the books and stories and articles that kept on and on (so many that it would take several years just to read all she wrote in her lifetime). In her seventies, she still kept grinding them out. This is but a sampling: "Temple of Fame," "Curse of Education," "Ignoble Martyr," "Country Girls in Town," "The Disease of Money-Getting," "Is It All for Nothing?" "In the Grey Cabins of New England" (about the "starved, coffined" lives of spinsters), "New Traits of the New American," "Under the Old Code," "The Black North" (about the furor aroused by President Roosevelt's inviting Booker T. Washington to dine at the White House—nothing so delighted Rebecca as exposing northern racist hypocrisy), "Recovery of Family Life," "Story of a Few Plain Women," "Undistinguished Americans," "Unwritten History."

She died in 1910, age seventy-nine, writing almost to the last moment. No literary journal noted her passing.

Life in the Iron Mills and *Margret Howth* were already so obliterated by 1891 that Eleanor Marx and Edward Aveling, in their *The Working Class Movement in America,* could write:

> . . . one of these days the Uncle Tom's Cabin of Capitalism will be written.
>
> And here we are tempted to ask, "Where are the American writers of fiction?" With a subject, and such a subject, lying ready to their very hands, clamoring at their very doors, not one of them touches it . . . there are no studies of factory-hands and of dwellers in tenement houses; no pictures of those sunk in the innermost depths of the modern *Inferno.*

On the occasion of her death, *The New York Times did* resurrect the fact that a half century before—before the Inferno had emerged as the overwhelming dominant of American life—a work on the subject had appeared. In its newsstory-obituary ("Mother of Richard Harding Davis Dies at Son's Home in Mt. Kisco, Aged 79"), it told how:

> In 1861 she sent to the *Atlantic Monthly* a story entitled "Life in the Iron Mills," depicting the grinding life of the working people around her. . . . It attracted attention from all over the country

... many thought the author must be a man. The stern but artistic realism of the picture she put alive upon paper, suggested a man, and a man of power not unlike Zola's.

They did not mention that she had preceded Zola by two decades.*

The *Dictionary of American Biography* memorializes her in an estimate denying stern and artistic merit altogether:

... without guidance or knowledge of literary art save as she had gained it from voluminous reading, she began early to write fiction. . . . Though often crude and amateurish in workmanship, these stories were nevertheless remarkable productions, distinct landmarks in the evolution of American fiction. Written when the American novel was in all its areas ultra-romantic and over-sentimental, they are Russian-like in their grim and sordid realism.

Landmarks, unless they loom large in landscapes often visited, tend to become weed-grown tombstones over the forgotten dead, noticed only by accident.

Even the sense of landmark has been obliterated. Rebecca Harding Davis is a name known today only to a handful of American Studies people and literary historians. Few have read any of her work; fewer still teach any of it.**

---

*The newsstory-obituary erred as to when *Life in the Iron Mills* was written, saying that Rebecca "was then less than 20 years old." The lead paragraph and the account as a whole gave as much space to her family as to her: "Mrs. Rebecca Harding Davis, 79 years old, widow of the late L. Clarke Davis, at one time editor of The Philadelphia Public Ledger, mother of Richard Harding Davis, the novelist and dramatist, and herself a novelist and editorial writer of power, died here to-night of heart disease."

**Since 1971 when this was written and published with *Life in the Iron Mills* in the Feminist Press reprint series, there has been a revival of interest in her work. *Life in the Iron Mills* is increasingly taught in literature courses, American Studies and Women's Studies classes. I first taught it, in Xerox copies made from the 1861 *Atlantic,* at Amherst College in 1969.

Myriads of human beings—those who did the necessary industrial work in the last century—lived and died and little remains
from which to reconstruct their perished (vanished) lives. About
them as about so much else, literature was largely silent, and the
charge can be levied: *Nowhere am I in it.*

> No picture, poem, statement, passing them to the
>   future
> Unlimn'd, they disappear.*

To those of us, descendants of their class, hungry for any
rendering of what our vanished people were like, of how they
lived, Rebecca Harding Davis's *Life in the Iron Mills* is immeasur-
ably valuable. Details, questions, Vision, found nowhere else—
dignified into literature.

She never wrote anything of its near-classic quality after.

Once, at Harvard's Widener Library, in that time of my trying to trace what had happened to Rebecca Harding, out of
one of her books—*John Andross?*—fell an undated presentation
card:

> For Mr. C. E. Norton
>   from R. H. D.
>   Judge me—not by what I have done,
> but by what I have hoped to do.**

Poor Rebecca. The cry of every artist (of every human). But
Proust is right. There are no excuses in art. Including having been
born female in the wrong time/place.

A scanty best of her work is close to the first rank; justifies
resurrection, currency, fame. Even that best is botched.

Here or there in even her most slipshod novels, stage-set plots,
moldering stories: a grandeur of conception ("touches, grand
sweeps of outline"), a breathing character, a stunning insight, a

---

*From Walt Whitman's "Yonnondio."

**C. E. Norton was Charles Eliot Norton, editor, man of literature, Harvard
professor. He left his library to that university.

scene as transcendent as any written in her century, also confirm for us what a great writer was lost in her.

Even in the tons of her ephemera, of the topical nonfiction, there is vitality, instructive range—and a fascinating native quality in its combination of radicalism, reaction, prophecy, piecemeal insight, skepticism, idealism—all done up in a kind of exasperated plain-spokenness.

The strong pulse of her work quoted herein evidences that—botched art or not—a significant portion of her work remains important and vitally alive for our time.

What Virginia Woolf wrote of Elizabeth Barrett Browning characterizes Rebecca as well: "a true daughter of her age: passionate interest in social questions, conflict as artist and woman, longing for knowledge and freedom." With Rebecca, much could be only longing.

She is more than landmark, of contemporary interest only to literary historians—though she is that too. There is an untraced indebtedness to her in the rise of realism.* She maintained that fiction which incorporates social and economic problems directly, *and in terms of their effects on human beings.*

She was more than realist. In the most scrupulous sense, she followed Emerson's dictum:

> I ask not for the great, the remote, the romantic. . . . I embrace the common, I explore and sit at the feet of the familiar, the low.
>
> The foolish man wonders at the unusual; the wise man at the usual.

---

*Only Elizabeth Stuart Lyon Phelps, herself largely forgotten, acknowledged the debt, the influence, paying tribute to Rebecca as "writing with an ardor that was human, and a passion that was art." In her reminiscences, *Chapters in a Life,* she writes of *Life in the Iron Mills* as: "a distinct crisis for one young writer at the point where intellect and moral nature meet. . . . One could never again say that one did not understand. The claims of toil and suffering upon ease had assumed a new form. For me they acquired a force which has never let me go." Phelps's "The Twelfth of January" (*Atlantic Monthly,* November 1868), in which 112 mill girls are burned to death in a textile mill fire (an actual incident), and her *Silent Partner* (1871) were directly inspired by Rebecca's work. So, less directly, were the *Story of Avis* and *Dr. Zay.*

The complexity of that wonder at the usual illumines her best pages.

She was not derivative. Her pioneering firsts in subject matter are unequaled in American literature. She extended the realm of fiction.

Without intention, she was a social historian invaluable for an understanding access to her time. On her pages are people and situations that are discovery, not only of the past, but of ourselves.

From her work—like *"the figure of the mill-woman cut in korl. . . . [kept] hid behind a curtain,—it is such a rough, ungainly thing"*—her epoch looks through *"with its thwarted life, its mighty hunger, its unfinished work."*

It is time to rend the curtain——

My primary sources have been the writings of Rebecca
Harding Davis, everything of hers accessible to me for reading.
In addition, I relied on Gerald Langford's *The Richard Harding Davis Years* (1961) for some biographical facts (not interpretation); on Helen Woodward Schaeffer's *Rebecca Harding
Davis, Pioneer Realist* (a superb, as-yet-unpublished doctoral
dissertation, 1947); on Charles Belmont Davis's *The Adven-
tures and Letters of Richard Harding Davis* (1917); and—as is
evident—on other reading of many years, coincidentally related
to the period in which Rebecca lived. I regret there was not
means to go to the archives of the University of Virginia to
read her collected papers there.

I first read *Life in the Iron Mills* in one of three water-stained,
coverless, bound volumes of the *Atlantic Monthly,* bought for ten
cents each in an Omaha junkshop. I was fifteen. Contributions to
those old *Atlantics* were published anonymously, and I was ignorant of any process whereby I might find the name of the author
of this work which meant increasingly more to me over the years,
saying, with a few other books, "Literature can be made out of the
lives of despised people," and "You, too, must write."

No reader I encountered had ever heard of the story, let alone
who might have written it. It was not until the collected *Letters
of Emily Dickinson* came out in 1958 that, in the reference room
of the San Francisco Public Library where I went lunch hours
from work to read them, I learned who the author was. Appended
to a note from Emily to her sister-in-law,

> Will Susan please lend Emily "Life in the Iron Mills"—and accept
> blossom

was this citation:

> Rebecca Harding Davis' "Life in the Iron Mills" appeared in the
> April 1861 issue of the *Atlantic Monthly.*

It did not surprise me that the author was of my sex. At once
I eagerly looked for other works by her. But there was no Rebecca
Harding Davis in the library's card catalogue. It did not occur to
me to try the index of periodicals, as it dated only from the 1890s

and I assumed that she had been dead long before. No other library, even had I had time, was accessible to me then.

Only when I received an appointment to the Radcliffe Institute in 1962 did I begin to have occasional time for and access to her other work. There they were, in Harvard's Widener Library, in the Cambridge and Boston public libraries—old volumes, not taken out for years.

So began my knowledge of her contribution and its woeful deterioration; my attempt to understand what had happened to the Rebecca Harding who had once written with such power, beauty, comprehension.

I never envisioned writing of her until Florence Howe and Paul Lauter, to whom I had introduced *Life in the Iron Mills,* suggested that The Feminist Press issue it and I write the afterword. This is the result. If I have quoted so extensively from her work, it is because it is neither readily available nor known. If this came to be more biographical interpretation and history ("human story") than critical afterword, it is because I am convinced that that is what is most needed. I have brought to her life and work my understanding as writer, as insatiable reader, as feminist-humanist, as woman.

Rebecca Harding Davis's correspondence, some of the correspondence with her, and other references used are scattered through a number of volumes. As for years, until the writing of this manuscript, I was reading for myself only, and had had no academic training in notation, I copied out material usually without troubling to record exact pages, publishers, dates of publication, sometimes even the titles of books or magazines. This explains the few instances in which the exact source is not cited; but in every case it can be authenticated. Where no source is indicated, and it is Rebecca Harding Davis who is being quoted, the material comes either from correspondence, articles, or is a phrase from her fiction, usually from *Life in the Iron Mills*—and the context should make the difference clear.

PART TWO

Acerbs, Asides, Amulets, Exhumations,
Sources,
Deepenings, Roundings, Expansions ▲

Much of this aftersection is the words
of others—some of them unknown or
little known, others of them great and
famous. Each quotation, as each reference to lives, is selectively chosen for
maximum significance; to become—or
to again become—current; to occur and
recur; to aim.

The organization follows the order of
thought in the original essays, page by
page, and is so keyed. ▲

▲ ESSAY PAGE NUMBER TO WHICH EACH REFERS.

PART TWO

The silences I speak of here are unnatural; the unnatural thwarting of what struggles to come into being . . . when the seed strikes stone; the soil will not sustain; the spring is false; the time is drought or blight or infestation; the frost comes premature.

SILENCES IN LITERATURE—II

SILENCES OF THE GREAT IN ACHIEVEMENT:
(Primarily in Their Own Words)

Thomas Hardy (1840–1928) ▲

> *"Less and less shrink the visions then vast in me," writes Thomas Hardy in his thirty-year ceasing from novels after the Victorian vileness to his* Jude the Obscure *("so ended his prose contributions to literature, his experiences . . . having killed all his interest in this form.")*

It was a twenty-eight year killing. Every aim and aspiration of Hardy's in the writing of fiction (except for the getting of his living by it) was thwarted. He had sought to write "the substance of life only"—(of working people, of women; illuminating their constricted circumstances; according them and their lives full dimension and tragedy)—and to create fiction "near to poetry." Tenaciously though he fought, always he ended up not being able to attain—or having to damage—"his artistic whole."

In the earlier writing years, he had had neither the confidence (by reason of origin) nor the means, to write what or how he wished. Later, even with *Tess,* even with *Jude,* the great mature novels written when he was financially less at the mercy of publishers, there yet remained the massive class and sexual (i.e., sexist) censorship of his time; the rigidly circumscribed form of the novel as then practiced, to continue to defeat him. He was fifty-eight when he was "grated to pieces by the constant attrition," gave up imaginative prose, thirty years of writing vitality still in him.

The record is in his own statements, understatements rather— for he was the most reticent of writers. Whether in first or third person, these are all Hardy's own words:*

1873

He perceived that he was . . . committed by circumstances to novel-writing as a regular trade; and that hence he would, he deemed, have to look for material in manners—in ordinary social and fashionable life, as other novelists did. Yet he took no interest in manners, but in the substance of life only. So far, what he had written had not been novels at all as usually understood.

1884

Hardy fancied he had damaged [his *Mayor of Casterbridge*] more recklessly as an artistic whole in the interest of the newspaper in which it appeared serially, than perhaps any of his other novels; his aiming to get an incident into almost every week's part, causing him . . . to add events to the narrative somewhat too freely.

1887

The ending of [*The Woodlanders*] hinted rather than stated . . . that the heroine is doomed to an unhappy life with an inconstant husband. I could not accentuate this strongly in the book, by reason of the conventions of the libraries, etc. Since it was written, however, truth to character is not considered quite such a crime in literature as it was formerly.

1889–1890

In October [1889], as much of *Tess of the d'Urbervilles* as was written was offered . . . to *Murray's Magazine*. It was declined and returned . . . virtually on the score of its improper explicitness. . . . The editor of *Macmillan's Magazine* . . . declined [it] for practically the same reason.

---

*Mostly from *The Life of Thomas Hardy*, ostensibly by Florence Emily Hardy, but actually dictated, or selected from notebooks and letters, by Hardy himself (except for the account of the last of his life).

Hardy would now have much preferred to finish the story and bring it out in volume form only, but there were reasons why he could not afford to do this. . . . Some chapters or parts of chapters [were] cut out . . . till they could be put back in their places at the printing of the whole in volume form. In addition several passages were modified. . . . But the work was sheer drudgery.

1890

If the true artist ever weeps, it is at the fearful price he has to pay for the privilege of writing in the language, no less a price than the complete extinction of sympathetic belief in his personages in the mind of every mature and penetrating reader.*

1891

. . . During the publication of *Tess of the d'Urbervilles* as a serial in *The Graphic* . . . the editor objected to the description of Angel Clare carrying in his arms, across a flooded lane, Tess and her three dairymaid companions. He suggested that it would be more decorous and suitable for the pages of a periodical intended for family reading if the damsels were wheeled across the land in a wheelbarrow. This was accordingly done.

The Graphic [also] refused to print the chapter describing the christening of Tess's illegitimate infant. This . . . was afterwards restored to the novel, where it was considered one of the finest passages.

1892

. . . The tediousness of the alterations and restorations had made him weary of [*Tess*].

1893–1895, during the writing of *Jude the Obscure* ("the tragedy of unfulfilled aims"), eight years in the gestation and closest of all his novels to his heart, Hardy again had to continuously alter, invent substitute scenes and prose suitable for magazine serial publication.

1894

. . . Restoring the Ms. of *Jude the Obscure* to its original state.
. . . On account of the labour of altering [it] to suit the magazine,

---

*Hardy's "Candour in English Fiction."

and then having to alter it back, I have lost energy for revising and improving the original as I meant to do.

1895

You have hardly an idea how poor and feeble the book seems to me, as executed, beside the idea of it that I had formed in prospect.

1896, in the midst of his private despair over his failure to make *Jude* the book he had wished, and of the public revilement of it, he wrote in his notebooks:

Poetry. Perhaps I can express more fully in verse, ideas and emotions which run counter to the inert crystallized opinion—hard as a rock—which the vast body of men have vested interests in supporting. . . . If Galileo had said in verse that the world moved, the Inquisition might have let him alone.

1897

. . . So ended his prose contributions to literature . . . his experiences of the few preceding years having killed all his interest in this form of imaginative work (which had ever been secondary to his interest in verse).

1897–1898

. . . [All] wellnigh compelled him, in his own judgment at any rate, if he wished to retain any shadow of self-respect, to abandon at once [this] form of literary art. . . .

. . . The change, after all, was not so great as it seemed. It was not as if he had been a writer of novels proper, and as more specifically understood, that is, stories of modern artificial life and manners showing a certain smartness of treatment. He had mostly aimed at keeping his narratives as close to natural life and as near to poetry in their subject as the conditions would allow, and had regretted that those conditions would not let him keep them nearer still.

How deeply he lived his books in their creating—the younger writer so possessed that in

. . . writing *Far From the Madding Crowd*—sometimes indoors, sometimes out—when he would occasionally find himself without a scrap of paper at the very moment that he felt volumes . . . he would use large dead leaves, white chips left by woodcutters, or pieces of stone or slate that came to hand.

How ineradicably his creations lived on in him; notebook entries of incidents, or people seen, reminding him of them; other instances of recalling. And the old, old Hardy, close to eighty-six, at a special performance in his home of *Tess of the D'Ubervilles*, sitting there with tears in his eyes, his lips mutely repeating by heart the words he had written thirty-seven years before; after the performance, "insisting on talking to us until the last minute. He talked of Tess as if she was someone real." He spoke of her so to Virginia Woolf, too, when she visited him: "I used to see women now and then with the look of her."

But the great poetry he wrote to the end of his life was not sufficient to hold, to develop, the vast visions which for twenty-eight years had had expression in novel after novel. People, situations, interrelationships, landscape—they cry for larger life in poem after poem.

Gerard Manley Hopkins (1844–1889) ▲

It was not visions shrinking with Hopkins, but a different torment. For seven years he kept his religious vow to refrain from writing poetry, but the poet's eye he could not shut, nor win "elected silence to beat upon [his] whorled ear." "I had long had haunting my ear the echo of a poem which now I realised on paper," he writes of the first poem permitted to end the seven years' silence. But poetry ("to hoard unheard; be heard, unheeded") could be only the least and last of his heavy priestly responsibilities. Nineteen poems were all he could produce in his last nine years—fullness to us, but torment pitched past grief to him, who felt himself become "time's eunuch, never to beget."

In briefest summary, the making of that torment:

—Years in which poetry begged to be written, had to be denied.
—Scarcely ever the slightest circumstances for writing—a life of sheer, hard, tasking work.
—When he did write, the sense of it as sin—betrayal of his highest convictions and responsibilities as a Jesuit priest.
—The crushing burden of the terrible circumstances for "common humanity" felt during his work in Liverpool, Glasgow, Dublin.
—The sense of exile: "*To seem the stranger lies my lot, my life Among strangers.*"
—Lonely knowledge of his great and original achievement—unvalidated outside himself. *To hoard unheard.*
—Aborted hopes for publication in his lifetime; ineradicable hunger for esteem, recognition of his achievement, if only in the form of comprehending appreciation of his work by a selected few poets of standing. *To be heard, unheeded.*

Each selection that follows could be multiplied many times over. All are from letters to those selected few poets of standing.

In each case, Hopkins initiated, and maintained, the correspondence.*

1876, when he began to write poetry again, to 1879 were years of favorable circumstances for Hopkins. He was stationed in Wales, which he loved and where he created almost with his early fluency—twenty-five poems in three years. It was in this time that he began to send work to the poet Robert Bridges; having to explain and defend it, he began writing to Richard Watson Dixon as well.

1877, to Bridges

> There is no conceivable license I shd. not be able to justify. . . . With all my licences, or rather laws, I am stricter than you and I might say than anybody I know. With the exception of the Bremen stanza, which was, I think, the first written after 10 years' interval of silence, and before I had fixed my principles, my rhymes are rigidly good to the ear. . . .

1878, the year Hopkins was ordained, to Dixon

> . . . if I had written and published works the extreme beauty of which the author himself the most keenly feels and they had fallen out of sight at once and been . . . almost wholly unknown; then, I say, I should feel a certain comfort to be told they had been deeply appreciated by some one person, a stranger at all events, and had not been published quite in vain. Many beautiful works have been almost unknown and then have gained fame at last . . . but many more must have been lost sight of altogether. . . .

---

*There is strong parallel between Hopkins and Emily Dickinson; both almost unpublished in their lifetime; both among the most original and greatest poets of their time; both obsessed by fame which they knew rightfully belonged to them (fame as Hopkins defined: "recognition belonging to the work itself"); both reaching out and clinging to the few recognized persons in letters who took them seriously, accorded them response. Obloquy continues to be heaped upon Thomas Wentworth Higginson (in my view, undeservedly) in regard to not getting Dickinson published—none upon Bridges, who became Poet Laureate of England. In addition to what becomes evident in the correspondence quoted here, Bridges waited twenty-nine years after Hopkins's death to begin to publish the poems, and then, in an apologetic and patronizing preface, expounded on Hopkins's "bad faults."

1878, also to Dixon

> When I spoke of fame I was not thinking of the harm it does to men as artists: it may do them harm, as you say, but so, I think, may the want of it, if "Fame is the spur that the clear spirit doth raise To shun delights and live laborious days"—a spur very hard to find a substitute for or to do without. . . .
>
> What I do regret is the loss of recognition belonging to the work itself. . . .
>
> . . . For disappointment and humiliations embitter the heart and make an aching in the very bones.

1878, also to Dixon

> You ask, do I write verse myself. What I had written I burnt before I became a Jesuit and resolved to write no more, as not belonging to my profession, unless it were by the wish of my superiors; so for seven years I wrote nothing but two or three little presentation pieces which occasion called for. But when in the winter of '75 the Deutschland was wrecked in the mouth of the Thames and five Franciscan nuns, exiles from Germany by the Falck Laws, aboard of her were drowned, I was affected by the account and happening to say so to my rector he said that he wished someone would write a poem on the subject. On this hint I set to work and, though my hand was out at first, produced one. I had long had haunting my ear the echo of a new rhythm which now I realised on paper.

1880, the beginning of heavy duties in Manchester, Liverpool, and Glasgow, to Dixon

> I do not think I can be long here; I have been long nowhere yet. I am brought face to face with the deepest poverty and misery in my district. . . .
>
> . . . The parish work of Liverpool is very wearying to mind and body and leaves me nothing but odds and ends of time. There is merit in it but little Muse, and indeed 26 lines is the whole I have writ in more than half a year, since I left Oxford.

1881, to Bridges

> Every impulse and spring of art seems to have died in me, except for music, and that I pursue under almost an impossibility of getting on. . . .

1881, also to Bridges

... The vein urged by any country sight or feeling of freedom or leisure (you cannot tell what a slavery of mind or heart it is to live my life in a great town) soon dried and I do not know if I can coax it to run again. One night, as I lay awake in a fevered state, I had some glowing thoughts and lines, but I did not put them down and I fear they may fade to little or nothing. I am sometimes surprised at myself how slow and laborious a thing verse (now) is to me. ...

1881, to Dixon

My vocation puts before me a standard so high that a higher can be found nowhere else. The question then for me is not whether I am willing (if I may guess what is in your mind) to make a sacrifice of hopes of fame (let us suppose), but whether I am not to undergo a severe judgment from God for the lothness I have shewn in making it, for the reserves I may have in my heart made, for the backward glances I have given with my hand upon the plough, for the waste of time the very compositions you admire may have caused and their preoccupation of the mind which belonged to more sacred or more binding duties, for the disquiet and the thoughts of vain-glory they have given rise to. A purpose may look smooth and perfect from without but be frayed and faltering from within. I have never wavered in my vocation, but I have not lived up to it. I destroyed the verse I had written when I entered the Society and meant to write no more; the Deutschland I began after a long interval at the chance suggestion of my superior, but that being done it is a question whether I did well to write anything else. However I shall, in my present mind, continue to compose, as occasion shall fairly allow, which I am afraid will be seldom and indeed for some years past has been scarcely ever. ...

1881, to Bridges

My Liverpool and Glasgow experience laid upon my mind a conviction, a truly crushing conviction, of the misery of the poor in general, of the degradation even of our race, of the hollowness of this century's civilisation: it made even life a burden to me to have daily thrust upon me the things I saw. ...

1883, to Bridges

Some of my rhymes I regret, but they are past changing, grubs in amber; there are only a few of these; others are unassailable. ...

. . . Some others again there are which malignity may munch at but the Muses love.

1884, to Bridges

Mr. Patmore [Coventry Patmore, the poet] did not on the whole like my poems [which had been sent him], was unconverted to them. . . . AND WHAT DOES ANYTHING AT ALL MATTER? . . . I am in great weakness.

1885, to Baillie

The melancholy I have all my life been subject to has become of late years not indeed more intense in its fits but rather more distributed, constant, and crippling. One . . . is daily anxiety about work to be done, which makes me break off or never finish all that lies outside that work. It is useless to write more on this: when I am at the worst, though my judgment is never affected, my state is much like madness. I see no ground for thinking I shall ever get over it or ever succeed in doing anything that is not forced on me to do of any consequence.

1885, to Bridges, enclosing fragments of a poem, "St Winefred's Well"

. . . I once thought well of the pieces, I do not know that I do now. But A and B please me well enough. You will see that as the feeling rises the rhythm becomes freer & more sprung. I think I have written nothing stronger than some of these lines. . . .

. . . if I were otherwise than I am it would brisk me up and set me to work, but in that coffin of weakness and dejection in which I live, without even the hope of change, I do not know that I can make, or, making, could keep up the exertion of learning better. . . .

1885, also to Bridges

Dearest Bridges—I must write something, though not as much as I have to say. The long delay was due to work, worry, and languishment of body and mind—which must be and will be; . . . I think that my fits of sadness, though they do not affect my judgment, resemble madness. Change is the only relief and that I can seldom get.

. . . we compose fragmentarily and what I had here and there done I finished up and sent as samples to see if I cd. be encouraged to go on—and I was encouraged; that is by your last [letter], for before you thought they wd. not do. There is a point with me in matters of any size when I must absolutely have encouragement as much as crops rain; afterwards I am independent. However, I am in my ordinary circumstances unable, with whatever encouragement, to go on with *Winefred* or anything else. I have after long silence written two sonnets . . . if ever anything was written in blood one of these was. . . .

1885, also to Bridges

If I could but get on, if I could but produce work I should not mind its being buried, silenced, and going no further; but it kills me to be time's eunuch and never to beget. After all I do not despair, things might change, anything may be; only there is no great appearance of it. Now because I have had a holiday though not strong I have some buoyancy; soon I am afraid I shall be ground down to a state like this last spring's and summer's, when my spirits were so crushed that madness seemed to be making approaches—and nobody was to blame, except myself partly for not managing myself better and contriving a change. . . .

1886, to Dixon

. . . I have written a few sonnets; that is all I have done in poetry for some years.

. . . It is not possible for me to do anything, unless a sonnet, and that rarely, in poetry with a fagged mind and a continual anxiety: but there are things at which I can, so far as time serves, work, if it were only by snatches.

1887, to Bridges

It was quite right to tell me what Woolridge thought—that is what I wanted to know—and to use it as a dissuasive, if you liked; but not as a discouragement (yr. own word): discouragement is not what my complaint, in my opinion, needs. Our institute provides us means of discouragement, and on me at all events they have had all the effect that could be expected or wished and rather more. . . .

1887, also to Bridges

Tomorrow morning I shall have been three years in Ireland, three

hard wearying wasting wasted years. . . . They should see my heart
and vitals, all shaggy with the whitest hair. In those I have done
God's will (in the main) and many many examination papers.
. . . I only need one thing—a working health, a working strength. . . .

1888, to Bridges

I laughed outright and often, but very sardonically, to think you
and the Canon [Dixon] could not construe my last sonnet; that he
had to write to you for a crib. It is plain I must go no farther on
this road: if you and he cannot understand me, who will?

Hopkins died in 1899 at the age of forty-five.

> . . . Only what word
> Wisest my heart breeds, dark heaven's baffling ban
> Bars or hell's spell thwarts. This to hoard unheard,
> Heard unheeded, leaves me a lonely began.*

> . . . See, banks and brakes
> Now, leavèd how thick! lacèd they are again
> With fretty chervil, look, and fresh wind shakes
> Them; birds build — but not I build; no, but strain,
> Time's eunuch, and not breed one work that wakes.
> Mine, O thou lord of life, send my roots rain.**

---

*From "To seem the stranger lies my lot, my life."
**From "Thou art indeed just, Lord."

Herman Melville (1819–1891) ▲

"O who shall reveal the horrors of poverty in authorship that is high?":

1849

> When a poor devil writes with duns all around him, and looking over the back of his chair, and perching on his pen, and dancing in his inkstand—like the Devils about St. Anthony—what can you expect of that poor devil? What but a beggarly *Redburn?*

1851

> I am so pulled hither and thither by circumstances. The calm, the coolness, the silent grass-growing mood in which a man ought always to compose,—that, I fear, can seldom be mine. Dollars damn me; and the malicious Devil is forever grinning in upon me, holding the door ajar. My dear Sir, a presentiment is on me,—I shall at last be worn out and perish, like an old nutmeg-grater, grated to pieces by the constant attrition. . . . What I feel most moved to write, that is banned,—it will not pay. Yet, altogether, write the *other* way I cannot. So the product is a final hash, and all my books are botches.

1863 All attempts at making a living from writing had failed. Melville yielded himself to silence, except for occasional poetry; burned the work no one had cared to publish ("Have I not saved you from the drear/Theft and ignoring?") and wrote to it—and to work that sought to be written, the poem "Immolated."

> Children of my happier prime,
> When one yet lived with me, and threw
> Her rainbow over life and time,
> Even Hope, my bride, and mother to you!
>   O, nurtured in sweet pastoral air,
> And fed on flowers and light, and dew
> Of morning meadows—spare, Ah, spare
> Reproach; spare, and upbraid me not
> That, yielding scarce to reckless mood,
> But jealous of your future lot,
> I sealed you in a fate subdued.

▲ SILENCES, PP. 7–8

1865–1885 (Fragments from the years of occasional poetry)

From Camoëns
(Before)

And ever must I fan this fire?
Forever in flame on flame aspire?
Ever restless, restless, craving rest—
The Imperfect toward Perfection pressed!
Yea, for the God demands thy best.
The world with endless beauty teems,
And thought evokes new worlds of dreams:
Hunt then the flying herds of themes!
And fan, yet fan thy fervid fire,
Until the crucibled gold shall show . . .

(After)

What now avails the pageant verse,
Trophies and arms with music borne?
Base is the world; and some rehearse
How noblest meet ignoble scorn.
Vain now thy ardor, vain thy fire,
Delirium mere, unsound desire:
Fate's knife hath ripped thy chorded lyre. . . .

From The American Aloe on Exhibition
[flowering once every hundred years]

But few they were who came to see
The Century-Plant in flower:
Ten cents admission—price you pay
For bon-bons of the hour. . . .

But lone at night the garland sighed
While moaned the aged stem:
"At last, at last! but joy and pride
What part have I with them?

Let be the dearth that kept me back
Now long from wreath decreed;

But, Ah, ye Roses that have passed
Accounting me a weed!"

From Thy Aim, Thy Aim?

Thy aim, thy aim?
. . . By some deed shall ignite the acclaim?
Then beware, and prepare thee
Lest . . . yearning be sequelled by shame.
. . . Then if, living, you kindle a flame,
Your guerdon will be but a flower,
Only a flower,
The flower of repute,
A flower cut down in an hour.
. . . And, dying, you truly ennoble a name—
Again but a flower!
Only a flower,
A funeral flower,
. . . The belated funeral flower of fame.

The belated funeral flower of fame.

Willa Cather (1876–1947) ▲

In 1906, when the thirty-two-year-old Willa Cather's first book of fiction, *The Troll Garden,* was published (in it, two imperishable Nebraska and Pittsburgh-inspired stories: "Wagner Matinee" and "Paul's Case"), she had been writing and publishing for years. (Assorted earlier writings, now being collected, already fill two thick volumes.) A future of steady, ever more distinguished productivity seemed assured.

Yet that year the abundant flow ceased. For the next five years she produced one (mostly Jamesian) story a year, stories which she later repudiated, forbidding their ever being republished. In 1912, there was a novel (also Jamesian), *Alexander's Bridge,* which—as with the stories—she later rejected, characterizing it as an attempt to be acceptably literary, that is, "genteel" in treatment, milieu; written because

> . . . usually the young writer must have his affair with the external material he covets; must imitate and strive to follow the masters he most admires, until he finds he is starving for reality and cannot make this go any longer. Then he learns that it is not the adventure he sought, but the adventure that sought him, which has made the enduring mark upon him.

The master she most admired in 1906 was Henry James. Cather had sent *The Troll Garden* to him on its publication, with a letter. James never responded. When Cather learned that her friend Witter Bynner knew him (as a result of having sent James *his* first book), she asked that he inquire of its reception. Bynner did so, in spite of remarks from James on "lady novelists who victimize the supine public." James wrote back:

> I have your graceful letter about "The Troll Garden" which only reached me some time ago (as many works of fiction duly reach me), and if I brazenly confess that I not only haven't read it, but haven't even been meaning to (till your words about it thus arrived), I do no more than register the sacred truth. That sacred truth is that, being now almost in my 100th year [he was sixty-three], with a long and weary experience of such matters

behind me, promiscuous fiction has become abhorrent to me, and I find it the hardest thing in the world to read almost *any* new novel. Any is hard enough, but the hardest from the innocent hands of young females, young American females perhaps above all. This is a subject—my battered, cynical, all-too-expert outliving of such possibilities—on which I could be eloquent, but I haven't time and will be more vivid and complete some other day. I've only time now to say that I *will* then (in spite of these professions) do my best for Miss Cather—so as not to be shamed by your so doing yours.

Cather was given the reply; waited. No letter ever came. (Perhaps, or so I wish to believe out of regard for his literary judgment, James did not open the book.)

It was after this that the constriction of writing (a true hidden silence) began.

The course of Willa Cather's development had not been as that of the young writer she describes above. She had not had to work her way through imitation; she had *begun*—unselfconsciously—with writing the "reality" that had made "the enduring mark" on her. But her landscapes and people, her developing vision of what was significant in them, even her direct, vigorous voice, were outside the prevalent, the admired, as was increasingly being impressed upon her.* James himself, the model, was in massive contradiction—attitude, content, form (not excellence)—to all that was deepest in her to write. By the time she sent him *The Troll Garden,* she was starving for validation that her "reality" was material for art; for encouragement to go on. His seeming disesteem was the last heaviness added to the other near-unendurable pressures to scorn, deny her own material and vigor—write in the manner

---

*"The 'novel of the soil' had not then come into fashion in this country. The drawing room was considered the proper setting for a novel, and the only characters worth reading about were smart people and clever people . . ." —Willa Cather, "My First Novels, There Were Two."

and of what was not hers; almost give up on herself as a serious writer.*

There is a postscript. Another "master," another decisive letter. Sara Orne Jewett (of the classic *Country of the Pointed Firs*) whose work Cather treasured for, among other qualities, "revealing in ordinary country people the treasure of life and feeling that lay below the pinched surfaces." Jewett befriended Cather in the constricted years, believed in her, and it was her letter (partially quoted in "One Out of Twelve") with its concern that Willa Cather quit *McClure's Magazine,* manage "time and quiet" to "perfect her work . . . write life itself," which reread in print when the Jewett letters were issued after her death in 1911, gave Cather the "courage" (confidence) to fight again for writing circumstances, again begin writing her "reality"—its first flowering, *O Pioneers.*

William Blake (1757–1827) ▲

About 1807–1827, in the "years of obscurity," and the last years.

Class reasons, and the repressive times.

---

*Cather became so ashamed in this time of *The Troll Garden* that she hid its existence. When her friend Elizabeth Sargeant *(Willa Cather: A Memoir)* heard of it, and asked for a copy to read, Cather refused, dismissing it as "unfledged stories." Cather "would say disparagingly, ironically [to her], that she could never write stories of Nebraska—Swedes and Bohemians were just a joke in New York—everybody would laugh."

Years later, in "My First Novels, There Were Two" (1931), Willa Cather reiterated this: "*O Pioneers* was set in Nebraska, of all places. As everyone knows, Nebraska is distinctly *déclassé* as a literary background. *O Pioneers* was not only about Nebraska farmers, the farmers were Swedes! Since I wrote *O Pioneers* for myself, I ignored all the situations and accents that were then thought to be necessary."

Jane Austen (1775–1817) ▲

The years 1800–1811.

Woman reasons: she was powerless in all major decisions deciding her life, including the effecting of enabling circumstances for writing.

*If the acknowledged great in achievment, possessing inner con-
firmation of their achievement; sometimes the stout retainer of
habituated productivity and/or outside recognition as well, can be
silenced—what, inescapably, does this bespeak of the power of circumstance?*

*What does it explain to the rest of us of possible causes—outside
ourselves—of our founderings, failures, unnatural silencings?*

SILENCES—ITS VARIETIES

> And now in age I bud again,
> After so many deaths I live and write;
> I once more smell the dew and rain,
> And relish versing. O my only Light,
> It cannot be
> That I am he
> On whom Thy tempests fell all night.
>
> —George Herbert, 1593–1633

Censorship Silences ▲

Immoral! Immoral!

Immoral! Immoral! Under this cloak hide the vices of wealth as well as the vast, unspoken blackness of poverty and ignorance and between them must walk the little novelist, choosing neither truth nor beauty, but some half-conceived phase of life that bears no honest resemblance to either the whole of nature or to man.

—Theodore Dreiser, 1902

Having to Censor Self

If you do not tell the truth about yourself you cannot tell it about other people. As the nineteenth century wore on, the writers knew that they were crippling themselves, diminishing their material, falsifying their object. "We are condemned," Stevenson wrote, "to avoid half the life that passes us by." What books Dickens could have written had he been permitted! Think of Thackeray as unfettered as Flaubert or Balzac! What books I might have written myself.

—Virginia Woolf

Work Withheld: Not published in one's lifetime (Mark Twain); or held for years waiting for a changed atmosphere (E.M. Forster: *Maurice*). Has other work by other writers been put aside, or kept from burgeoning, because of fear that its content would deny its being published?

Publishers' Censorship: The silencing—or being driven to the novel form—of story or novella writers because "there is no market for stories."

Political Silences ▲

Involvement: When political involvement takes priority, though the need and love for writing go on. Every freedom movement has, and has had, its roll of writers participating at the price of their writing.

The Complete Silencing by Governments

Lives of the Poets

> Otto-René Castillo was born
> in Quezaltenango
> > Guatemala
> in 1936 and was killed there
> in March of 1967 while fighting
> with the Revolutionary
> Armed Forces.
> > The poem
> by Javier Heraud, written
> in 1963 in La Paz
> > Bolivia,
> was one of the last by the poet
> before his death.

                        Peruvian,
he was killed
at the age of 21
while fighting for the
                liberation
of his country.
Leonel Rugama, another young
                Latin American
martyr, was assassinated
in January 1970,
in Managua
                Nicaragua.
The house
where he and two comrades hid
was surrounded by 1500
national guardsmen and the battle
lasted 4 hours. Before
they went in
to finish him off, Rugama answered
the demand that he surrender
with "*¡Que se rinde*
                tu madre!"
Carlos Maria Gutierrez is
                Uruguayan,
well known
as a revolutionary journalist.
Diario del Cuartelo
came directly out of a
                prison
experience in 1969
and is his first
and only book of poems. His first
and only book
                of poems.*

---

*A "found poem." It comes from Margaret Randall's *Part of the Solution*, where it serves as a biographical introduction to Randall's translations of revolutionary Latin American poets, and was arranged as a poem by Lillian Robinson: "I have made no changes except to set Randall's words as verse, and to repeat the last phrase."

Political Silences. A woman form: [▲]

Anna Tsetsaeyva, also known as Marina Cvetaeva, the Russian poet, in exile

It is my notebook that keeps me above the surface of the waters. . . . It will soon be Christmas. To tell you the truth, I've been driven so hard by life that I feel nothing. Through these years (1917–1927) it was not my mind that grew numb, but my soul. An astonishing observation: it is precisely for feeling that one needs time, and not for thought. Thought is a flash of lightning, feeling is a ray from the most distant of stars. Feeling requires leisure; it cannot survive under fear. A basic example: rolling 1½ kilos of small fishes in flour, I am able to think, but as for feeling—no. The smell is in the way. The smell is in the way, my sticky hands are in the way, the squirting oil in the way, *the fish* are in the way, each one individually and the entire 1½ kilos as a whole. Feeling is apparently more demanding than thought. It requires all or nothing. There is nothing I can give to my own [feeling]: no time, no quiet, no solitude. I am always in the presence of others, from 7 in the morning till 10 at night, and by 10 at night I am so exhausted —what feeling can there be? Feeling requires *strength*. No, I simply sit down to mend and darn things: Mur's, S.'s, Alya's, my own. 11 o'clock. 12 o'clock. 1 o'clock. S. arrives by the last [subway] train, a brief chat, and off to bed, which means lying in bed with a book until 2 or 2:30. The books are good, but I could have written even better ones, if only . . .

"The knife of the perfectionist attitude in art and life."

This haunting sentence, not in the original talk, is from *What the Woman Lived* (1973), letters by the consummate poet, Louise Bogan—to me one of our most grievous "hidden silences." (Woman, economic, perfectionist causes—all inextricably intertwined.)

Silences of the Marginal ▲

*The writer of a class, sex, color still marginal in literature,
and whose coming to voice at all against complex odds is
exhausting achievement.*

"Only eleven [black writers] in the hundred years since 1850
have published novels more than twice."*

Nineteen fifty was evidently the watershed year. Since 1960, *any
single year* has seen more than nine novels by black writers that
are their second, third, or fourth books.

They are reaping the (hard-won) benefits of having been born
in the more favorable nineteen thirties, forties, fifties, instead of
into their parents' generations. They grew into a time of rising
economic levels (still low, but for more, above an all-conditioning
economic imperative); ever higher levels of literacy and education
(however painfully gotten); shorter work hours; great mass migra-
tions seeking more humane conditions of life; visible struggle; and,
with the fifties, a resurgence of black consciousness—all providing
a more enabling soil and climate.

Bone did not take into account fiction privately published, nor
did he have the advantage of recent bibliographies (such as those
by Rush, Myers, Arata: *Black American Writers,* 1973) which
disclose a wealth of writers, most of them born since 1920—and
indicating eloquently what was silenced in the generations before
—(and their own generation)—("lives that never came to writing").

These bibliographies also indicate how vulnerable nearly all
(especially first-generation writers) were to lessenings and silencings; revealing numbers of poems and stories that never came to
books—and long interims between works. *Marks of all marginal
writers.*

They do not, except by inference, reveal "the complex odds."
No one has as yet written *A Room of One's Own* for writers, other
than women, still marginal in literature. Nor do any bibliographies exist for writers whose origins and circumstances are marginal. Class remains the greatest unexamined factor.

---

*Robert Bone. *The Negro Novel in America,* 1958.

"The sacrifice of talent, in pieces, to preserve its essential value"▲

Scott Fitzgerald: "But one hundred and twenty stories":

> The roller skates rain down the streets.
> The black cars shine between the leaves.
> Your voice, far away . . .
>
> I have asked a lot of my emotions—one hundred and twenty stories. The price was high, right up with Kipling, because there was one little drop of something—not blood, not a tear, not my seed, but me more intimately than these, in every story. It was the extra I had. Now it has gone and I am just like you now.
>
> Once the phial was full—here is the bottle it came in.
>
> Hold on, there's a drop left there. . . . No, it was just the way the light fell.
>
> . . . If I hadn't abused words so, what you said might have meant something. But one hundred and twenty stories. . . .
>
> April evening spreads over everything the purple blur left by a child who has used the whole paint box.
>
> —"An April Letter" in *The Crack-Up.*

Absences That Are a Kind of Silence ("But one hundred and twenty stories. . . .")

"A professional makes the pot boil," said Henry James who certainly did. "It's the only basis of sanity and freedom."

Some writers, happily, are able to do so—and by writing their best (sometimes *the* best) work. (Think of, in our time, Ernest Hemingway, Thornton Wilder, Robert Penn Warren, John Hersey, Saul Bellow, John Cheever, Bernard Malamud, Nabokov, Salinger, Joyce Carol Oates, John Updike, E.L. Doctorow, bestsellers all.)*

There is another kind of professional who, also beginning with aspiration and capacity, ends up making the pot boil—but by Fitzgerald's "sacrifice of talent, in pieces, to preserve its essential value."

---

*I see: one out of twelve.

Easily distinguishable from the meretricious, the sleazy (along with the conscientious, capable free lancer), they are the producers of the good in the daily stream of publishing: the made-to-order, the topical, the popular, the entertainment, the ghost writing—the current staples. Like Rebecca Harding Davis, they remain serious writers—committed to substance, respecting language and craftsmanship. If they cannot make each piece art, they make it as readable, believable, and rewarding as possible. Sometimes—notably with science fiction, Gothic, detective, mystery—their work is so distinguished, they establish a new form in literature.

Able to reach and touch people, they often directly affect their time as few "quality" writers are able to. But many are a Silence —that is, an *Absence* from deeper, more lasting literature.*

Virulent Destroyers: Premature Silencers ▲

> But o! each visitation
> Suspends what nature gave me at my birth,
> My shaping spirit of Imagination.
> > —Coleridge in his "wilder'd and dark,"
> > "my head is cloudy, mazy" time . . .
>
> Morality and its philistine judgments have nought
> to do with me. . . . But I have learned this:
> it is not what one does that is wrong, but what one
> becomes as a consequence of it.**
> > —Oscar Wilde, *De Profundis*

---

*Gail Godwin writes of one such professional, her mother, who wrote true confessions and women's fiction to support her children and herself. She made her stories "true to life" problems, fought (unsuccessfully) for true endings, wrote the best she dared (sometimes borrowing a phrase from Katherine Mansfield or Woolf). (In an essay deploring the lack of strong female models in fiction, Godwin did not realize she had just described one—in life.) What the mother was not free to accomplish, the daughter is.

**No, Wilde was not referring to homosexuality, but a disordered, narcissistic, insulated way of life.

▲ SILENCES, PP. 9–10

Malign mystique surrounds and protects those virulent destroyers of capacity, those premature Silencers: alcoholism, drug use to dependency, suicide. Contrary to the actual lives of most writers of achievement, these are not intrinsic to the artist being—though certain "savage god" humans batten on the belief that it is so.

The Seasons in Hell of Coleridge, Baudelaire, Rimbaud, Artaud —their agony over "what one becomes as a consequence" (evidenced in their own testimony and in that of their lives, deaths, yes, and in the lives, deaths of too many other writers—Dylan Thomas, John Berryman—living others I will not name)—are obscured. It is not new forms, intensities, enhanced visionary sense, that comes: it is the ravaging and obliteration of the capacity for them; loss of power for work, impairment of critical judgment, logorrhea, blurredness, or aridity; premature death; suicide.

"I am suffering from a frightful malady of the mind," writes Antonin Artaud when coherence was still possible for him:

> . . . a kind of erosion. My thoughts evade me in every way possible. There is something that is destroying my thinking, something that does not prevent me from being what I might be, but which leaves me in abeyance; a something furtive which takes away the words I have found, which step by step destroys in its substance my thinking as it evolves, which diminishes my intensity, which takes away from me even the memory of the devices and figures of speech by which one expresses oneself. What will restore to me the concentration of my forces, the cohesion that my mind lacks, the constancy of its tension, the consistency of its own substance?

And again Rimbaud:

> Had I not once a youth pleasant, heroic, fabulous enough to write on leaves of gold; too much luck. Through what crime, what error have I earned my present weakness? You who maintain that some animals sob sorrowfully, that the dead have dreams, try to tell the story of my downfall and my slumber . . . I no longer know how to speak.

I no longer know how to speak.

Baudelaire's own account is required reading. Capacity for sustained work was essential to him.

I've never possessed either facility in conception or in expression. It should be self-evident that the small amount of work I've produced has been the result of long and painful labour . . . labour by which a revery becomes a work of art.

But sustained work became more and more impossible,*

When the nerves of a man are strained by an infinite amount of anxiety and suffering, the devil, in spite of all the good resolutions, slips every morning into his brain in shapes like: why not enjoy or rest one day more in oblivion of these things? Tonight at one fell swoop I'll accomplish them. And then night comes and the mind reels at the thought of the number of things left undone again, overwhelming melancholy induces sterility, and next day there is the same old comic-tragedy, the same resolution, honesty, confidence.

There began endless timetables of work to be accomplished; then the revenant desolation of *My Heart Laid Bare,* when—added to the harm of years—even the physical basis for carrying through will or work was gone. The humiliating litany of "Hygiene. Morality. Conduct. Method." could not avail. "Too Late!"**

Foreground Silences ▲

The Emerson letter to Whitman (from which my phrase comes), July 1855:

I am not blind to the worth of the wonderful gift of *Leaves of Grass.* I find it the most extraordinary piece of wit and wisdom that America has yet contributed. I am very happy in reading it, as great power makes us happy. It meets the demand I am always making of what seemed the sterile and stingy nature, as if too much handiwork, or too much lymph in temperament, were making our west-

---

*He was also not capable of—and therefore more vulnerable to damage from— "the need to wrest from his art means of carrying on his daily life."—Enid Starkie, in the biography of Baudelaire.

**Excerpts from *My Heart Laid Bare* appear on pages 287–289.

▲ SILENCES, P. 10

ern wits fat and mean. I give you joy of free and brave thought. I
have great joy in it. I find incomparable things said incomparably
well, as they must be. I find the courage of treatment which so
delights us, and which large perception only can inspire. . . .

I greet you at the beginning of a great career, which yet must
have had a long foreground somewhere for such a start. . . . It has
the best merits, namely, of fortifying and encouraging.

Silences Where the Lives Never Come to Writing ▲

What has humanity not lost by suppression and subjection? We
have a Shakespeare; but what of the possible Shakespeares we might
have had who passed their life from youth upward brewing currant
wine and making pastries for fat country squires to eat, with no
glimpse of the freedom of life and action necessary even to poach
on deer in the green forests; stifled out without one line written,
simply because being of the weaker sex, life gave no room for action
and grasp on life? Here and there, where queens have been born as
rulers, the vast powers for governance and the keen insight have
been shown; but what of the millions of the race in all ages whose
vast powers of intellect and insight and creation have been lost to
us because . . . their line of life was rigidly apportioned to them.
What statesmen, what leaders, what creative intelligence have been
lost to humanity because there has been no free trade in the powers
and gifts.*

---

*Olive Schreiner, *From Man to Man,* 1883. (An unnoted ancestor of Virginia
Woolf's classic imagining—in *A Room of One's Own*—of what Shakespeare's life
would have been, had he been born into a female body.)

THE WORK OF CREATION AND THE CIRCUMSTANCES IT DEMANDS FOR FULL FUNCTIONING

In placid hours well-pleased we dream
Of many a brave unbodied scheme.
But form to lend, pulsed life create,
What unlike things must meet and mate:
A flame to melt—a wind to freeze;
Sad patience—joyous energies;
Humility—yet pride and scorn;
Instinct and study; love and hate;
Audacity—reverence. These must mate,
And fuse with Jacob's mystic heart,
To wrestle with the angel—Art.
                                          —Herman Melville

THE WORK OF CREATION AND THE CIRCUMSTANCES IT DEMANDS FOR FULL FUNCTIONING ▲

Among journals, accounts, letters of "the practitioners them-selves." (A personal selection): ▲

Virginia Woolf: *A Writer's Diary.* (We are now beginning to have the letters as well.)

Anton Chekhov: certain letters; his *Notebooks.*

Katherine Mansfield: *Journal, Letters.*

Franz Kafka: *Diaries,* all letters (*Letters to Milena,* etc.).

Albert Camus: *Notebooks (Actuelles).*

Joseph Conrad on Fiction; the prefaces; certain of his let-ters.

Herman Melville: passages in *Pierre;* certain letters and margin-alia.

André Gide: *Journals.*

Rainer Maria Rilke: letters; passages in *Malte Laurids Brigge* and in the poems.

Henry James: *Notebooks;* the prefaces.

Scott Fitzgerald: *The Crack-Up.*

Gustave Flaubert: many of the letters.

Cesare Pavese: *The Burning Brand.*

Jessamyn West: *Hide and Seek.*

Also invaluable: Thoreau's *Journals;* Van Gogh's *Letters* (*Dear Theo* remains the best collection if the three volume *Collected Letters* is unavailable); Käthe Kollwitz's *Diaries and Letters.* Many collections of letters of writers, among them: Sherwood Anderson; the younger D.H. Lawrence; Malcolm Lowry on *Under the Vol-cano;* Louise Bogan. Reading the Dostoyevsky *Notebooks for*

The Idiot, or *Notebooks for Crime and Punishment* or Gide's for *The Counterfeiters,* along with the books themselves, is fascinating and suggestive.

"Constant toil is the law of art, as it is of life" ▲

If an artist does not spring to his work as a soldier to the breach, if once within the crater he does not labor as a miner buried in the earth, if he contemplates his difficulties instead of conquering them one by one, the work remains unachieved, production becomes impossible, and the artist assists the suicide of his own talent. . . . The solution of the problem can be found only through incessant and sustained work . . . true artists, true poets, generate and give birth today, tomorrow, ever. From this habit of labor results a ceaseless comprehension of difficulties which keep them in communion with the muse and her creative forces.

—Balzac, *Cousin Bette*

Unconfined Solitude ▲

I doubt I shall succeed in writing here, I have not the sense of perfect seclusion which has always been essential to my power of producing anything.

—Nathaniel Hawthorne at Brook Farm

The Homely Underpinning for It All (to Add to the Conrad Truth) ▲

You know how much I used to love Plato. Now I realize he lied. The things of this world are not a reflection of the ideal, but the product of human blood and hard labour. It is we who built the pyramids, hewed the marble for the temples and statues, we who pulled the oars in the galleys and dragged wooden ploughs for their food, while they wrote dialogues and dramas. . . . We were filthy,

and died early deaths. They were aesthetic, and carried on subtle
debates, and made art.

—"Letter from Auschwitz" (a young poet to two poet friends)
in Tadeusz Borowski, *This Way for the Gas, Ladies and
Gentlemen* *

The Constant Toil; The Terrible Law; The Frightful Task

From eight o'clock in the morning till half-past four in the evening, Pierre sits there in his room;—eight hours and a half!

In the midst of the merriments of the mutations of Time, Pierre
hath ringed himself in with the grief of Eternity. Pierre is a peak
inflexible in the heart of Time.

He will not be called to; he will not be stirred. . . .

Is there then all this work to one book, which shall be read in
a very few hours; and, far more frequently, utterly skipped in one
second; and which, in the end, whatever it be, must undoubtedly
go to the worms?

Not so; that which now absorbs the time and the life of Pierre,
is not the book, but the primitive elementalising of the strange stuff,
which in the act of attempting that book has upheaved and up-
gushed in his soul. Two books are being writ; of which the world
shall only see one, and that the bungled one. The larger book, and
the infinitely better, is for Pierre's own private shelf. That it is,
whose unfathomable cravings drink his blood; the other only demands his ink.

Who shall tell all the thoughts and feelings of Pierre in that
desolate and shivering room when at last the idea obtruded, that
the wiser and profounder he should grow, the more and more he
lessened the chances for bread. . . .

But his is the famishing which loathes all food. He cannot eat but
by force. He has assassinated the natural day; how then can he eat
with an appetite? He cannot sleep, he has waked the infinite wake-
fulness in him, then how can he slumber? Still his book, like a vast

---

*Viking edition, 1965. This is expressed in its own way on the last pages of
George Orwell's *The Road to Wigan Pier*.

lumbering planet, revolves in his aching head. He cannot command the thing out of his orbit; fain would he behead himself, to gain one night's respose. At last the heavy hours move on, and sheer exhaustion overtakes him, and he lies still—not asleep as children and day laborers sleep—but lies still from his throbbing and for that interval holdingly sheathes the beak of the vulture in his hand, and lets it not enter his heart. Morning comes; again the dropt sash, the icy water, the flesh brush, the breakfast, the hot brick, the ink, the pen, the from eight o'clock to half-past five, and the whole general inclusive hell of the same departed day.

Ah shivering thus day after day in his wrappers and cloak, is this the warm lad that once sang to the world the Tropical Summer?

—Herman Melville, *Pierre*

I sit down religiously every morning, I sit down for eight hours, and the sitting down is all. In the course of that working day of eight hours I write three sentences which I erase before leaving the table in despair. Sometimes it takes all my resolution and power of self control to refrain from butting my head against the wall. After such crises of despair I doze for hours, still held conscious that there is that story that I am unable to write. Then I wake up, try again, and at last go to bed completely done up. So the days pass and nothing is done. At night I sleep. In the morning I get up with that horror of that powerlessness I must face through a day of vain efforts. . . .

I seem to have lost all sense of style and yet I am haunted by the necessity of style. And that story I cant write weaves itself into all I see, into all I speak, into all I think, into the lines of every book I try to read . . . I feel my brain. I am distinctly conscious of the contents of my head. My story is there in a fluid—in an evading shape. I cant get hold of it. It is all there—to bursting, yet I cant get hold of it any more than you can grasp a handful of water. . . .

I never mean to be slow. The stuff comes out at its own rate. I am always ready to put it down . . . the trouble is that too often, alas, I've to wait for the sentence, for the word. . . . The worst is that while I'm thus powerless to produce, my imagination is extremely active; whole paragraphs, whole pages, whole chapters pass through my mind. Everything is there: descriptions, dialogue, reflection, everything, everything but the belief, the conviction, the only thing needed to make me put pen to paper. I've thought out a volume a day till I felt sick in mind and heart and gone to bed, completely done up, without having written a line. The effort I put out should give birth to Masterpieces as big as mountains, and it brings forth a ridiculous mouse now and then. . . .

They [the ideas and words] creep about in my head and have got to be caught and tortured into some kind of shape.

—from Letters of Joseph Conrad

This Incomprehensible Master: Work

As regards work, he [Cezanne] says that up to his fortieth year he had lived as a Bohemian. Only then, in his friendship with Pissarro, did work dawn on him—to such an extent that he did nothing but work for the last 30 years of his life. Without real pleasure it seems, in continual rage, ever at odds with his every endeavour, none of which appeared to him to achieve what he regarded as the ultimate desirable. . . .

Old, ill, wearied every evening to the point of unconsciousness by the regularity of his daily work (so much so that he often went to bed at six o'clock as soon as it became dark after a supper mindlessly eaten) surly, mistrustful . . . he hoped from day to day still to attain that triumph . . . and does not know whether he has really succeeded. And sits in the garden like an old dog, the dog of this work which calls him again and again and beats him and lets him go hungry. And still he clings with all his strength to this incomprehensible master.

—Rainer Maria Rilke

Subterranean Forces ▲

Before subterranean forces will feed the creator back, they must be fed, passionately fed, what needs to be worked on. . . . A receptive waiting that means, not demands which prevent "an undistracted center of being." And when the response comes, availability to work must be immediate. If not used at once, all may vanish as a dream; worse, future creation be endangered, for only the removal and development of the material frees the forces for further work.

Something probably lurks in it, something that I have only to woo forth. Let me live with it a while, let me woo it, even if I sit here in mere divine leisure every patient morning for a week or two.

—Henry James

These poems are the fruit of long labor: trials, repetitions, rejections, choices—months, even years of reflection.

—Paul Valéry

Your work is unbeautiful, alright let it be unbeautiful. It will grieve you, but it must not discourage you. Nature demands a certain devotion, and she demands a period of struggling with her. . . . It is the experience and hard work of every day which alone will ripen in the long run and allow one to do something truer and more complete. . . . You will not always do well, but the days you least expect it, you will do that which holds its own with the work of those that have gone before.

—Vincent Van Gogh

Look sharply after your thoughts. They come unlooked for like a bird seen on your trees, and if you turn to your usual task, disappear, and you shall never find that perception again. Never, I say, but for years perhaps, and I know not what events and worlds may lie between you and its return.

—Emerson

One sentence follows another, is born of the other, and I feel as I see it being born and growing within me an almost physical rapture. This artesian welling up is the result of my long subconscious preparation.

—André Gide

SUBTERRANEAN FORCES—
AND THE WORK OF CREATION
IN CIRCUMSTANCES ENABLING
FULL FUNCTION

The writing of The Waves (1926–1931)
partial selections from Virginia Woolf's
A Writer's Diary

1927 June

> . . . I read—any trash . . . Slowly ideas began trickling in . . . the
> Moths,* which I think I will write very quickly. . . . the play-poem
> idea; the idea of some continuous stream, not solely of human
> thought, but of the ship, the night etc. all flowing together: inter-
> sected by the arrival of the bright moths. A man and a woman are
> to be sitting at table talking. Or shall they remain silent? It is to be
> a love story; she is finally to let the last great moth in. . . . But it
> needs ripening. I do a little work on it in the evening when the
> gramophone is playing late Beethoven sonatas.

1928 November

> As for my next book, I am going to hold myself from writing till
> I have it impending in me: grown heavy in my mind like a ripe pear;
> pendant, gravid, asking to be cut or it will fall. *The Moths* still
> haunts me, coming, as they always do, unbidden, between tea and
> dinner, while L. plays the gramophone. I shape a page or two; and
> make myself stop. . . .

---

*Later, *The Waves*.

1929 December

. . . Blundering on at *The Waves*. I write two pages of arrant nonsense, after straining; I write variations of every sentence; compromises; bad shots; possibilities; till my writing book is like a lunatic's dream. Then I trust to some inspiration on re-reading; and pencil them into some sense. Still I am not satisfied. . . . I press to my centre. I don't care if it all is scratched out . . . and then, if nothing comes of it—anyhow I have examined the possibilities. But I wish I enjoyed it more. I don't have it in my head all day like the *Lighthouse* and *Orlando*.

1930 January

"And now I can think of nothing else." Thanks to my pertinacity and industry, I can now hardly stop making up *The Waves* . . . after 6 months' hacking.

1930 January

. . . I cannot yet write naturally in my new room, because the table is not the right height and I must stoop to warm my hands. Everything must be absolutely what I am used to. . . . I am stuck fast in that book—I mean glued to it, like a fly on gummed paper. Sometimes I am out of touch; but go on; then again I feel that I have at last, by violent measures—like breaking through gorse—set my hands on something central. . . . But how to pull it together, how to comport it—press it into one—I do not know . . .

1930 February

. . . If I could stay in bed another fortnight (but there is no chance of that) I believe I should see the whole of *The Waves*. . . . [in] these illnesses . . . something happens in my mind. It refuses to go on registering impressions. It shuts itself up. It becomes chrysalis. I lie quite torpid, often with acute physical pain. . . . Then suddenly something springs.

. . . Ideas rush in me; often though this is before I can control my mind or pen. . . . My mind works in idleness. To do nothing is often my most profitable way.

1930 March

Yes, but this book is a very queer business. I had a day of intoxication when I said, "Children are nothing to this": . . . felt the pressure of the form—the splendour, the greatness—as perhaps I have never felt them. But I shan't race it off in intoxication. I keep pegging away; and find it the most complex and difficult of all my books. . . . I have not yet mastered the speaking voice . . . and I propose to go on pegging it down, arduously, and then re-write, reading much of it aloud, like poetry. . . . At any rate, I have taken my fence.

1930 April

. . . I have never written a book so full of holes and patches; that will need re-building, yes, not only re-modelling.

1930 May

. . . I begin to see what I had in my mind; and want to begin cutting out masses of irrelevance and clearing, sharpening and making the good phrases shine. One wave after another.

1931 February

Here in the few minutes that remain, I must record, heaven be praised, the end of *The Waves.* I wrote the words O Death fifteen minutes ago, having reeled across the last ten pages with some moments of such intensity and intoxication that I seemed only to stumble after my own voice, or almost, after some sort of speaker (as when I was mad) I was almost afraid, remembering the voices that used to fly ahead. Anyhow, it is done; and I have been sitting these 15 minutes in a state of glory, and calm, and some tears. . . . How physical the sense of triumph and relief is! Whether good or bad, it's done; and, as I certainly felt at the end, not merely finished, but rounded off, completed, the thing stated—how hastily, how fragmentarily, I know; but I mean that I have netted that fin ' in the waste of water which appeared to me over the marshes out of my window at Rodmell when I was coming to an end of *To the Lighthouse.* *

---

*September 30, 1926.

Subterranean Forces ▲

> It is the great quantity of what is not done that lies with all its weight on what wants to come out of the soil.
>
> —Rainer Maria Rilke

"The quiet, patient, generous mornings (yielding to 'the surging chaos of the unexpressed') will bring it," James wrote in his *Notebooks.* If there had been "other claims, other responsibilities so that writing could not be first"; if he (or Woolf) had had only occasional mornings or none; if Conrad had not been able to "sit down religiously every morning . . . for eight hours" with his "crises of despair"—would they have created a body of work? If Pierre (Melville) had gone out to a job that 8:00 to 4:30 instead of into his desolate and shivering room, how long would his unfinished book have revolved in his head?

WHEN THE CLAIMS OF CREATION CANNOT BE PRIMARY▴

What if there is not that fullness of time, let alone totality of self?
—The situation for most writers:

> The dissatisfaction about bad work, the failure of things, the difficulties of technique . . . and then to swallow that despair and that melancholy, to bear oneself as one is, not in order to sit down and rest, but to struggle on notwithstanding thousands of shortcomings and faults and the uncertainty of conquering them. Then this struggle with one's self, the trying to better one's self, the cry for energy —all this complicated by material difficulties. . . . One works hard, but still one cannot make ends meet.
>
> —Vincent Van Gogh

> I am absolutely going to pot. What a fine form of torture, the objective impossibility of thinking and consequently of writing can be, for here we work the whole day, for seven deadly hours on end, and afterward I walk, and then I eat, and at dessert I fall fast asleep from fatigue.
>
> —Paul Valéry

> Material anxieties frighten me because I feel how mysteriously independent of myself is my power of expression. . . . I am not as the workmen who can take up and lay down their tools. I am, so to speak, only the agent of an unreliable master.
>
> —Joseph Conrad

> . . . I know that I haven't powers enough to divide myself into one who earns and one who creates. And even if I had all the powers in the world, I would have to give *all* my powers to the important

thing in me: it has a right to that. . . . I know I am not exhausted;
but the little and continual thoughts of every day and its most
unimportant things confuse me so that I can no longer recollect my
own. . . . Before I used to hear all my voices in me; now it is as if
someone had closed the window toward the garden in which my
poems live; far, far away I hear something and listen and can no
longer distinguish it. My head is full of ridiculous additions. And
hardly have I been paid for one job and am thinking that I may now
collect myself for my own work, when it is already time again to
think of the *next* and of where it is to be found and by what efforts
obtained and my nervous strength is slipping away; my time, my
courage, and I fail to catch up with myself day after day and am
somewhere out of reach, full of flowers past their bloom, whose
fading scents fill me with dead weight.

. . . But now I scarcely have plans any more; now it seems to me
an infinite presumption to have plans when the very next stage is
so dismaying, so dark, and so full of the tiniest questions. It seems
as if I were in the midst of nets; I feel these nets on my hands with
every gesture that would arise freely.

. . . I look for some person who will understand my need without
taking me for a beggar. . . .

It is clear to me that I need help in order to continue on my way. . . .

What can one who wants a great deal say of this wanting (that
deep wanting which goes toward my work and toward its continuous realization) without betraying it and becoming a boaster? Here
every word involves a false note and an affront to what it means.
One can only say that one comes more and more to protect this
wanting which goes toward deep and important things, that one
longs more and more sincerely and wholeheartedly to give it all
one's strength and all one's love and to experience worries through
it and not through the little harassing accidents of which life in
poverty is full. . . . This winter, for the first time, it [poverty] stood
before me for months like a specter, and I lost myself and all my
beloved aims and all the light out of my heart and came near taking
some little official post that would have meant dying and setting
out on a spiritual transmigration full of homelessness and madness.

I am indeed no longer a beginner who throws himself at random
into the future. I have worked for years, and if I have worked out
anything for myself, it is the belief in the right to raise the best I
have in me and the awareness of the treasures in the sesame of my
soul which I can no longer forget. And after all, I know that my

pen will be strong enough to carry me: only I may not misuse it too
early and must give it time to attain its full growth.

> —Rainer Maria Rilke, from two letters, 1903 and 1902

Always to be doing work that one did not wish to do, while that
one gift which it was death to hide (my writing powers), perishing,
and with it, myself. A rust eating away the bloom of spring, destroy-
ing the tree at its heart.

> —Virginia Woolf

Eight hours a day I have paid, working as an advertising writer the
last five years while trying to save nerve force and courage enough
to admit other writing. It has cost me dearly in rare projects gone
wrong.

> —Sherwood Anderson

I have done nothing as far as serious literature for a year—must
stop—go someplace—straighten out my burdened spirit and do
some real writing. Above all the fact that my only hope for salvation
lies in my not having to earn money . . . I need help to get myself
out of this snare. . . .

Money that I can get only for work, the wrong work, and right
now I'm so worn out and distracted I can't work.

> —Isaac Babel

I am not getting the needful hours to ripen anything in myself. . . .

. . . I have had very little time left over from the day's work to
give to it [poetry]. . . .

But a long poem like that ["The Bridge"] needs unbroken time
and extensive concentration and my present routine of life permits
me only fragments. (There are days when I simply have to 'sit on
myself' at my desk to shut out rhythms and melodies that belong
to that poem and have never been written because I have succeeded
only too well during the course of the day's work in excluding and
stifling such a train of thoughts . . . & then there are periods when
the whole world couldn't shut out the plans and beauties of that
work—& I get a little of it on paper.)

> —Hart Crane

I think I've only spent about ten percent of my energies on writing.
The other ninety percent went to keeping my head above water.
> —Katherine Anne Porter

When the Claims of Creation Cannot be Primary: The Literary Situation ▲

It is the great quantity of what is not done that lies with all its weight on what wants to come out of the soil.

Money that I can get only for work, the wrong work.

I know that I haven't powers enough to divide myself into one who earns and one who creates.

I could not live by literature if only to begin with, because of the slow maturing of my work and its special character.

The sacrifice of talent, in pieces, to preserve its essential value.

> I have no patience with this dreadful idea that whatever you have in you has to come out, that you can't suppress true talent. People can be destroyed; they can be bent, distorted and completely crippled. . . . In spite of all the poetry, all the philosophy to the contrary, we are not really masters of our fate. We don't really direct our lives unaided and unobstructed. Our being is subject to all the chances of life.
>
> —Katherine Anne Porter

The cost to literature of its sporadic, occasional, week-end or sabbatical writers (it may take an entire sabbatical to undo damage and to recover power for work) *is* unfinished work, minor effort and accomplishment, silences—where might be a great flowering.

And some writers are grated to pieces by the constant attrition. Lost forever.

("What if writers must work regularly at something besides their own own work—as do nearly all in the arts in the United States today?") ▲

THE LITERARY SITUATION* (1976)

John Leonard of the *New York Times* estimates that there are only 100 or so writers in this country who can actually make a living from their books. According to Leonard, 1,300 to 1,400 serious novels are nevertheless published every year by trade publishers (2,000—if westerns, mysteries, science fiction and Gothics are counted). *A Directory of American Fiction Writers* (by no means all-inclusive) lists over 800 writers of serious fiction.

—*Poets & Writers Newsletter,* 1976

In 1971–72, P.E.N. surveyed its membership. These were writers of professional status (biographers, poets, essayists, journalists, as well as fiction writers) of sufficient reputation to have been invited into P.E.N.

In a year when $7,300 was the *minimum* adequate standard of living for a family of four, a third of these established writers had not earned $3,000; more than half earned less than $6,000. A third were able to earn $10,000 or over.

An earlier survey (1969) of writers-in-residence at The Mac-Dowell Colony (some demonstration of achievement is required for admission) showed half of the writers earned $1,000 a year or less from their writing; a quarter earned from $1,000

---

*Title of a fine book by Malcolm Cowley, 1954. What follows confirms his earlier findings. It's no better.

to \$5,000, and only a fourth were able to bring in more than \$5,000.*

"The remarkable fact of the economics of the artist's life is not how little he [she] earns, but how much he [she] manages to create in spite of the niggardly earnings," the article comments. " 'Art,' as one of the colonists [me!] accurately said, 'is subsidized by artists' "—with their lives.

As for foundation help, fewer than one in ten of the MacDowell writers had ever received grants of any sort, and half of the grants were for less than \$2,500. One and a half percent got grants of \$5,000 or more.

Nearly all had, or answered that most of their artist friends had, been "habitually forced by pressure for adequate income to put aside their creative work."

Remember that the above figures are for writers accorded some recognition. What would a similar survey of the 800 writers listed in CODA's *Directory of American Fiction Writers* (which requires only some kind of publication for listing), or of a cross-section of *all* writers reveal?

It is the same with Individuals as Nations; works of Art can only be produc'd in Perfection where the Man is either in Affluence or is Above the Care of it. Poverty is the Fool's Rod, which at last is turn'd on his own back; this is A Last Judgment—when Men of Real Art Govern & Pretenders Fall. Some People & not a few Artists have asserted that the Painter of this Picture would not have done so well if he had been properly Encourag'd. Let those who think so, reflect on the State of Nations under Poverty & their incapability of Art; tho' Art is Above Either, the Argument is better for Affluence than Poverty; & tho' he would not have been a greater Artist, yet he would have produc'd Greater works of Art in proportion to his means. A Last Judgment is not for the purpose of making Bad Men better, but for the Purpose of hindering them from oppressing the Good with Poverty & Pain by means of such Vile Arguments & Insinuations. . . .

---

*Russell Lynes, "The Artist as Uneconomic Man," *Saturday Review,* February 28, 1970.

Who will Dare to Say that Polite Art is Encouraged or Either
Wished or Tolerated in a Nation where The Society for the Encouragement of Art Suffer'd Barry to Give them his Labour for Nothing, A society composed of the Flower of the English Nobility &
Gentry Suffering an Artist to Starve while he Supported Really
what They, under Pretence of Encouraging, were suppressing. . . .

Liberality! we want not Liberality. We want a Fair Price &
proportionate Value & a General Demand for Art.
Let not that Nation where Less than Nobility is the Reward,
Pretend that Art is Encouraged by that Nation. Art is First in
Intellectuals & Ought to be First in Nations.
                                    —William Blake, 175 years ago

What follows is the blues. Writer, don't read it. You know it
anyway, you live it; and have probably read it in one way or place
or another before and said better. This is for readers to whom it
may be news. An unrevised draft is all I can bring myself to.

When Van Gogh, quoted earlier, said:

The dissatisfaction about bad work, the failure of things, the difficulties of technique . . . and then to swallow that despair and that
melancholy . . . to struggle on notwithstanding thousands of short-
comings and faults and the uncertainty of conquering them. . . . All
this complicated by material difficulties. . . . One works hard, but
still one cannot make ends meet

he was speaking for most dedicated writers. Ah, if that were all.

"Who will read me, who will care?" It does not help the
work to be done, that work already completed is surrounded
by silence and indifference—if it is published at all. Few books
ever have the attention of a review—good or bad. Fewer stay
longer than a few weeks on bookstore shelves, if they get there
at all. New books are always coming in. Quality or ephemera
—if the three- or four-week-old one hasn't yet made best-sell-
erdom or the book clubs (usually synonymous)—Out! Room
must be made. It is always fall in the commercial literary
world, and books are its seasonal leaves. Even fewer books
(again, regardless of merit) are kept alive by critics or academics who could be doing so. "Works of art" (or at least books,

stories, poems, meriting life) "disappear before our very eyes because of the absence of responsible attention," Chekhov wrote nearly ninety years ago. Are they even seen? Out of the moveable feast, critics and academics tend to invoke the same dozen or so writers as if none else exist worthy of mention, or as if they've never troubled to read anyone else. Anthologies, textbooks, courses concerned with contemporary literature, tend to be made up of living writers whose names will immediately be recognized (usually coincident with writers whom publishers have promoted). A prize or good-foundation-fellowship seal of approval helps. Public libraries, starved for funds, buy less and less books. Published writers of good books, if their books haven't been respectable money-makers, more and more find themselves without a publisher for their latest one. Younger writers (that is, new ones of any age) find that fewer and fewer first books are being published. The magazine market for fiction has shrunk—what? 75 percent?—in the last two decades.

I see there is a lot of "fewer and fewer" and "less and less."

At a time when there is more reading and *writing* of imaginative literature than any time in the human past (and an indiscriminate glut of books on the market), and a greater potential audience than ever before, it is harder and harder for the serious writer to get published or get to readers once published.

Another way of saying it:

Writers in a profit making economy are an exploitable commodity whose works are products to be marketed, and are so judged and handled. That happier schizophrenic time when publishers managed profit necessities in combination with some commitment to literature of quality and content, is less and less possible. Almost *all* publishing houses are now owned by conglomerates who bought them for investment purposes (oh, they knew about the high costs of printing, paper, mailing, etc.) and whose only concern (necessarily) is high profit return. Why diversify, take risks, settle for modest returns, take trouble—and literature *is* trouble. Salability—as *maximum*-profit defined—leads to, well too much of what has been said here already, and other ramifications there is no room or spirit to discuss here.

The pressure to publish, "to keep before the public"

> Nowadays if you don't want to be forgotten, you must produce
> a masterpiece a year.
> —Jules and Edmond Goncourt

> Literature is an occupation in which you have to keep proving
> your talent to people who have none.
> —Jules Renard

The literary atmosphere

> This miserable bartering of fame, this coveting of it, fighting for
> it, tearing it from mouth to mouth . . . this continual talking
> about literature in ignorance as if it were some sort of com-
> merce; this constant criticizing, denigrating, envying, self-prais-
> ing, exalting people and writings that deserve contempt—all this
> depresses me to such a degree that if I had not got the refuge of
> posterity, and the certainty that in the course of time, every-
> thing does fall into its right place, I would send all literature to
> the devil a thousand times over.
> —Giacomo Leopardi, 1835

The literary atmosphere that sets writers against one another, breeds the feeling that writers are in competition with
each other. (In its extremest sense, Hemingway's feeling that
the measure of success would be "to knock Tolstoy out of the
prize ring": literature as prize ring!) The prize-givings that are
barterings and tradings-off more often than true honorings.
The foundation grants, starvingly few in number, for the aston-
ishingly many demonstrably worthy* —grants now so associated with honor, status, credentials, that those who do not
need them to get their work done, seek (and sometimes receive) them at the expense of those who do need them; the
harm of the applyings, the trying not to feel the being passed
over as condemnation of capacity. The "major/minor" pigeon-

---

*. . . *and to whom denial of circumstances is irremediable lessening of literature.*

holing. The judgings having nought to do with true criticism; the unjustified malignity and ignorance of much "reviewing," its superior tone, its tendency to follow the leader: *New York Times Book Review* and the *New York Review of Books.*

> Disappointment and humiliations embitter the heart and make an aching in the very bones. . . .

> . . . There is a point with me in matters of any size when I must absolutely have encouragement as much as crops rain; afterwards I am independent. . . .

> . . . When I spoke of fame I was not thinking of the harm it does to men as artists: it may do them harm . . . but so, I think, may the want of it, if "Fame is the spur that the clear spirit doth raise To shun delights and live laborious days"—a spur very hard to find a substitute for or to do without.
>
> —Gerard Manley Hopkins

Writer's isolation, loneliness.

The attitude: nobody owes you (the writer) anything; the world never asked you to write.

My long ago and still instinctive response: What's wrong with the world then, that it doesn't ask—and make it possible—for people to raise and contribute the best that is in them.

— — —

I can't go on.

I can't leave it there either. I sound like certain established writers at forums and conferences (and sometimes even in classes) eagerly bringing the news to unestablished ones of how frightful and hard and impossible it is—not in an emboldening spirit of solidarity and resistance either—or even balancing it with the rest, the joys and rewards which keep writers going.

— — —

(Writers, you can start reading again here.)

> O ye dead poets who are living still
> Immortal in your verse though life be fled,
> And ye, O living poets who are dead

Though ye are living, for neglect can kill,
Tell me if in the darkest hours of ill
With drops of anguish falling fast and red
From the sharp crown of thorns upon your head
Ye were not glad your errand to fulfil?

Yes, for the gift and ministry of Song
Have something in them so divinely sweet
It can assuage the bitterness of wrong.
                —the scarcely-ever-now-quoted Longfellow

Yes.

> In art, as in no other form of endeavour,
> there is meaning apart from success.
>   —Conrad

(I believe that to be true for all forms of human endeavor, but let it stand.)

The *rapture;* the saving comfort; the joyous energies, pride, love, audacity, reverence in wrestling with the angel, Art—

> This dear old blessed healing
>
>   —James

> I walk, making up phrases, sit, contriving scenes; am, in short, in the thick of the greatest rapture known to me.
>
>   —V. Woolf

> One sentence follows another, is born of the other, and I feel as I see it being born and growing within me, an almost physical rapture.
>
>   —Gide

> The strange mysterious perhaps dangerous perhaps saving comfort there is in writing; it is a leap out of the murderers' row; it is a seeing of what is really taking place.
>
>   —Kafka

Yes.

> The American bards shall be marked for generosity and affection
> and for encouraging competitors. They shall be Kosmos, without
> monopoly or secrecy, glad to pass anything to anyone—hungry for
> equals by night and by day.*
>
> —Whitman

O yes.

The truth under the spume and corrosion. Literature is a place
for generosity and affection and hunger for equals—not a prize-
fight ring. We are increased, confirmed in our medium, roused to
do our best, by every good writer, every fine achievement. Would
we want one good writer or fine book less? The sense of writers
being pitted against each other is bred primarily by the workings
of the commercial marketplace, and by critics lauding one writer
at the expense of another while ignoring the existence of nearly all.
What—in addition to all the preceding—disheartens, weakens,
can poison, is the existence, and sometimes success, of the sleazy,
the corrupt, the tricky.

Hungry for equals. The sustenance some writers are to each
other personally, besides the help of doing their best work.

Hungry for equals. The spirit of those writers who have
worked longer years, solved more, are more established; reaching out to the newer, the ones who must carry on the loved
medium.

The small presses, magazines, making work accessible.

Established writers trying to get unestablished ones known or

---

*Re-affirmed newly in the 1974 National Book Awards, when prizewinner in
Poetry Adrienne Rich "refused the terms of patriarchal competition," rejecting
the award as an individual, but accepting it in the name of all women (in a
statement written with Audre Lord and Alice Walker, two other nominees): "We
. . . together accept this award in the name of all the women whose voices have
gone and still go unheard in a patriarchal world, and in the name of those who,
like us, have been tolerated as token women in this culture, often at great cost
and in great pain. . . . We symbolically join here in refusing the terms of
patriarchal competition and declaring that we will share this prize among us, to
be used as best we can for women. . . . We dedicate this occasion to the struggle
for self-determination of all women, of every color, identification or deprived
class . . . the women who will understand what we are doing here and those who
will not understand yet: the silent women whose voices have been denied us, the
articulate women who have given us strength to do our work."

published. Or, a different form of concern; serving on committees for other writers.

Poets and Writers (CODA) building a sense of community among writers through their *Newsletter,* directory, services. *Margins.*

Even in the publishing world, those who are drawn there because of their love for literature, who still do what they can.

The exceptional publisher, anthologist, critic, bookstore.

The teacher and librarian who incite to literature.

Our caring readers—co-partners.

The sustaining existence of writers whose work and lives we can respect—and love.

A little-known writer:

> Some of what I know to be my best writing will never be published . . . many of my most cherished projects will never come to fruition; many of my aspirations forever unfulfilled. I am always surprised when a stranger recognizes my name . . . but for more than half a century I had had my work published . . . at 77 I am busier with my writing than ever before and expect to continue until I die. . . . When I was young I was going to be a great poet . . . now I am happy that at long last I did get one volume [of poetry] published . . . I was also going to be a famous short story writer and novelist. How many years of disappointment and rebellion and grief to realise that I was never going to be anything of the kind; [there are only] my dozen books, my moderate recognition in two or three specialized fields.
>
> *It is what you aspire to rather than what you attain that brings into being even what you do attain. Never set your sights too low. . . .*
>
> There is no disgrace in joining us Almosters. At least a little of what we had to say has been said and a few have heard and even listened.
>
> —Miriam Allen De Ford, 1973

And a famous one:

> I spent so much of my life teaching and lecturing and reading . . . that I had not time or energy to write the things that I have really begun. I have 3 unfinished books which were the main objects of my life. I am 85 years old, I am working ferociously trying to

make a deadline, being a little late of course, but this time, thank God, my deadline is my own. I rather enjoy driving myself. It brings back the old times when I was like, not an ox, but a horse on a treadmill, being urged at a dead run always. And, without seeming to grow roses on a past that was full of briars and cactus, it was not so bad; I did survive. I have enjoyed my work, it has been my only happiness. . . . It was worth living for and I still have what might seem a wild hope that I shall finish at least this book I am working on. And the other 2 are still alive and beginning to agitate for attention like very healthy children in an uncomfortable cradle.

My dear fellow artists, I suggest that you go ahead and do your work and do it as you please and refuse to allow any force, any influence (that is to say, any editor or publisher) to tamper with your life or to debase your work. You are practicing an art and they are running a business and just keep this in mind.

—Katherine Anne Porter, 1976

"We are the injured body. Let us not desert one another."

The Literary Situation.

THE WRITER-WOMAN:
ONE OUT OF TWELVE—II

Acerbs, Asides, Amulets, Exhumations, Sources,
Deepenings, Roundings, Expansions

. . . And yet the tree did bear fruit.

BLIGHT▲

Its Earliest Expression (Early 1600s)

I never rested on the Muses bed,
Nor dipt my quill in the Thessalian fountaine,
My rustick Muse was rudely fostered
And flies too low to reach the double mountaine.

Then do not sparkes with your bright Suns compare,
Perfection in a Woman's work is rare.
From an untroubled mind should verses flow,
My discontents make mine too muddy show.

And hoarse encumbrances of householde care,
Where these remain, the Muses ne'er repaire.
>   —Mary Oxlie of Morpet to
>   William Drummond of Hawthornden

*Compared to men writers of like distinction and years of
life, few women writers have had lives of unbroken productivity, or leave behind a "body of work." Early beginnings, then silence; or clogged late ones (foreground silences); long periods between books (hidden silences);
characterize most of us.*

A SENSE OF WRONG VOICED*

Background

*Linked with the old, resurrected classics on women, this movement
in three years has accumulated a vast new mass of testimony, of new
comprehensions, as to what it is to be female. Inequities, restrictions,
penalties, denials, leechings, have been painstakingly and painfully
documented; damaging differences in circumstances and treatment
from that of males attested to; and limitations, harms, a sense of
wrong voiced.*

The three years had also shaped a swelling indictment of literature, in its beginning around Images of Women in Literature.
Virginia Woolf had once called it "Women in Fiction—and in
Fact." *Sexual Politics* is how Kate Millett defined the difference
in 1969. Tentatively phrased, exploratory questions in the beginning:

> Is women's character in fiction a function of cultural values? of
> male subjectivity? and not an accurate portrayal of woman's real
> situation and reactions?

> Are women portrayed only in terms of relationships to men; men
> in a variety of situations?

became arraignment:

> There is a wide discrepancy in American culture between the life
> of women as conceived by men and the life of women as lived by
> women.*

---

*Lilian Schissel.

Literature has unwittingly aided the conspiracy of silence, neglect, as to the nature of women's lives and services.

Throughout much of our literature, fanciful constructs of the female, her character and psychology, have obscured the limitations suffered by actual women. Worse, they have encouraged expectations and behavior that only strengthen the real oppression.*

A search began for different (truer) Images of Women in Literature.** Women writers, previously scarcely included in the literary curriculum, began to be hungrily read and studied in increasing number; "Women in Literature" classes, teaching now mostly writing by women, proliferated,† became (often interdisciplinary) Women's Studies courses. They had to be argued and fought for.

There are practical and intellectual reasons for establishing some separate courses dealing with women writers. We cannot change literary history or reinterpret a tradition overnight. We cannot create women writers where they do not exist, and few existed before the Nineteenth Century. . . . Women writers should not be studied as a distinct group on the assumption that they write alike, or even display stylistic resemblances distinctively feminine. But women do have a special literary history, susceptible to analysis, which includes such complex considerations as the effects of social and political changes in women's status upon individuals, and the implications of stereotypes on the woman writer and restrictions on her artistic autonomy.‡

The contribution of women writers has been ignored too long—the addition of a few women to reading lists is not sufficient. An entire course makes more sense, because when studied in succession, their writing and experience reveal patterns which are almost impossible to perceive if they are studied only in relation to male writers.§

---

*Lillian Robinson.

**Title of a pioneering anthology textbook; Mary Ann Ferguson, editor.

†Some 110 in 1970–71. (By 1973 there were 600 courses in literature alone.)

‡Elaine Showalter.

§I cannot identify the author of this quotation or all previous quotations, but they were copied (in 1971) out of course descriptions or *Female Studies* (K.N.O.W. and Feminist Press).

"By what standards should literature (itself) be judged?" came into question. "Should viciousness or falseness of portrayal affect the evaluation of literature?" asked one course description. An older touchstone for literature—truth—re-entered the classroom to reside along with critical analysis. Classes themselves became profound experiences, charged with intellectual-emotional discovery. ("For a tear is an intellectual thing."*)

Feminist literary criticism came into practice.

The woman writer herself became a special field of exploration (one to which an increasing number of women writers contributed, some in fictional form).

Realization of the "staggering exclusions from the male-stream of literature,"** roused and emboldened diverse expression: poetry, fiction, biography, personal accounts, criticism, anthologies.

Five years later (1976), it is unmistakable that out of the sense of wrong has come substantial yields for literature: its enlargement and vivification through reclamation of obscured writers and intensified rereading of classic ones; new insights and perspectives; an enhancement and deepening of literary scholarship, criticism, theory; an opening up and freeing for already existing writers; the coming into being and encouragement of new ones;—and an outpouring of writing in every field and form of literature.

All while "still in the egg life, chafing the shell."

Women in Fiction and in Fact: 1815–1975

1815: Jane Austen: "I will not allow books to prove anything"

> "Yes, we certainly do not forget you as soon as you forget us. It is perhaps our fate rather than our merit. We cannot help ourselves. We live at home, quiet, confined, and our feelings prey upon us. You are forced on exertion. You have always business of some sort or other to take you back to the world

---

*William Blake.

**Adrienne Rich in her preface to Susan Griffin's *Voices*, 1976.

immediately, and continual occupation and change soon weaken impressions. . . ."

"But let me observe that all histories are against you—all stories, prose and verse."

"Please, if you please, no reference to books. Men have had every advantage of us in telling their own story. Education has been theirs in so much higher a degree; the pen has been in their hands. I will not allow books to prove anything."

> —The exchange between Anne and Captain Harville in
> Jane Austen's, *Persuasion*

1871: Walt Whitman early on noted the discrepancy between "Women in Fiction—and in Fact." In *Democratic Vistas* ("Literature has never recognized the common people") he counterposes against

the stock feminine characters of the current novelists (Ophelias, Enids, princesses, ladies of one kind or another) [presented] as supreme ideals of feminine excellence to be sought after

four "typical" American women:

A young American woman, one of a large family of daughters, who, some years since, migrated from her meagre country home to one of the northern cities to gain her own support . . . an expert seamstress . . . cook . . . her presence itself healthy and bracing . . . preserves her independence. . . .

. . . another woman who, from taste and necessity conjoin'd, has gone into practical affairs, carries on a mechanical business, partly works at it herself, dashes out more and more into real hardy life, is not abash'd by the coarseness of contact, knows how to be firm and silent at the same time, holds her own with unvarying coolness and decorum, and will compare, any day, with superior carpenters, farmers, and even boatmen and drivers. . . .

The wife of a mechanic, mother of two children, a woman of merely passable English education, but of fine wit. . . . Never abnegating her own proper independence, but always genially preserving it, and what belongs to it. . . .

. . . a resplendent person, . . . known by the name of the Peacemaker . . . well toward eighty years old, had always lived on a farm . . . an invariable and welcom'd favorite, especially with young married women . . . numerous children and grandchildren . . .

uneducated, but possess'd of a native dignity. She had come to be a tacitly agreed upon domestic regulator, judge, settler of difficulties, shepherdess, and reconciler in the land.

"The foregoing portraits," adds Whitman, "are frightfully out of line from [the] imported models of womanly personality."

1975

Shortly after the publication of Philip Roth's *Portnoy's Complaint*, Charlotte [Baum] attended a meeting of a Jewish women's "reading club" to participate in a discussion of the book. Although Charlotte's experience in no way paralleled Alexander Portnoy's, she intended to defend Roth's point of view, and to support his right to demythicize the legendary Jewish family.

Most of the women in the group were in their sixties. They were the daughters of Eastern European Jews, either born here, or having immigrated as children. They were now upper-middle class women whose husbands, none of whom had attended college, were manufacturers or owners of medium-sized businesses. Their sons were university-educated professionals, or associated with the family businesses. Their daughters were themselves all active in Jewish philanthropic organizations like Hadassah, ORT, B'nai B'rith, and synagogue sisterhoods.

The women began to defend themselves against Roth's highly critical view of Jewish women, as embodied in his character Sophie Portnoy. They described their sacrifices, struggles, and hardships, and Charlotte knew she was hearing the truth. She remembered stories from her own past, about her aunts' involvement in the labor movement, her mother's friends who had taken in boarders to supplement the family's income and her own mother who worked in the grocery store eighteen hours a day. She found herself agreeing with these Jewish women that if anyone had complaints to make, it was they! . . .

Why were there no Jewish women novelists recording their experiences and hers? Had the daughters of these women been so psychologically damaged that they were incapable of generating a voice of their own?

> —from the preface to *The Jewish Woman in America*,
> Michel, Hyman, Baum-Sheedy, 1975

LITERACY[▲]

Two-thirds of the illiterate in the world today are women.

Frederick Douglass was able to leave for us the legacy of his life and thoughts as he chose to write it; Harriet Tubman and Sojourner Truth (Truth one of the most eloquent users of spoken words in her time)* come to us filtered through the words of others: words they were not able to read to correct or change.

Faulkner's "real life" Dilsey lived and died (one hundred seven years old) walking distance from the world-famous writer to whose books, language (and self) she contributed so much—never enabled to read a word he had written, let alone write; tell in her own powerful language, her own imaginings, reality.

Camus, Dreiser, had unlettered mothers. Remarkable women by their son's testimony. Lost writers?

How many of us who are writers have mothers, grandmothers, of limited education; awkward, not at home, with the written word, however eloquent they may be with the spoken one? Born a generation or two before, we might have been they.

The dying Ellen Glasgow writes in *The Woman Within* of the "Mammy" of her childhood who first roused, nurtured, her love of language, her imagination; taught her endless stories and encouraged her to create her own. They had a compact: when the

---

*Her famous "And Ain't *I* A Woman?" speech is a perfect statement of "real life" Women in Fiction—and in Fact.

little girl learned to read and write, she would teach her too. It never came to be. Glasgow's tears, the half-century after, are felt on the page.

These last few decades, we have begun to have an impressive body of prison writing by men previously near-illiterate (or the kind of illiteracy consisting of never reading books, and inarticulateness in written expression). Men writers, not women. Even in prison circumstances, there is a marked difference in circumstances and encouragement.

ONE OUT OF TWELVE—THE FIGURES FOR WRITERS ACCORDED RECOGNITION▲

Proportion of Women Writers to Men Writers*

Included in Twentieth-Century Literature Courses: One Out of Seventeen (6% women, 94% men)

> In 223 *undergraduate* course offerings and bibliographies (1970–1976) at community, state, private, colleges and universities, one woman writer was studied to every seventeen men writers. The disparity would have been even more marked, if the proportions of women writers studied at the graduate level, or permitted as subjects for master's theses and doctoral dissertations, had been included. As a guess: 2% women, 98% men?

Criticism and Critical Surveys in Fiction: One Out of Thirteen to One Out of Thirty

> *Authors, editors of works of criticism: One out of Fifteen (7% women, 93% men):*
> Of seventy-six works listed in the *Poets and Writers Directory*, seventy were written or edited by men, four by women, and two co-edited. One of the four by women was on writers who are women, and so identified by the title. Not one of the books con-

---

*These are round figure, rough estimates that include both the 1971 findings used in the original talk, and 1976 ones which confirm. As only the conclusions remain from 1971, most titles herein are 1976 work, in or on what was readily accessible in limited time.

sidering only men writers included "male" in the title to similarly define their content, nor would it have occurred to their authors to do so.*

Inclusion in critical works:
Name in a list, no discussion of work: One out of Thirteen
*Page-space accorded: One page out of Thirty***

To illustrate: in Tony Tanner's *City of Words—American Fiction 1950–1970,* there are 445 pages. Plath is written of on two pages, mentioned three times otherwise; Sontag is given four pages and three mentions. No other women are discussed. In Alfred Kazin's 317 page *Bright Book of Life,* forty-three concern women writers. They are segregated into one chapter, not for purposes of illumination, discovery, or because of similarities in theme or style—legitimate reasons for grouping and a different matter from segregation —but simply because they are women. One page in the chapter on Southern writers includes O'Connor and McCullers.
No more than 10 percent of the women writers named in "One Out of Twelve" are discussed in the critical works surveyed.

Critical Reference Works: About One Out of Eleven (9% women, 91% men)

Contemporary World Literature: 2,519 entries, 178 of them on women. One out of fourteen or fifteen on a world scale.
Contemporary Literary Criticism; Cumulative Index to Authors: 540 entries, 87 on women.
Contemporary Novel; A Checklist of Critical Literature in Britain and America Since 1945: 181 listed, 30 of them women.
Modern American Literature; A Library of Literary Criticism: about 290 entries, 42 women.
With the exception of a few authors, the page space accorded women is comparatively meager.

---

*Among their titles: *Adversity and Grace: Studies in Recent American Literature; Beyond the Wasteland, A Study of the American Novel in the 1960s; Contemporary American-Jewish Literature, Critical Essays; Literary Disruptions: The Making of a Post Contemporary American Fiction.*

**The proportion would have been more accurate had the number of pages in books concerned only with male writers also been figured in.

Interviews (selection according to critical judgment): *One Out of Ten (10% women, 90% men)*

> As instance, the *Paris Review* interviews—considered a literary honor. In seventy-four interviews—to the end of 1975—only seven were women.

Anthologies, Textbooks: One Out of Eleven (9% women, 91% men)

> *The Anthologies Themselves:* Ninety books were in the 1976 sampling; twelve included only men authors.* A listing of forty-three anthologies by title, editor, and percentage, is on pages 190–192. *Editors: Close to One out of Thirteen (8% women, 92% men):* Sixty-four anthologies are listed in the *Writers Directory* (CODA); five were edited by women, one co-edited.

Inclusion in Selective Writers Directories: About One Out of Seven (13% women, 87% men)**

> These include *Contemporary Novelists* (all advisers male); *200 Contemporary Authors; Twentieth Century Authors: World Authors (1950–1970)*—of the latter, 960 writers, 125 of them women.

Prizes, Awards—One Out of Six? Seven? Eight? (Difficult to come to a figure, because some awards are considered weightier honors than others.)

---

*I am looking forward to the anthologies (and works of criticism) which, though including women writers only, will be titled: *The Major Young Poets; Innovative Fiction, Stories for the Seventies; American Literature, 1950–1975;* or: *Critical Studies in Recent American Literature.* Or conversely, when only men writers are being discussed, *The Male Imagination* or *Literary Men.*

**The percentage figure is misleading. Page space accorded women writers is considerably less than that given to writers who are men; on rough estimate—one out of eighteen.

Especially in view of some of the men included, the omission of women writers whose work is far more vital, substantial, important is indefensible. Noticeably absent are black women writers. (Even among women authors chosen for inclusion, several of the directories—in disadvantageous contrast—have a preponderance of popular, genre, "fluff" women writers.)

Nobel Prize for Literature, 1920–1972   49 recipients,
5 women

Bollingen Poetry Prize, 1950–1973   24 recipients,
4 women

Pulitzer Prizes:
  Fiction, 1920–1973 . . . . 47 recipients,
16 women
  Drama, 1920–1973 . . . . 45 awards,
56 recipients,
6 women
  Poetry, 1922–1973 . . . . 51 recipients,
11 women

National Book Awards:
  Fiction (1950–1973) . . . . 26 recipients,
3 women
  Poetry (1950–1973) . . . . 26 recipients,
3 women

Guggenheim Fellowships for Fiction,
Drama and Poetry (mixed), 1926–1972 . . . . 419 recipients,
79 women
                 1975 . . . . . . 21 recipients,
6 women
                 1976 . . . . . . 30 recipients,
6 women

American Academy/National Institute
  of Arts & Letters:
    Gold Medal, 1922–1973 . . . . 39 recipients,
7 women
    Award of Merit Medal, 1944–1973 . . . 16 recipients,
7 women
    Awards in Literature, 1941–1973 . . . . 224 recipients,
48 women

Academy of American Poets Awards,
1946–1975 . . . . 33 recipients,
5 women
O. Henry Awards, First Prizes, 1919–1973 . . 54 recipients,
20 women

Book Review Index (sampling in 1974, 1975, 1976): Between One
out of Six and Seven.

Books in Print, 1975 (sampling from 100 pages): One out of Five or Six. (A like sampling in 1971 indicated One out of Four or Five. I would welcome a computer study.)

Memberships: About One out of Four.

> P.E.N. American Center, 1970, 1971, 1975, about One out of Four. Listed in CODA Poets and Fiction Writers Directories, between One out of Four and Five (20% to 25% women).

All Fiction Published:

> Fiction Catalog (sampling) 1971–1974, about One out of Four.

Anthologies of Student Work (prose, poetry): Less than One out of Three.

> These include *Intro, New Campus Writing,* and *Twenty Years of Stanford Stories.* (What happened with those young women?)

Films, Videotape (as listed in the *Directory of American Fiction Writers):*

> Of 123 films whose subjects are writers, only nine are of women; five others include women; of 287 videotapes, fifty-eight are of women.

A Sampling of the Ratio of Women Writers to Men Writers in Anthologies and Textbooks*

Literature for Our Time, Waite, Atkinson, eds.	5 out of 107
How We Live, Contemporary Life in	
Contemporary Fiction, Hills and Hills, eds.	4 out of 51
Modern Age Literature, Lief and Light, eds.	8 out of 106
Modern Occasions, Rahv, ed.	prose 1 out of 10
	poetry 1 out of 6

---

*Most of these titles listed in Poets and Writers Directory.

Scenes from American Life: Contemporary
  Short Fiction, Oates, ed.   5 out of 20
The Single Voice: An Anthology of
  Contemporary Fiction, Charyn, ed.   2 out of 32
Southern Writing in the Sixties: Fiction,
  Corrington and Williams, eds.   3 out of 20
Statements: New Fiction from the Fiction
  Collective, Horowitz et al., eds.   2 out of 27
Writer's Choice: Twenty American Authors
  Introduce Their Own Best Story, Hills,
  ed.   1 out of 20
Short Story Masterpieces, Warren and
  Erskine, eds.   8 out of 36
Great English Short Stories, Isherwood, ed.   2 out of 12
New Directions in Prose and Poetry, Laughlin,
  ed.   2 out of 21
Twelve From the Sixties, Kostelanetz, ed.   2 out of 12
Innovative Fiction, Stories for the Seventies,
  Klinkowitz and Somer, eds.   No women, 16 men
Stories of Modern America, Gold and
  Stevenson, eds.   4 out of 23
The World of Short Fiction, Albrecht, ed.   2 out of 21
Statements: New Fiction from the Fiction
  Collective, Horowitz, ed.   2 out of 27
The Realm of Fiction, Hall, ed.   6 out of 45
Ten Modern Masters, Davis, ed.   1 out of 10
Fifty Best American Stories, O. Henry Prize
  Awards 1915–1965, Abrahams, ed.   13 out of 50
Fifty Years of the American Short Story,
  Foley, ed.   8 out of 36

Fiction—Anthologies, Ethnic (CODA, Poets and Writers Directory, classification)

Black Writers of America: A Comprehensive
  Anthology, Barksdale and Kinnamon, eds.   17 out of 80
The Chicanos: Mexican American Voices,
  Ludwig and Santibanez, eds.   2 out of 18
From the Roots: Short Stories by Black
  Americans, James, ed.   4 out of 22
Literature of American Jews, Gross, ed.   3 out of 39
The Man to Send Rain Clouds: Contemporary
  Stories by American Indians, Rosen, ed.   3 out of 8

Out of Our Lives: A Selection of
    Contemporary Black Fiction, Stadler, ed.   7 out of 17
Tales and Stories for Black Folks: Written by
    Black Authors, Bambara, ed.   8 out of 15
Voices of Aztlan: Chicano Literature of Today,
    Harth and Baldwin, eds.   1 out of 24
Soul Script, Jordan, ed.   14 out of 54

Poetry Anthologies

Anthology of New York Poets,
    Padgett and Shapiro, eds.   1 out of 27
Best Poems of 1973, Borestone Mountain
    Poetry Awards.   26 out of 74
Chief Modern Poets of Britain and America,
    Sanders, ed.   6 out of 57
Contemporary American Poets, Strand, ed.   12 out of 92
Contemporary American Poetry, Hall, ed.   2 out of 25
A Controversy of Poets: An Anthology of
    Contemporary American Poetry, Leary and
    Kelly, eds.   8 out of 59
The Norton Anthology of Contemporary
    Poetry, Ellmann and O'Clair, eds.   13 out of 96
The Major Young Poets, Lee, ed.   No women, 8 men
New American Poetry, Monaca, ed.   5 out of 21
Quickly Aging Here; Some Poets of the
    1970's, Hewett, ed.   8 out of 35
31 New American Poets, Schreiber, ed.   8 out of 31
Naked Poetry, Berg and Mazey, eds.   2 out of 19
The Voice That Is Great Within Us,
    Carruth, ed.   23 out of 114

A recent New York Times *reviewer (April 1976), making the prevalent (unexamined) assumption, chastised Ellen Moers, author of the superb* Literary Women, *for limiting her subject matter to women and "exiling the other half of the writing race." As these figures establish, women are the exiled. By the most generous estimate, simply the percentage of fiction of all manner and kind published, men are three-quarters of the writing race; in the more selective and indicative estimates, they are 88% to 98%.*

The leeching of belief, of will, the damaging of capacity, begin so early.

THE BABY; THE GIRL-CHILD; THE GIRL; THE YOUNG WRITER-WOMAN ▲

Little put-upon sisters . . .

What keyhole have we slipped through,
What door has shut? . . .

Everything has happened.*

[Baby] Bess who has been fingering a fruit-jar lid—absently, heed-lessly drops it—aimlessly groping across the table, reclaims it again. Lightning in her brain. She releases, grabs, releases, grabs. I can do. Bang! I did that. I can do. I! A look of neanderthal concentration is on her face. That noise! In triumphant, astounded joy she clashes the lid down. Bang, slam, whack. Release, grab, slam, bang, bang. Centuries of human drive work in her; human ecstasy of achievement, satisfaction deep and fundamental as sex: *I can do, I use my powers, I! I!* Wilder, madder, happier the bangs. The fetid fevered air rings with . . . Bess's toothless, triumphant crow. Heat misery, rash misery transcended.**

---

* "The Babysitters," Sylvia Plath.

**From *Yonnondio,* by the young (twenty-year-old) mother-writer who was myself.

Was the beginning sexual?
I remember a girlboy in one
(Although haunted by father pain)
Sexless like tree shoots, roving
Along seemingly flowerless trees

So sensual, she lay on tree trunk
Or quick-changed, burrowed into
Silts and banks. I remember her bridling
In the sex of a stallion (never the mare)
Driven along by string reins, mouthbit.

Did He draw She? (In her sleep
She heard them argue, never in her
Dreams dare he come.) . . . I don't doubt
Him, snake swaying like a man, in the tree
Drawing her away from her true god.*

Looking back at poems I wrote before I was twenty-one, I'm star-
tled because beneath the conscious craft are glimpses of the split I
even then experienced between the girl who wrote poems, who
defined herself in writing poems, and the girl who defined herself
by her relationships with men . . .

—Adrienne Rich

. . . Oh, the jealous and anxious passion I had for solitude, O
solitude of my young days! You were my refuge, my panacea,
the citadel of my youthful pride. With what might and main
did I cling to you—and how afraid I was even then of losing
you! I trembled at the mere thought of the more ruthless and
less rare ecstasy of love! At the thought of losing you I felt already demeaned. And yet . . . who can resist the pull of love?
To become only a woman—how paltry! Yet I hastened eagerly
toward that common goal.

---

*From "Adam and Eve and the Child" in *Ladder of the World's Joy,* Sarah
Appleton.

Did I hesitate a minute, one solitary minute, standing between your beloved specter, O solitude, and the menacing apparition of love? . . . I don't know.

—Colette

As lonely in her trouble as if she had been the only girl in the civilised world of that day who had come out of her school life with a soul untrained for inevitable struggles; with no other part of her inherited share in the hard won treasures of thought which generations of painful toil have laid for the race of men, than shreds and patches of feeble literature and false history.

—George Eliot

And in all the usual college teaching . . . little to help that young woman understand the source or nature of this inexplicable draining self-doubt, loss of aspiration, of confidence.

It is in these years that another significant turn to silencing takes place. What was needed to confirm and vivify has been meager— and occasional, accidental. The compound of what actively denies, divides, vitiates, has been powerful—and continuous, institutionalized. The young unhelped "sexless, bound in sex" being is now in

. . . the glade
Wherein Fate sprung Love's ambuscade, . . .
To flush me in this sensuous strife. . . .

Of that which makes the sexual feud
And clogs the aspirant life.*

---

*From Melville's "After the Pleasure Party."

How many making up the eleven in the possible twelve founder here?

(With more than is recognized, it has not been a leaving of literature, but an attempt at solution, a keeping and using of it within precedented woman ways. So is born the enabler, the encourager, the wife, the helper; where there is economic imperative—that mammoth silencer only indicated in this book—the teacher, librarian, editor. And still the want to write does not die; it waits, unsleeping, sleeping, unsleeping.)

There was that . . . conception, which I'd been brought up to and wanted to believe, that I should find the *solution* to my life, not just companionship, in a single, other person. . . .

At Iowa . . . a classmate told me he believed that to be a woman poet was "a contradiction in terms." . . .

Princeton . . . intensified my own sense of dichotomy between "woman" and "poet." I knew a number of men who wrote, but no women. Work by women was still sparsely represented in contemporary poetry anthologies. . . . Men's praise of poetry didn't seem to go much beyond Marianne Moore and Elizabeth Bishop, whose work I admired but couldn't then *use,* in the deep sense that writers use the discoveries of other writers as steps toward their own growth.

. . . From the age of twenty-two to the age of twenty-six, I worked strenuously and perfectly seriously on a book of poems (a *book,* not just poems), then "gave up poetry" and never tried to publish but one of them.

"Didn't anyone ever tell you it was all right to write?" asked the psychiatrist who came along much later: "Yes, but not to be a writer." Behind me lay the sort of middle-class education that encourages writing, painting, music, theater, so long as they aren't taken too seriously, so long as they can be set aside once the real business of life begins. . . .*

> Now she is still not beautiful but more
> Moving than before, for time has come
> When she shall be delivered; some-
> one must have, move her, or the doors
> Be shuttered over, the doorlids shut, her
> Eyes' lies shattered. In the spume
> Of a triple wave she lives: sperm,
> Man and life's mate break like flags upon her shore.
>
> Marriage must take her now, or the sly
> Inquirer, inviting her to ship for his sake,
> Will share all islands inland with her, her sky

---

*Jane Cooper. *Maps and Windows.*

No one else shares, will slake
Conquerlust. Seas wash away her ties
While through her thigh-trees water strikes like a snake.*

Everything has happened!

---

*"Eve," written in 1947 when Jane Cooper was twenty-three, was put away with other poems, and not published until *Maps and Windows,* in 1974.

THE DAMNATION OF WOMEN*

I. Within the Injunction

> Perfection is terrible.
> It cannot have children.
> It tamps the womb.

Was it so that "most women writers of distinction never questioned, or at least accepted [a few sanctified] the patriarchal injunction;* this different condition for achievement not imposed on men"?

A few sanctified, yes. Willa Cather:

> Art of every kind is an exacting master, more so than Jehovah. He says only "Thou shalt have no other gods before me." Art, Science, Letters cry: "Thou shalt have no other gods at all." They accept only human sacrifices.

For Ellen Glasgow there was not even a question. She answered the literary man who told her,

> The best advice I can give you is to stop writing and go back to the South and have some babies. The greatest woman is not the woman

---

*"You must choose between your art and fulfillment as a woman, full personal life." "Them lady poets must not marry, pal."

who has written the finest book, but the woman who has had the finest babies

that "all I ever wanted was to write books. And not ever had I felt the faintest wish to have babies."

Henry Handel Richardson (quoted in "Silences") and Katherine Anne Porter acquiesced; it was one or the other:

There are enough women to do the childbearing and the childrearing. I know of none who can write my books,

wrote Richardson. Porter told an interviewer:

Now I am all for human life, and I am all for marriage and children and all that sort of thing, but quite often you can't have that and do what you were supposed to do, too. Art is a vocation, as much as anything in the world, not as necessary as air and water, perhaps, but as food and water. . . . We really do lead almost a monastic life, you know.

In that long roll of childless women writers who paid the cost of being able to do their best work, was there not one who felt it as damnation? Not one? Silence, reticence, until with Katherine Mansfield and Virginia Woolf, in our century, an anguish, a longing to have children, breaks into expression. In private diaries and letters only.

Virginia Woolf, writing of the causes of her descent into madness as a young woman:

. . . and all the devils came out—heavy black ones—to be 29 & unmarried—to be a failure—childless—insane too, no writer . . .

At thirty-eight:
Why is life so tragic; so like a little strip of pavement over an abyss? . . . It's having no children, living away from friends, failing to write well. . . .

At forty-four:
Woke up perhaps at 3. Oh it's beginning, it's coming—the horror —physically like a painful wave swelling about the heart—tossing

me up. I'm unhappy, unhappy! Down—God, I wish I were dead.
Pause. But why am I feeling this? Let me watch the wave rise. I
watch. Vanessa.*   Children. Failure. Yes. Failure. Failure. The
wave rises.

She was one month to forty-six before she could write
   ... And yet oddly enough I scarcely want children of my own now.
   This insatiable desire to write something before I die, this ravaging
   sense of the shortness and feverishness of life, make me cling, like
   a man on a rock, to my own anchor. I don't like the physicalness
   of having children of one's own. This occurred to me at Rodmell,
   but I never wrote it down. I can dramatise myself as a parent, it
   is true. And perhaps I have killed the feeling instinctively; or perhaps nature does.

Or perhaps nature does. Only at forty-eight, on
   a day of intoxication ... when I sat surveying the whole book [*The
   Waves*] complete ... felt the pressure of the form—the splendour,
   the greatness—as perhaps I have never felt them

could she write, unqualifiedly:

   Children are nothing to this.

Not until 1971, is there poetry:

> My body knows it will never bear children.
> What can I say to my body now,
> this used violin?
> Every night it cries out desolately
> from its secret cave.
>
> Old body, old friend,
> why are you so unforgiving? . . .
> —Jane Cooper, *Maps and Windows.*

---

*Her artist-sister, and mother of three.

Might There Not Have Been Other Marvels?▲

What possible difference, you may ask, does it make to literature whether or not a woman writer remains childless—free choice or not —especially in view of the marvels these childless women have created.

Might there not have been other marvels as well, or other dimensions to these marvels? Might there not have been present profound aspects and understandings of human life as yet largely absent in literature?

That was not all I said at the MLA in 1971, nor was it phrased as question—but as based conviction.

I spoke not only of the loss in literature, but to other fields of human knowledge and action as well, because comprehensions possible out of motherhood *(including,* among so much invaluable else, *the very nature, needs, illimitable potentiality of the human being—and the everyday means by which these are distorted, discouraged, limited, extinguished)* have never had the circumstances to come to powerful, undeniable, useful expression—have had instead to remain inchoate, fragmentary, unformulated (and alas, unvalidated).

But I scarcely began on what needed to be said. Not only its seeming digression or the time limitation. I was entering into an almost taboo area; the last refuge of sexism; what has been, is, the least understood, least and last explored, tormentingly complex *core* of woman's oppression (and, I believe, transport as woman) —motherhood. No context had been established.

I was conscious, too, of the many childless women present (professionals! having to obey the patriarchal injunction), and that to speak to them of yields possible in circumstanced motherhood, unless placed in context, might come only as more of its familiar traditional (mis)use to rebuke and belittle the hard-won achievement of their lives; more of the societal coercion to conform; family as the only suitable way of life for a female.

I was not able to reconstitute my remarks satisfactorily by the *College English* deadline. (They remain unpublished.)

▲ ONE OUT OF TWELVE, P. 32

II. Writer-Mothers: The Fundamental Situation

". . . that only at the sacrifice of their best work can they bear and rear children . . ."*

When a man becomes an author, it is merely a change of employment to him. He takes a portion of that time which has hitherto been devoted to some other pursuit . . . and another merchant or lawyer or doctor steps into his vacant place and probably does as well as he. But no other can take up the quiet regular duties of the daughter, the wife or the mother. . . . A woman's principal work in life is hardly left to her choice; nor can she drop the domestic charges evolving on her as an individual for the exercise of the most splendid talents that were ever bestowed. And yet she must not shrink from the extra responsibility implied by the very fact of her possessing such talents. She must not hide her gift in a napkin; it was meant for the use and service of others. In an humble and faithful spirit she must labor to do what is not impossible.

—Mrs. Elizabeth Gaskell, *Life of Charlotte Brontë*,
1857—and still:

(The very fact that these are real needs, that one feels them as one's own, *that there is no one else responsible for these needs,* gives them primacy.)

—"Silences," 1962

The Fundamental Situation: Its earliest expression (1838)

"Come Harriet," said I, as I found her tending one baby and watching two others just able to walk, "where is that piece for the 'Souvenir' which I promised the editor I would get from you? You have only this one day left to finish it, and have it I must."

"And how will you get it, friend of mine. . . . You will at least have to wait till I get housecleaning over and baby's teeth through."

"As to housecleaning, you can defer it one day longer; and as to baby's teeth, there is to be no end to them, as I can see . . ."

"But . . . there is a great baking down in the kitchen, and there

---

*W.E.B. Du Bois, "The Damnation of Women" again.

is a 'new girl' for 'help' besides preparations for housecleaning next week. It is really out of the question."

". . . I do not know what genius is given for, if it is not to help a woman out of a scrape. . . . Just take your seat at the kitchen table with your writing weapons, and while you superintend Mina, fill up the odd snatches of time with the labors of your pen."

In ten minutes she was seated (the baby in her lap); a table with flour, rolling-pin, ginger, and lard on one side, a dresser with eggs, pork, and beans, and various cooking utensils on the other, near her an oven heating . . .

". . . Mina, you may do what I told you, while I write a few minutes till it is time to mould up the bread. Where *is* the ink-stand?"

"Here it is, on top of the tea-kettle."

[interruptions]

"Come, come, you see how it is. . . . We must give up the writing for today."

"No, no; you can dictate as easily as you can write. Come, I can set the baby in this clothes-basket and give him some mischief or other to keep him quiet; you shall dictate and I will write. Now . . . what shall I write next?"

"Mina, pour a little milk into this pearlash."

. . . and etc.

—the twenty-seven-year-old Harriet Beecher Stowe (1811–1896) making light of her attempts to get writing done.

Writer-Mothers: Harriet Beecher Stowe and A Room of One's Own

Another child and two years later (1840) ("for a year I have held the pen only to write an occasional business letter such as could not be neglected"), she had a near-breakdown. Away from home, "confiding to her husband some of her literary plans and aspirations," to his (yes) "my dear, you must be a literary woman," she answered:

Our children are just coming to the age when everything depends on my efforts. They are delicate in health, and nervous and excitable and need a mother's whole attention. *Can* I lawfully divide my attention by literary efforts?

. . . [But] If I *am* to write, I must have a room to myself, which shall be *my* room. I have in my own mind pitched on Mrs. Whipple's room. We can put the stove in it. I have bought a cheap carpet for it, and there is furniture enough at home to furnish it comfortably, and I only beg in addition that you will let me change the glass door from the nursery into that room and keep my plants there, and then I shall be quite happy.

All last winter I felt the need of some place where I could go and be quiet and satisfied. I could not there [the dining room], for there was all the setting of tables, and clearing up of tables, and dressing and washing of children, and everything else going on, and the continual falling of soot and coal dust on everything in the room was a constant annoyance to me, and I never felt comfortable there, though I tried hard. Then if I came into the parlor where you were, I felt as if I were interrupting you, and you know you sometimes thought so, too.

Now this winter let the cooking stove be put into that room, and let the pipe run up through the floor into the room above. . . . You can study by the parlor fire, and I and my plants will take the other room. I shall keep my work and all my things there and feel settled and quiet. I intend to have a regular part of each day devoted to the children, and then I shall take them in there.

[1841]

Plans. Plans. Sporadic writing for magazines, and, furthermore, only what would add to family income.

Six children and "cares endless" later (1846, she was thirty-five) —like Rebecca Harding Davis, "having lived too much in relations . . . she became a stranger to the resources of her own nature" —"broke down." While a sister took over at home, she stayed for eleven months in Vermont, giving "the renovating fountains time to rise up."

There was the death of one child; the birth of another. The sporadic writing went on—under the same old circumstances—

I can [now] earn four hundred dollars a year by writing, but I don't want to feel that I must, and, when weary with teaching the children, and tending the baby, and buying provisions, and mending dresses, and darning stockings, sit down and write a piece for some paper.

Like Rebecca she became more and more habituated to rapid, unripened (usually made-to-order) work. The book she wanted to write "to make this whole nation feel what an accursed thing slavery is" waited and waited. "As long as the baby sleeps with

me nights I can't do much at anything, but I will do it at last,"
she vowed in a letter.

There was "many a night weeping, the baby sleeping beside me,
as I thought of the slave mothers whose babes were torn from
them," but nothing was translated onto paper.

Stowe was thirty-nine before she got to *Uncle Tom's Cabin*—
at last. She wrote it in magazine serial installments—in between
—when weary with teaching the children and tending the baby
and buying provisions and mending and darning; much of it on
the kitchen table as the younger Harriet Beecher Stowe had, when
trying to get writing done fourteen years before. The firm, flawless
style of her girlhood letters was gone.

If—

Another Early Writer-Mother in the Fundamental Situation
  Elizabeth Stuart Phelps (1815–1852), as seen in reminiscences
by her similarly named daughter:

> Now she sits correcting proof-sheets, and now she is painting apos-
> tles for the baby's first Bible lesson. Now she is writing her new
> book, and now she is dyeing things canary-yellow in the white oak
> dye—for the professor's salary is small, and a crushing economy [is
> necessary] . . . Now—for her practical ingenuity is unlimited—she
> is whittling little wooden feet to stretch the children's stockings on,
> to save them from shrinking; and now she is reading to us from the
> old, red copy of Hazlitt's *British Poets* up on a winter night. Now
> she is a popular writer, incredulous of her first success, with her
> future flashing before her; and now she is a tired, tender mother,
> crooning to a sick child while the Ms. lies unfinished on the table,
> and the publishers are wishing their professor's wife were a free
> woman, childless and solitary, able to send copy as fast as it was
> wanted.
>
> > —from Elizabeth Stuart Lyon Phelps's autobiography,
> > *Chapters from a Life*

Not until she was in her mid-thirties, was the mother able to begin
on her writing. She was stunningly successful, first with fiction for
the young. But within a few years, she was dead. Her attempt "to
achieve the difficult reconciliation between genius and domestic
life" ("her last book and her last baby came together, and they

killed her'') is unforgettably fictionalized in the daughter's classic
Story of Avis.

The mother's pioneering story of this (then) insoluble situation,
"The Angel Over the Right Shoulder,"* tells the woman's side
of Coventry Patmore's nineteenth-century cherished angel-in-the-
house** for it limns the toll exacted. There are *two* angels in
Phelps's story: the angel over the right shoulder who records for
God every evidence of right mothering, of "performing faithfully
all those little household cares and duties on which the comfort
and virtue of her family depend"; and the awful angel over the left
shoulder who, weeping, records for God every bit of time not so
used, every lapse and deficiency. Though in the mother's view, "it
is right and important for her to cultivate her own mind and
heart," in actuality, even "the little fragments of broken time"
made with such enormous effort (as well as the very toll of making
the effort), "rob her little ones." Eventually she can no longer keep
up the struggle.

Sitting by the bedside of her young sleeping daughter, her tears
"falling fast,"

> most earnestly did she wish that she could shield [her] child from
> the disappointment and mistakes and self-reproach from which
> [she] was suffering; that the little one might take up life where she
> could give it to her—all mended by her own experience. It would
> have been a comfort to have felt that, in fighting the battle, she had
> fought for both.†

Sustaining Interruption; Postponing (1877)
"Where [now] is the strength and glory of the vision?"

> Scarcely had the palette-knife struck the cobalt to the Naples yel-
> low, when the studio-door shivered, stirred and started with a
> prolonged and inspiriting creak. Van admitted his little nose on

---

*Written in 1850; collected in 1868. In embryo it is Rebecca Harding Davis's
"The Wife's Story," as well as *Story of Avis.*

**Known to us in our time because of Virginia Woolf's reference to it.

†Such efforts—such trying—do fight for both. But the battle, continued throughout her daughter's long lifetime, is still to be won. The bounteous, productive,
and successful Elizabeth Stuart Lyon Phelps never had children.

probation into the crack and heaved a heart breaking sigh. "Shut the door, Van."

His pretty mamma had an unhappy habit of expecting to be obeyed, which was a source of serious disorder to Van's small system. He shut the door in—nose and all—with a filial haste and emphasis, the immediate consequences of which fell heavily upon both parties. . . . When the outcry is over, and the sobbing has ceased, and the tears are kissed away, and the solid little sinner lies soothed upon the cramped and forgiving arm, where is the strength and glory of the vision? Where are the leaping fingers that quivered to do its bidding in the fresh life of the winter morning hour?

"Run away again, Van: mother must go to work now."

"Mamma," faintly, "I've sat down on—something. I'm all blue and colors, Mamma, on my sack behind. I didn't know it was your palette, Mamma. I didn't mean to."

By and By

Avis left the unfinished sketch or painting patiently. She said, "By and by. After a while. I must wait a little." She was still able to allure herself with the melody of this refrain, to which so many · hundreds of women's lips have shaped themselves trembling; while the ears of a departing hope or a struggling purpose were bent to hear. Life had become a succession of expectancies. . . .

Women understand—only women altogether—what a dreary will-o'-the-wisp is this old, common, I had almost said commonplace, experience, "When the fall sewing is done," "When the baby can walk," "When house-cleaning is over," "When the company has gone," "When we have got through with the whooping-cough," "When I am a little stronger," then I will write the poem, or learn the language, or study the great charity, or master the symphony; then I will act, dare, dream, become.

—from *Story of Avis* by Elizabeth Stuart Lyon Phelps, 1877—a century or so ago.

Sustaining interruption—a century later

a child with untameable curly blond hair. i call her kia, pine nut person, & her eyes so open as she watches me try to capture her, as I try to name her . . .

. . . what of the lonely 7 year old (7½ mommy!) watching tv in the front room? what of her?

what of yesterday when she chased the baby into my room & I
screamed
OUT OUT GET OUT & she ran
right out but the baby stayed,
unafraid. what is it like to have
a child afraid of you, your own
child, your first child, the one
who must forgive you if either of you are to survive . . .

& how right is it to shut her out of the room so i can write about
her?
how human, how loving? how can
i even try to
: name her.
           —from Alta's *Momma: A Start on All the Untold Stories,* 1971

Writers, Mothers: It is humanly impossible for a woman who is a
wife and mother to work on a regular teaching job and write

> People ask me how I find time to write with a family and a teaching
> job. I don't. That is one reason I was so long with *Jubilee.* A writer
> needs time to write a certain number of hours every day. This is
> particularly true with prose fiction and absolutely necessary with
> the novel. Writing poetry may be different, but the novel demands
> long hours every day at a steady pace until the thing is done. It is
> humanly impossible for a woman who is a wife and mother to work
> on a regular teaching job and write. Weekends and nights and
> vacations are all right for reading but not enough for writing. This
> is a full-time job, but for me such full attention has only been
> possible during the three Depression years I was on the Writers'
> Project and during that one [graduate] school year in which I
> finished *Jubilee.*
> —Margaret Walker, thirty years (1938–1968) from the inception of
> *Jubilee* to its completion: four children and twenty-six years in "the
> teaching harness" in that time.

And yet I do not regret the shape my life has taken.
Three contemporary writer-mothers speak:

> My grandmother, who wrote and sold short stories at one point in
> her life, before raising six children, used to claim with some bitter-
> ness that bearing and raising children drained a woman's creativity.
> Her disappointment reminds me of my own failure to solve the

problems of raising children and carrying on a fulltime career. I haven't lost my sap, but I have certainly lost time: five out of the past ten years, at least, have been "lost" to bearing and raising three boys, and the end is not yet in sight. My work is reduced to five or six hours a week, always subject to interruptions and cancellations; and yet I do not regret the shape my life has taken, although it is not the one I would have chosen, ten years ago.

I don't believe there is a solution to this problem, or at least, I don't believe there is one which recognizes the emotional complexities involved. A life without children is, I feel, an impoverished life for most women; yet life with children imposes demands that consume energy and imagination as well as time, and that cannot all be delegated—even supposing there were a delegate available. . . .

A woman's response to a child's illness is part of her whole involvement with that child; it is not logical, perhaps, and yet it may be essential to that child's belief that his mother cares for him. I cannot imagine continuing to work when one of my children is running a high fever or is in pain; my mind would be totally distracted. Nor can I easily imagine leaving him in someone else's care; my thoughts would still be preempted.*

—Sallie Bingham, author of the memorable *The Way It Is Now*, 1972—and no book since

Why discourage women from the colossal swallowing up which is the essence of all motherhood, the mad love (for it is there, the love of a mother for her child), and the madness that maternity represents? For her to feel like a man, free from the consequences of maternity, from the fantastic shackles that it implies? That is probably the reason. But if I answer that men are sick precisely because of this, because they do not have the only opportunity offered a human being to experience a bursting of the ego, how would I be answered? That it was man who made motherhood the monstrous burden it is for sure. But to me the historical reasons for the burden

*". . . Again I feel as I used to when the children were sick, after the cause for real anxiety had passed and I stayed close by them, did everything for them, did not even think about my own work and was concerned only with being near them, physically, spiritually. Tending them back to health. This glorious feeling then of reconquest, the profound sense of happiness overlaying the lingering tremors of anxiety; they will stay; I shall keep them."

—Käthe Kollwitz, a diary entry, in her fifties

and the drudgery seem the most superficial, because for those there is a remedy. And even if men are responsible for this enslaving form of motherhood, is this enough to condemn maternity itself?

—Marguerite Duras, in an interview

The meaning of work, and the need to learn to insistently be an artist in the midst of family is what I am now always trying to understand, and after each moment of understanding to painstakingly, always with great attention to detail, structure my time. In Adrienne Rich's book on motherhood [read in galleys]* she uses portions of early diaries kept when her boys were young. She is always planning her time. I must not accept any social engagements. I must not do anything but work when not with the children. I must learn to sleep less. That is what it is like. I feel still caught in the middle, between that time when women will be able to devote themselves to work and have children and love . . . and the past, the physical and emotional crampedness. I have my desk in the middle of the living room and the apartment is mine at least four days a week for four hours each day** (not enough) but emotionally, I sneak off into a corner to grab an idea and promise to transform it into something whole. There is so much to be written about this motherhood and its holds on us. . . . My children are only two and six years old, still babies, whose bodies I yearn for every afternoon around four when I must go and get them.

—a letter from Jane Lazarre, author of *The Mother Knot,* 1976

Integration—and a Looking Back: A Question

> *As you, the children of my body, have been
> my tasks, so too are my other works.* †

I am gradually approaching the period in my life when work comes first. When both the boys were away for Easter, I hardly did anything but work. Worked, slept, ate, and went for short walks. But above all I worked.

---

*Of Woman Born.

**Circumstances that still few mother-writers have.

†Diary, *Käthe Kollwitz, Life in Art.* Integration: that word "other."

And yet I wonder whether the "blessing" is not missing from such work. No longer diverted by other emotions, I work the way a cow grazes. . . . Perhaps in reality I accomplish a little more. The hands work and work and the head imagines it is producing God knows what, and yet formerly, in my so wretchedly limited working time, I was more productive, because I was more sensual; I lived as a human being must live, passionately interested in everything. . . . Potency, potency is diminishing.*

Käthe Kollwitz, forty-three, rare in being great artist and mother. One wonders what work was lost to us, undone, in that "wretchedly limited" time. Her greatest work was still ahead, but then the strength began to be "wretchedly limited."

IF—needed time *and* strength were available simultaneously with "the blessing," the "living as a human being must live" . . . (as, with changes, now could be).

---

*Diaries and Letters of Käthe Kollwitz.

THE ANGEL IN THE HOUSE*

Virginia Woolf and the Angel

> It was she who used to come between me and my paper . . . who
> bothered me and wasted my time and so tormented me that at last
> I killed her.*

But Virginia Woolf never killed that aspect of the angel "extremely sensitive to the needs and moods and wishes of others":
she remained—an essential part of her equipment as writer ("I
think writing, my kind of writing, is a species of mediumship; I
become the person"). And—as is evident in Woolf's diary and the
reminiscences of those close to her—was usually characteristic of
her personal relationships as well.

More important to remember, Woolf recognized in the angel an
artist-being having to be expressed for and through others; understood her human value in a patriarchal structure (had herself been
a beneficiary).

In *Mrs. Dalloway* and *To the Lighthouse,* (Mrs. Ramsay) enduring portraits of women constricted to the angel (and shown in
their true powerlessness, division, exhaustion, narrowness), she
celebrated—in anguish—their creative power ("making the moment something permanent . . . [making] the individual more
whole and present"); their active professional qualities ("Domestic life is a *profession* and should be *paid;* motherhood is an
exacting task." "The difficult *arts* of family life"); their longings,
latencies; their having to find fulfillment vicariously in varied

---

*"Professions for Women."

contributions to others at a time when achievement for nearly all
women could be only through others. She did not see them as
submissive, passive, nor despise them for their constricted development. She knew, that born into her mother's generation, almost
inescapably her capacities and life would have gone as theirs; that
in her own generation, too, she was an exception—and that chan-
cily; barely.

Some Manifestations of the Angel, 1800–1970:

The Answering and Echoing Movements

> . . . the exceeding sympathy, always ready and always profound, by
> which she made all that one could tell her reverberate to one's own
> feelings by the manifest impression that it made on hers. The pulses
> of light were not more quick nor inevitable in their flow and undula-
> tion than were the answering and echoing movements of her sympa-
> thizing attention.
>
> —Thomas De Quincey on Dorothy Wordsworth, 1827

A perfect mother's life—the life of a perfect wife

> She is no more of an angel today than she had always been; but I
> can't believe that by the accident of her death all of her unspeakable
> tenderness is lost to the beings she so dearly loved. . . . One can feel
> forever, the inextinguishable vibration of her devotion. I can't help
> feeling that in those last weeks I was not tender enough with her
> —that I was blind to her sweetness and beneficence. . . .
>
> When I came back from Europe I was struck with her being worn
> and shrunken, and now I know that she was very weary. She went
> about her usual activities, but the burden of life had grown heavy
> for her, and she needed rest. There is something inexpressibly
> touching to me in the way in which, during these last years, she
> went on from year to year without it. If she could only have lived
> she should have had it, and it would have been a delight to see her
> have it. But she has it now, in the most complete perfection! Sum-
> mer after summer she never left Cambridge—it was impossible that
> father should leave his own house. The country, the sea, the change
> of air and scene, were an exquisite enjoyment to her; but she bore

with the deepest gentleness and patience the constant loss of such opportunities. She passed her nights and her days in that dry, flat, hot, stale and odious Cambridge, and had never a thought while she did so but for father and Alice. It was a perfect mother's life—the life of a perfect wife. To bring her children into the world—to expend herself, for years, for their happiness and welfare—then, when they had reached full maturity and were absorbed in the world and in their own interests—to lay herself down in her ebbing strength and yield up her pure soul to the celestial power that had given her this divine commission.

—Henry James in his *Notebooks,* after the death of his mother
(1882)

William Butler Yeats, "On Woman"

> May God be praised for woman
> That gives up all her mind,
> A man may find in no man
> A friendship of her kind
> That covers all he has brought
> As with her flesh and bone,
> Nor quarrels with a thought
> Because it is not her own.

Sparing Him, And So On

Ida, I want you if you can to come to me. But like this. We should have to deceive Jack. Jack can never realize what I have to do. He helps me all he can but he can't help me really and the result is I spend all my energy, every bit, in keeping going, I have none left for work. All my work is behindhand and I can't do it. I simply stare at the sky. I am too tired even to think. What makes me tired? Getting up, seeing about everything, arranging everything, *sparing him,* and so on. That journey nearly killed me, literally. He had no *idea* I suffered at all, and could not understand why I looked "so awful" and why everybody seemed to think I was terribly ill. . . .

—Katherine Mansfield (a letter to her friend, Ida Baker)

Katherine Anne Porter, on being asked:

. . . But haven't you found that being a woman presented to you, as an artist, certain special problems? It seems to me that a great deal of the upbringing of women encourages the dispersion of the self in many small bits, and that the practice of any kind of art demands a corralling and concentrating of that self and its always insufficient energies.

I think that's very true and very right. You're brought up with the . . . curious idea of feminine availability in all spiritual ways, and in giving service to anyone who demands it. And I suppose that's why it has taken me twenty years to write this novel; it's been interrupted by just anyone who could jimmy his way into my life.

—*Writers at Work, The Paris Review Interviews*

FREEING THE ESSENTIAL ANGEL*

Virginia Woolf's vision of the future

> I think of Sussex in five hundred years to come.... Things will have been scorched up, eliminated. There will be magic gates. Draughts fan-blown by electric power will cleanse houses. Lights intense and firmly directed will go over the earth, doing the work....
>
> ... And then there was the sudden dancing light, that was hung in the future ... "Look, I will make a little figure for your satisfaction.... Does this little figure advancing ... to the economical, powerful, and efficient future when houses will be cleansed by a puff of hot wind satisfy you?" ... We cried out together: "Yes, yes," as if affirming something, in a moment of recognition.*

Charlotte Perkins Gilman (*Women & Economics* [1898], *The Home, Its Work and Influence* [1907]) is the pioneer and still almost the only exponent of ways whereby "this technologically and socially obsolete, human-wasting drudgery" could be eliminated (the essential angel freed), while still preserving human maintenance-of-life satisfactions where they are intrinsic. But as free, voluntary, expression of the self, not life-consuming necessity.

---

*"Evening over Sussex: Reflections in a Motor-car," *Collected Essays.*

WIVES, MOTHERS, ENABLERS▲

To My Wife, Without Whom . . .

> My portion was to see to it that he [Thomas Mann] had the best circumstances for his work.
> —Katia Mann, of her husband

> All Gertrude had to do was be a genius.
> —Alice B. Toklas, of her services to Gertrude Stein

Few have been the writer-women who have had George Eliot's luck of "the perfect happiness of living with a being who protects and stimulates in me the health of highest productivity,"—but the writer-men in like circumstances are and have been many. And not only wives: mothers, sisters, daughters, lovers, helper women, secretaries, housekeepers, watchers and warders.

Not here the place to list the myriad women whose contribution was significant, sometimes decisive, to the development and productivity of writers.* *But how many were of the silenced in the possible twelve?*

Remember the young women writers, their aspirant lives clogged in Love's ambuscade—those who let their work go (his gifts are more important than mine**) in the belief that they would become of the tradition-hallowed "inspirer-beloved"; and

---

*As any discerning reading of biographies discloses.

**—their sense of their own potentialities, their self-confidence already so robbed: not recognizing everyday enabling differences in circumstances for males, let alone superior advantages since birth.

those who had every intention of going on writing—and tried; both usually subsumed into the server-enablers; wives; mothers of children.* Mothers alone (in my not-exhaustive knowledge) who wrote seriously when girls, young women (or late in life) would fill a page.**

Think too of the helper women, the famous enablers: Margaret Anderson, Jane Heap, Harriet Monroe, Sylvia Beach, who—if only in autobiography or occasional pieces—disclosed a writing self of capacity. Yes, and Edith Mirrielees (founder of the Stanford Creative Writing Center) and nameless other magnificent teachers, way openers. And Martha Foley (of the *Best American Short Story* Annuals) who, more than any other single individual in my lifetime, has nurtured the story. "All I ever wanted to do was write." In earlier years she did. But (common circumstance) there was a child and herself to support.

I am haunted by the writer-wives (or long-time wives) of notable literary men: Eleanor Clark, Janet Lewis, Caroline Gordon, Jane Bowles,† Elizabeth Hardwick, Mary Ellmann, Diana Trilling, Hope Hale Davis, Ann Birstein, Helen Yglesias.‡ Nearly every one, in their own distinguished way, evidencing quality, vision, capacity to contribute to literature, greater or as great as that of their men—but with marked contrast in productivity, influence, recognition.

---

*—and, I might add, perhaps discarded.

**A sampling of famous sons, this century, includes T.S. Eliot, Jorge Luis Borges, Allen Ginsberg, John Updike. Remember also, Woolf's ". . . whenever one reads of a remarkable man who had a mother, then I think we are on the track of a lost novelist, a suppressed poet . . ."

†"In the 20 years that we've lived here [Morocco], I have written only two short stories and nothing else. It's good for Paul, but not for me."

‡The husbands: Robert Penn Warren, Yvor Winters, Allen Tate, Paul Bowles, Robert Lowell, Richard Ellmann, Lionel Trilling, Robert Gorham Davis, Alfred Kazin, José Yglesias.

Wives, Mothers, Enablers: As with Her Flesh and Bone

Melville's Pierre *again:*

> . . . Delly brings still another hot brick to put under his inkstand, to prevent the ink from thickening. Then Isabel drags the camp-bedstead nearer to him, on which are the two or three books he may possibly have occasion to refer to that day, with a biscuit or two, and some water, and a clean towel, and a basin. Then she leans against the plank by the elbow of Pierre, a crook-ended stick. . . .—Pierre, if in his solitude, he should chance to need anything beyond the reach of his arm, then the crook-ended cane drags it to his immediate vicinity.
>
> Pierre glances slowly all round him; everything seems to be right; he looks up with a grateful, melancholy satisfaction at Isabel; a tear gathers in her eye; but she conceals it from him by coming very close to him, stooping over, and kissing his brow. 'Tis her lips that leave the warm moisture there; not her tears; she says.
>
> "I suppose I must go now, Pierre. Now don't, don't be so long to-day. I will call thee at half-past four. Thou shalt not strain thine eyes in the twilight."

Jorge Luis Borges:

> . . . My mother has always had a hospitable mind. She translated Saroyan, Hawthorne, [Herbert] Read, Melville, Woolf, Faulkner. She has always been a companion to me and an understanding and forgiving friend. For years she handled all my secretarial work, answering letters, reading to me, taking down my dictation and also traveling with me. . . . It was she who quietly and effectively fostered my literary career. . . .

Of Edmund Wilson:

> You would have loved the Wilson *ménage.* Elena has really effected a tremendous change in Edmund's way of living. She really *loves* him, moreover! The little girl, Helen, is delightful; I must send her

an *Orlando* book. The house couldn't be more attractive; and Elena
has evidently put real elbow grease into decorating it; scraping
floors and walls and making curtains. There is a "parlor" with a
good deal of Federal mahogany (E.'s mother's) upholstered in yellow; a dining room with more mahogany against blue walls, plus
lovely blue Staffordshire and silver; a "middle room" with more
blue walls and blue chintz and linen; and Ed.'s magnificent study,
with a bathroom attached, and a stairway to an attic, filled with
overflow books. For the first time poor E. has attention, space and
effectively arranged paraphernalia of all kinds.—Mary never really
helped in the more practical ways; and E. has had a v. scrappy kind
of life, down the years. Now all moves smoothly: tea on a tray for
his "elevenses"; absolute silence in his working hours, and good
meals at appropriate intervals.   —Elena was v. hospitable, and fed
me enormous luncheons (one of lobster), with highballs at tea-time.
. . . They have a tiny sun-trap of a garden by the side-door, and
Elena has a little vegetable garden, v. European, with lettuces and
beans mixed with herbs and the zinnias.

> —The peerless poet, Louise Bogan (who had none of these
> things—except a daughter to raise, alone).

(From a letter to May Sarton, 1954, in *What the Woman Lived*)

INTERVIEWER: Was he writing very much when you were first
engaged?

MRS. WILLIAM CARLOS WILLIAMS: No; once in a while he would
send me a poem. But he was busy building up his practice. After
we were married he wrote more. I saw to it that he had time.

John Gardner:

. . . If I have any doubts about what a character would say or what
a room would look like, I ask my wife. She has the ability to go into
a room where she doesn't know anyone and tell you the first names
of several people because they seem the Raymond type or the Sheila
type. My writing involves these two imaginations in a very deep
way, page after page after page. My own imagination is poetic and
philosophical. I'm concerned with the rhythms of sentences and
paragraphs and chapters, and with ideas as they are embodied in
characters and actions. Joan's imagination is a very close psycho-
logical and sociological one. It informs everything I do. Perhaps I
should have used "John and Joan Gardner" on the titles all along;
I may do this in the future. But in modern times such a work is

regarded as not really art. The notion that art is an individual and unique vision is a very unmedieval and unclassical view. In the Middle Ages it was very common to have several people work on one thing; the thirteenth-century Vulgate cycle of Arthurian romances had hundreds of writers. I feel comfortable with this approach, but I haven't felt comfortable telling people it's what I do. As I get more and more into the medieval mode, I'll probably admit how many writers I have.

BELLAMY: You leave it sounding as if your wife is a collaborator. Has she actually written parts of your books?

GARDNER: . . . I use a lot of people, Joan in particular. She hasn't actually written any lines, because Joan's too lazy for that. But she's willing to answer questions. The extent of her contribution doesn't quite approach collaboration in the modern sense.*

—from *The New Fiction: Interviews with Innovative American Writers,* 1974

We Who Write Are Survivors—Only's; One Out of Twelve . . . and must tell our chancy luck, our special circumstances ▲

Fortunate are those of us who are daughters born into knowledgeable, ambitious families where no sons were born; fortunate are those in economic circumstance beyond the basic imperatives, thus affording some choice; fortunate are those in whose lives is another human being "protecting and stimulating the health of highest productivity";** fortunate are those of us to whom en-

---

*I have qualms in quoting Gardner; he expresses the situation forthrightly. The true "leech" writers—whom I would have preferred to quote—do not do so.

Furthermore, I share his "medieval" view: classical, medieval, or modern, we in art have all been contributed to, have "collaborators."

And—writer-woman (temerity) question: what makes someone with capacity "too lazy," that is a contributor, and not a doer in her own voice? Which is not to say that this question is necessarily pertinent in this instance or that everyone is or should be a writer—but that this is an essential question always to ask. We are only beginning to understand the process of discouragings, of silencings; of the making of enabled and of enablers.

**But no one's development should any longer be at the cost of another's.

couragement, approval, grants, publication, come at the founder-ing time before it is too late; fortunate as has been indicated here, are those born into the better climates, when a movement has created a special interest in one's sex, or in one's special subject; fortunate are those who live where relationships, opportunities, not everywhere available are.

The rule is simple: whenever anyone of that sex, and/or class, and/or color, generally denied enabling circumstances, comes to recognized individual achievement, it is not by virtue of special capacity, courage, determination, will (common qualities) but be-cause of chancy luck, combining with those qualities.

BLIGHT. THE HIDDEN SILENCER—
BREAKDOWN

Only by inference, present in the original talks:

From youngest years, the damaging of capacity; the leeching of will, of belief in self. Distraction, division, shame. Robbing of aspiration. The Angel and having to try to kill the Angel; and hoarse encumbrances of household care. The Damnation of Women. The Fundamental Situation. Economic Imperatives. Postponing; sustaining interruption, breaking concentration. Sporadic effort; unfinished work; unsatisfactory quality of work. Devaluation. Cruel climates. Critical Attitudes. Restriction. Constriction.

"Her mind must have been strained and her vitality lowered by the need to oppose this."

Yes. And sometimes—break down.

Breakdown (not genuine madness, rare among women writers; nor suicide, which is rarer).*

Extremity. When overborne, overworn—for a period—one breaks down, gives up, goes under, cannot go on.

Reality depression. Nullity. Survival withdrawal. Ragings. Or pain, harms, felt in—moved into, working in—the *body,* when there is no other way, place, to feel it, act upon it, remove the cause.

---

*In spite of the widely believed "savage God" theory that madness and suicide are the corollary of daring creative endeavor by women. In the few instances of madness or suicide, the hidden blights are scarcely or not at all considered as factors.

Not neuroses or symptoms of neuroses as commonly (mis)apprehended, (mis)treated. Natural. Extremity. Sanity. It would be unreal (insane) not to (re)act so.

They understood clearer in the last century. Termed it more accurately.

Fuller (already twice quoted):

> If any individual live too much in relations, so that [s]he becomes a stranger to the resources of [her] own nature, [s]he falls, after a while, into a distraction, or imbecility, which can only be cured by a time of isolation which gives the renovating fountains time to rise up.

[as happened with Fuller]

Emily Dickinson:

> Sweet Sister. Was that what I used to call you?
>
> I hardly recollect, all seems so different—
>
> I hesitate which word to take, as I can take but few and each must be the chiefest, but recall that Earth's most graphic transaction is placed within a syllable, nay, even a gaze—
>
> The Physician says I have "Nervous prostration."
>
> Possibly I have—I do not know the Names of Sickness. The crisis of the sorrow of so many years is all that tires me. . . .
>
> Please Sister to wait— . . .
>
> —Letter to Mrs. J. G. Holland, late 1883

> . . . Eight Saturday noons ago, I was making a loaf cake with Maggie, when I saw a great darkness coming and knew no more until late at night. . . . I had fainted and lain unconscious for the first time in my life. Then I grew very sick and gave the others much alarm, but am now staying. The doctor calls it "revenge of the nerves"; but who but Death had wronged them? . . .
>
> —Letter to Louise and Frances Norcross, early August 1884

Vincent Van Gogh:

> And perhaps the disease of the heart is caused by this. One does not rebel against things, it does no good; nor is one resigned to them; one's ill because of them and one does not get better. . . .

Olive Schreiner (writing of those who try to live ahead of their time, when the societal changes making it possible are not-yet, or only in, the process) ("a time when nothing can be done, except by inches"*):

> In times of modifying, of doing away with traditional ways, within the individuality itself of such persons goes on, in an intensified form, that very . . . conflict, disco-ordination which is going on in the society at large—and agonizing moments must arise when the individual, seeing the necessity for adopting new courses of action will yet be tortured by the hold [outer, inner] of traditional ways . . . [this is] almost bound to rupture the continuity of their psychological being.

> Because there was no other place to flee to,
> I came back to the scene of the disordered senses.
>
> Everyone has left me
> except my muse,
> *that good nurse.* **

"Flee on your donkey," Annes, Annes, Sweet Sisters,

> . . . In her work, as in her private problems, [Virginia Woolf] was always civilized and sane on the subject of madness. She pared the edges off this particular malady, she tied it down to being a malady, and robbed it of the evil magic it has acquired through timid or careless thinking; here is one of the gifts we have to thank her for.†

Yes.

In her life and in her diaries, the incomparable record (help for us all) of her preventing, staving off, countering, *bounding* the malady (sometimes true madness, sometimes breakdown); understanding, using, it.

---

*Adrienne Rich.

**Anne Sexton, "Flee on Your Donkey," from *Live or Die*.

†E.M. Forster. *Recollections of Virginia Woolf.*

The above are swiftings from an as yet unedited, unpublished talk given at M.I.T. in 1973 during the worst of the madness-suicide mystique. It began with this roll of names:

*Suicides**

Charlotte Mew
Amy Levy
Sara Teasdale

Perhaps a suicide

Sylvia Plath

Chosen death

Charlotte Perkins Gilman
Virginia Woolf

Not suicides
(though some, in time of extremity, may have tried or considered it)

Jane Austen
George Sand
The Brontës
Mrs. Gaskell
George Eliot
Emily Dickinson
Harriet Beecher Stowe
Elizabeth Barrett Browning
Kate Chopin
Olive Schreiner
Sarah Orne Jewett

Gertrude Stein
Willa Cather
Colette
Edith Wharton
Mary Austin
Ellen Glasgow
Susan Glaspell
Katherine Mansfield
Dorothy Richardson
Henry Handel Richardson
Edna St. Vincent Millay
Zora Neale Hurston
Dorothy Parker
Agnes Smedley
Dorothy Canfield Fisher
Louise Bogan
Gabriela Mistral
Elizabeth Madox Roberts
Elizabeth Bowen
(and many others)

With us still
(in their seventies or more)

Jean Rhys
Katherine Anne Porter
Nelly Sachs
Anaïs Nin
Kay Boyle
Christina Stead
Jessamyn West
Rebecca West

---

*Since then, we have lost Anne Sexton.

If I might but be one of those born in the future; then, perhaps to be born a woman will not be to be born branded.

—Lyndall, in Olive Schreiner's *Story of an African Farm*, 1883

*HIDDEN BLIGHT— PROFESSIONAL CIRCUMSTANCES*⁴

Treatment, circumstances for the writer-woman and her work, based not on capacities, attainment alone, but affected by her being of her sex: female.

"You will, I know, keep measuring me by some standard of what you deem becoming to my sex."

—Charlotte Brontë, 1849

"Nevertheless her mind must have been strained and her vitality lowered by her need to oppose this."

—Virginia Woolf

Devaluation; Critical Attitudes▲

The perpetual dancing dog phenomena:

Ozick's instance was 1969. A 1928 version is quoted in Virginia Woolf's *A Room of One's Own,* as is Dr. Johnson's of two hundred years before, the (in)famous

> Sir, a woman's preaching is like a dog's walking on his hind legs. It is not done well, but you are surprised to find it done at all

and the four hundred years ago (Shakespeare's time) original, Nick Greene's: "a woman acting puts me in mind of a dog dancing." Its current descendant is: breadth—or strength— or knowledge—or power—(or whatever) *"surprising in a woman."*

Reviewers

> A man who reviewed my *Procedures for Underground* . . . talked about the "domestic" imagery of the poems, entirely ignoring the fact that seven-eighths of the poems take place outdoors. . . . In his case, the theories of what women ought to be writing about, had intruded very solidly between reader and poems, rendering the poems themselves invisible to him.
>
> —Margaret Atwood

"Sexual Bias in Reviewing" (condensed from a study by Margaret Atwood's students, 1973):

> . . . by which we meant not unfavorable reviews, but points being added or subtracted by the reviewer on the basis of the author's sex and supposedly associated characteristics, rather than on the basis of the work itself. . . . Writers, half of them male, half female [were asked] had they ever experienced sexual bias . . . in a review? A large number of reviews from a wide range of periodicals and newspapers [were surveyed].
>
> Of the men, none answered Yes, a quarter answered Maybe, and three-quarters: No. Of women, half were Yeses, a quarter Maybes, and a quarter No's. The women replying Yes often wrote long

detailed letters, giving instances and discussing their own attitudes. All the men's letters were short. . . .

When we got round to the reviews, we discovered they [the women] were justified.

Areas of bias found included:

Assignment of reviews:

"Masculine" adjectives still most likely to be applied to the work of male writers; to female writers, . . . some version of "the feminine style" or "feminine sensibility" whether their work merits it or not. (Called the Quiller-Couch Syndrome after a turn-of-the-century essay defining masculine and feminine styles in writing.)

She Writes Like a Man:—a pattern in which good equals male, bad equals female. Meant as a compliment. . . . If a woman writer happens to be a good writer, she should be deprived of her identity as a female and provided with higher (male) status.*

The (usually male) habit of concentrating on domestic themes in the work of a female writer, ignoring any other topic she might have dealt with, then patronizing her for "interest in domestic themes." Critical space taken up with discussion of appearance.** Points for attractiveness. (Called the Sexual Compliment/Put-down Syndrome)

—Atwood's Paradoxes and Dilemmas,
The Woman as Writer, 1973

Critical Attitudes: Major Art Is . . .

"Major Art is about the activities of men." That's why so much of it is about women. But not by them. "Major Art includes where women can't go, or shouldn't, or never have." Childbed is not a place or an event; it is merely what women do. "Major Art is never

---

*"Power is not recognized as the power it is at all, if the subject matter is considered woman's."

**The definitive *Twentieth Century Authors,* first edition (1945), edited by Stanley Kunitz, was an example of this. Scarcely a woman writer escaped discussion of her appearance (and domestic habits).

about the activities of women." Except when it's by men. "Women are household artists." . . . Let's face it, dear ladies—a house is not a cosmic home. . . .

. . ."And look at women writer's *style!*" Critics of this type always know what major art is—and wish to discuss only major artists. That's how they know they're major critics. A Major Artist writes only in a "masculine" style. "Which uses short words." Like Faulkner. "Whose sentences don't inch forward on little iambs but are rough and clumsy." Like Hemingway's. "What a masculine and major art must never be is jeweled—beg pardon, lapidary. A jeweled fancy is always feminine." Like Shakespeare's. And Melville's. And Sir Thomas Browne's.

Most symptomatic of all, when I, or any woman, complains of male injustices—we must joke.

—Hortense Calisher, "No Important Woman Writer"

. . . Literature has never been so sexually polarized as it is today, and women, as subjects, images, and artists, have never been so inconsequential in the realms of high literary culture. There is not even a Dark Lady, a token, a high priestess to satisfy affirmative action requirements in the new lineup of Pynchon, Barth, Heller, Barthelme, Hawkes, Coover, Vonnegut, Elkin. In symposia like the one on "Ongoing American Fiction" in *Triquarterly* (Spring 1975), one searches in vain for female names. And the problem is not simply that women are not writing in the abstract, discontinuous, parodistic manner of postmodernist fiction; female fabulists and experimentalists like Susan Sontag,* Rosellen Brown, Rosalyn Drexler, and Carol Emshwiller seem not to be noticed. While we have been out looking for androgyny, a new regional literature, whose region is the library, has quietly taken over, and its subjects and themes—apocalypse, war, entropy, cybernetics, baseball, computers, and rockets—are not androgynous at all. As this new virtuoso fiction becomes the yardstick of what is serious and important in contemporary writing, women writers are being crowded once more into that snugly isolated inner space of art which they have often described as "the living centre," a space which always looks disturbingly like the kitchen.

—Elaine Showalter, *Signs,* Vol. 1, No. 2, 1976

---

*A small demur: Sontag seems to be that high priestess.

Remember that "eclipsing, devaluation, are the result of critical judgments, a predominantly male domain. The most damaging, and still prevalent, critical attitude remains 'that women's experience, and literature written by women are, by definition, minor.' Indeed, for a sizable percentage of male writers, critics, academics, writer-women are eliminated from consideration, consciousness, altogether."

Climate ▲

Writers know the importance of respect for one's vision and integrity; of comradeship with other writers; of being taken seriously; of being dealt with on the basis of one's work and not for other reasons. . . . Nearly all writers who are women are at a disadvantage here.

Appearance

Yes, it has a place here in the hidden blight.

Scarcely at all a factor for the man writer.

But for nearly all writers who are women, its harmful importance (enforced since infancy through unspoken penalties, or meretricious approvals—also a penalty). Admitted, unadmitted; acceded to—or fought to proportion—its toll in *time,* concentration, wholeness.

Its weaponry against un-self consciousness, naturalness; against based sense of self-worth.

Its use to demean or lessen achievement.

Appearance and Singleness

Patriarchal attitudes last century, with application to this.

> The poor little woman of genius! The fiery little eager brave tremulous homely-faced creature! I can read a great deal of her life as I fancy her in her book [*Villette*] and see that rather than have fame, rather than any other earthly good or mayhap heavenly one, she wants some Tomkins or another to love her and be in love with. But you see she is a little bit of a creature without a pennyworth of good looks, thirty years old I should think, buried in the country, and eating up her own heart there and no Tomkins will come. You girls with pretty faces will get dozens of young fellows fluttering about you—whereas here is one genius, a noble heart longing to mate itself and destined to wither away into old maidenhood with no chance to fulfil the burning desire.
>
> —Eminent novelist, Wm. Thackeray, explaining the pitiful situation of Charlotte Brontë—and her own infinitely preferable one—to a young friend, 1853

> There was but little feminine charm about her, and of this fact she was herself uneasily and perpetually conscious. . . . I believe she

would have given all her genius and all her fame to have been beautiful.

—Brontë's publisher, George Smith, summing her up in a reminiscence in 1900, forty-five years after her death

"Insights" unsupported by her work or life. Blinded by commonplace male attitudes, they did not see (missed!) the actual Charlotte Brontë. The little bit of a creature lacking feminine charm and perpetually conscious of it; eating up her heart because no Tomkins will come; as the Brontë glad to give up all her genius and fame to be thought beautiful and charming, are conjures, bred out of "judging by a standard of what is deemed becoming in her sex" and the (sexist) preconception that single women aren't complete. and, being women, what they must really care about, would give up anything for, is to be deemed attractive and to snare a man.

Think of Charlotte Brontë, that proud, lonely writer-self, coming to London "hungry for equals"; encountering instead this blindness to her actual being; this patronizing, subtle discounting of her very source-motivations, achievement, stature.

She knew this reductiveness well. In her work, as in her personal conduct, she fought it. The novels are, among so much else, proud, conscious refutations of it. Remember: it was *Jane Eyre* that first challenged the judging a woman on the basis of appearance or singleness; indeed the very standards for beauty, charm—and created the first heroine—fascinating and of substance—who was "plain."

> She once told her sisters that they were wrong—even morally wrong—in making their heroines beautiful as a matter of course. [When] they replied that it was impossible to make a heroine interesting on any other terms, her answer was "I will prove to you that you are wrong. I will show you a heroine as small and as plain as myself who shall be as interesting as any of yours." Hence Jane Eyre . . . but she is not myself, any further than that.
>
> —Harriet Martineau, a conversation with Brontë

Nevertheless: *"Her mind must have been strained and her vitality lowered by the need to oppose this."*

Climate: This Abasement

> Then why did she mind what he said? "Women can't write, women
> can't paint." . . . Why did her whole being bow, like corn under a
> wind, and erect itself again from this abasement only with a great
> and painful effort?
>
> —Virginia Woolf, *To the Lighthouse*

Without the semblance of a suspicion that I may be busy . . .

> And the egotism of men surprises and shocks me, even now. Is there
> a woman of my acquaintance who could sit in my armchair from
> 3 to 6:30 without the semblance of a suspicion that I may be busy,
> or tired or bored; and so sitting could talk, grumbling and grudging,
> of her difficulties, worries; then eat chocolates, then read a book,
> and go at last, apparently self-complacent and wrapped in a kind
> of blubber of misty self-salutation?
>
> —Virginia Woolf, *A Writer's Diary*

"Obliged to shut off three-fourths of their being": 1816–1916

1816: A woman, especially

> Where people wish to attach, they should always be ignorant. To
> come with a well-informed mind is to come with an inability of
> administering to the vanity of others, which a sensible person
> should always wish to avoid. A woman, especially, if she have the
> misfortune of knowing anything, should conceal it as well as she
> can.
>
> —Jane Austen, *Persuasion* nonsense!
>   *Northanger Abbey*

1916: The Literary Lion and young women writers

> With a flash of insight . . . she saw how very slight, how restricted
> and perpetually baffled must always be the communication between
> him and anything that bore the name of woman. Saw the price each
> one had paid with whom he had been intimate either in love or
> friendship, in being obliged to shut off . . . three-fourths of their
> being.
>
> What could any one of them be for him, beyond the fact that they

were providers of what he regarded as vitalizing physical contacts, or sounding-boards for his ideas; admirers, supporters? Either they were disciples . . . and were therefore not women at all, but the "intelligent emancipated creatures" for whom he expressed so much admiration while fighting shy of them in his leisure hours because of their awful consistency and conscientiousness . . . "a rush of brains to the head usually made them rather plain in the face"; or they played up whenever they were with him, . . . and lived for the rest of their time in their own deep world. . . .

There was no place in his universe for women who did not either sincerely, blindly, follow; or play up and make him believe they were following. All the others were merely pleasant or unpleasant biological material. Those who opposed: misguided creatures who must not be allowed to obstruct. The majority played up: for the sake of his society, his charm, the charm of enjoying and watching him enjoy the pranks of his lightning-swift intelligence. The temptation was great.

She knew she had not always resisted it.

—Dorothy Richardson, *Pilgrimage*

A man whose work I revered . . . [my] book a serious, original contribution

When *The Hours of Isis* was published I sent it to the greatest authority on Egyptology at that time, a man whose work I revered, and whose knowledge filled me with awe. I wanted to make some return for the inspiration his books had brought to me, and I was filled with astonishment and joy when he acknowledged the gift with an invitation to meet him. He asked me to come to his office in the late afternoon when he would be at leisure.

I was shown into a room which was not so much an office as a private library, with books from ceiling to floor, armchairs and reading lamps and a large desk on which I could see *The Hours of Isis* beside a great tome which I recognized as Sir Wallis Budge's *Osiris*. The sight of them together overpowered me and I could hardly stammer "How do you do?"

"Come here," he said. "I have something to show you."

I went round to his side to look down at the books.

"You know what all this is about, don't you?" he asked. "It's a phallic myth. You know what a phallus is?"

He proceeded to show me. The shock was enormous. Not so the

object. I had seen those before . . . indecent old men in the Paris métro exposing themselves at the rush hour in the hope of getting a reaction. Once a sturdy fishwife standing next to me turned the tables superbly by saying loudly: *"Quand on n'a pas de marchandise on n'ouvre pas sa boutique,"* which I suppose can be translated roughly: "If you're short on goods don't open up the shop." The crowd laughed and he edged over to the door and got out quickly at the next station.

What shocked me was that this great man could insult Isis and Osiris by behaving in that way. The book was a serious, original contribution to his own field.

By this time he had seized me and was pawing and nuzzling my breasts. I managed to squirm loose, shaking with rage and shame, and after a moment, during which he probably saw me clearly for the first time, he began to mutter something, excuses, justification. The gist of it was that no nice girl would fill her little mind with phallic myths. A girl who wrote a book about Osiris was fair game, obviously asking for it. . . .

—Evelyn Eaton's autobiography,
The Trees and Fields Went the Other Way, 1974

What They All Need . . .

One of them was complaining about the number of female writers.

"And they've all got three names," he said, "Mary Roberts Wilcox, Ella Wheeler Catheter, Ford Mary Rineheart . . ."

Then someone started a train of stories by suggesting that what they all needed was a good rape.

"I knew a gal who was regular until she fell in with a group and went literary. She began writing for the little magazines about how much Beauty hurt her and ditched the boy friend who set up pins in a bowling alley. The guys on the block got sore and took her into the lots one night. About eight of them. They ganged her proper . . ."

"That's like the one they tell about another female writer. When this hard-boiled stuff first came in, she dropped the trick English accent and went in for scram and lam. She got to hanging around with a lot of mugs in a speak, gathering material for a novel. Well, the mugs didn't know they were picturesque and thought she was regular until the barkeep put them wise. They got her into the back room to teach her a new word and put the boots to her. They didn't let her out for three days. On the last day they sold tickets to niggers . . ."

Miss Lonelyhearts stopped listening. His friends would go on telling those stories until they were too drunk to talk. . . .

—Nathanael West, *Miss Lonelyhearts*

Climate; Critical Attitudes; Exclusions

The Ground of Departure

I have a terrible confession to make—I have nothing to say about any of the talented women who write today. Out of what is no doubt a fault in me, I do not seem able to read them. Indeed I doubt if there will be a really exciting woman writer until the first whore becomes a call girl and tells her tale. At the risk of making a dozen devoted enemies for life, I can only say that the sniffs I get from the ink of the women are always fey, old-hat, Quaintsy Goysy, tiny, too dykily psychotic, crippled, creepish, fashionable, frigid, outer-Baroque, *maquille* in mannequin's whimsy, or else bright and stillborn. Since I've never been able to read Virginia Woolf, and am sometimes willing to believe it can conceivably be my fault, this verdict may be taken fairly as the twisted tongue of a soured taste, at least by those readers who do not share with me the ground of departure—that a good novelist can do without everything but the remnant of his balls.

—Norman Mailer (*Advertisements for Myself*), in "Evaluations

—Quick and Expensive Comments on the Talent in the Room"

(1959). This is the one paragraph considering women in ten pages, twenty-eight paragraphs.*

Subtler Exclusions

In the first stages of his development, before he has found his distinctive style, the poet is, as it were, engaged to language and, like any young man who is courting, it is right and proper that he should play the chivalrous servant, carry parcels, submit to tests and humiliations, wait hours at street corners, and defer to his beloved's slightest whims, but once he has proved his love and been accepted, then it is another matter. Once he is mar-

---

*(I tried to resist quoting this, but it belongs with the museum pieces.)

ried, he must be master in his own house and be responsible for their relationship. . . .

. . . The poet is the father who begets the poem which the language bears. At first sight this would seem to give the poet too little to do and the language too much till one remembers that, as the husband, it is he, not the language, who is responsible for the success of their marriage which differs from natural marriage in that in this relationship there is no loveless love-making, no accidental pregnancies. . . .

. . . Poets, like husbands, are good, bad and indifferent. Some are Victorian tyrants who treat language like a doormat, some are dreadfully hen-pecked, some bored, some unfaithful. For all of them, there are periods of tension, brawls, sulky silences, and, for many, divorce after a few passionate years.

—W.H. Auden, *Poets at Work*

Exclusion: Language Itself

"Language itself, all achievement, anything to do with the human [cast] in exclusively male terms."

> But "glory" doesn't mean "a nice knockdown argument," Alice objected.
>
> When *I* use a word, Humpty Dumpty said in a rather scornful tone, it means just what I choose it to mean—neither more nor less.
>
> The question is, said Alice, whether you can make words mean so many different things?
>
> The question is, said Humpty Dumpty, who is to be master—that's all.*

It is the saturation—the never ceasing, life-long saturation.

Man. The poet: he (his). The writer: he (his).

No, not simply a matter of "correct usage"; our inherited language; i.e., *man,* a generic term, defined as including, subsuming, woman, the entire human race.

The perpetuating—by continued usage—entrenched, centuries-old oppressive power realities, early-on incorporated into lan-

---

*Lewis Carroll. *Through the Looking Glass.*

guage: male rule; male ownership; our secondariness; our *exclusion.*

In reading Auden ("The poet is the father who begets the poem"), the effort having to be made in us somewhere to include ourselves as writer also. The reinforcement to the "ground of departure" attitudes: "a *real* writer has balls—is male. . . ."

The unconscious, conscious harm (as well, as ill), to a woman —when writing of writing or writers or of oneself as poet, as writer —of having to refer to oneself, and to one's activity, as masculine. As Willa Cather (quoted earlier):

> usually the young writer must have *his* affair with the external material *he* covets . . .

Or as Denise Levertov, from "The Poet in the World":

> He picks up crystal buttons from the ocean floor
> Gills of the mind pulse in unfathomed water.
>
> In the infinite dictionary he discovers
> gold grains of sand. . . .
>
> Blind to what he does not yet need,
> he feels his way over broken glass
> to the one stone that fits his palm . . .

Why is it so hard for us? So difficult to, naturally, state our presence in the "she" "hers" belonging to us?

(Precision of language—the writer's special tool and task. Exact to meaning.

Man, he, mankind—*only* if meaning: exclusively male.

Humanity (two more syllables) when meaning the human race. (Ascent of Humanity, not "Ascent of Man.") The individual (not he); the human being (not man); humankind (not mankind)—if that is what is meant. To write naturally: the poet, she; the writer, she—if the reference is to self, if that is what is meant.

The awkwardness (and often ridicule) if we try now to be accurate. To say: she/he; her/him; or the ungrammatical "they" when referring to both-sex poets, writers, or a writing activity.)

Marks of centuries-old entrenched power realities. Measure of the heaviness of our task no longer to abide by them,—to find and raise our various truths into truthful language.

Exclusions; Isolations; Patriarchal Atmospheres

Distinguished poet and editor A. Alvarez on assignment to meet and interview the new poet-sensation, Ted Hughes (1958):

> I was also told that he had a wife called Sylvia, who also wrote poetry, "but"—and this was said reassuringly—"she's very sharp and intelligent." . . .
>
> We arranged to take our kids for a walk . . . Ted went downstairs to get the pram ready while she [Sylvia] dressed the baby. I stayed behind a minute, zipping up my son's coat. Sylvia turned to me suddenly, without gush:
>
> "I'm so glad you picked *that* poem," she said. "It's one of my favorites but no one else seemed to like it."
>
> For a moment I went completely blank; I didn't know what she was talking about. She noticed and helped me out.
>
> "The one you put in *The Observer* a year ago. About the factory at night."
>
> "For Christ's sake, Sylvia *Plath* . . . I'm sorry. It was a lovely poem."
>
> "Lovely" wasn't the right word, but what else do you say to a bright young housewife? . . .
>
> I was embarrassed not to have known who she was. She seemed so embarrassed to have [had to remind] me, and also depressed. . . .
>
> After that I saw Ted occasionally, Sylvia more rarely. He and I would meet for a beer in one of the pubs. . . .
>
> Ted occasionally dropped in and I would hobble with him briefly to the pub. But I saw Sylvia not at all. . . .
>
> They had had a new baby in January, [this time] a boy, and Sylvia had changed. No longer quiet and withheld, a housewifely appendage to a powerful husband, she seemed made solid and complete. . . . Perhaps the birth of a son had something to do with this new confident air.
>
> —from "Sylvia Plath: A Memoir"

Restriction (Exclusion) Deprivation ▲

Limitation of circumstances (experience, knowledge) for scope, subject, context: the kind of comprehensions that can come only in situations beyond the private:

Restriction: Riveted to the Ground

Culture must be apprehended through the free action of a transcendence: that is, the free spirit with all its riches must project itself toward an empty heaven that it is to populate; but if a thousand persistent bonds hold it to earth, its surge is broken. . . . [The woman artist-writer] can today go out alone, but . . . eyes and heads [lie] in wait everywhere; if she wanders carelessly, her mind freely drifting, if she lights a cigarette in front of a cafe, if she goes alone to the movies, a disagreeable incident [may well] happen. She must inspire respect by her dress and manners. *But this preoccupation rivets her to the ground and to herself.* *

When women finally do begin to try to write . . . we write autobiographically. So autobiographically in fact that it is very hard to find any sense of any other reality. There is no other reality besides my house. There is no other reality outside Chattanooga. St. Louis is the only city that exists. This grammar school where me and my friends went, we chewed bubblegum, and went and got screwed the first time—that's all that happens. See, the whole thing is that our mobility is limited, our ability to read is limited, our ability to write is limited, our ability—or even the impulse—to dream is limited. . . . And the work has to move us to some other place.**

A culture fosters creativity to the extent that it provides an individual with the opportunity to experience its many facets. . . . A culture that limits a person's freedom to work, study or experience, that restricts [her] opportunity for exposure, that keeps [her] from learn-

---

*Simone de Beauvoir, *The Second Sex.*

**Ntozake Shange (author: *For Colored Girls Who Have Considered Suicide When the Rainbow Is Enuf*) speaking of limitations for women and for Third World youngsters in a panel on Women and Creative Process, Stanford University, 1975.

▲ ONE OUT OF TWELVE, P. 41

ing necessary media through which feelings and ideas could be contributed to others, decreases probability of creative contributions.

. . . Creativity is transactional between the individual and the environment in which [s]he lives.*

Christina Stead—no banker she, nor dweller in the realms of power—wrote the definitive novel on world banking *(House of All Nations)*. But for seven years she had had to work for a living in a bank, and long before that had made herself a peerless writer-observer (the acknowledged classic, *The Man Who Loved Children*, already years behind her). If—besides time—she had been able to move freely up and down the social scale, had all open to her, would a year have sufficed (as it did for Balzac, Zola)—and she been able to go on to other revealings? What rarest combinations of imaginative fiction might we not have had from her.

What rarest combinations might we not have had from Beatrix Potter, imaginative writer, excluded from the world of science she sought to enter, turned instead to *Peter Rabbit* and a garden patch.

From birth on, Virginia Woolf moved in personal-social relationship to men of power in her time—among them makers of British policy, "constantly affect[ing] the course of history."**

---

*Tumin and Stein: "A Study on Creativity." The arbitrary change of pronoun from male (him, he) to female is mine.

**"Molly has very unfairly, I think, laid upon me the burden of providing a memoir tonight. . . . But it is unfair. It is not my turn; I am not the oldest of you. I am not the most widely lived or the most richly memoried. Maynard, Desmond, Clive and Leonard all live stirring and active lives; all constantly brush up against the great; all constantly affect the course of history one way or another. It is for them to unlock the doors of their treasure-houses and to set before us those gilt and gleaming objects which repose within. Who am I that I should be asked to read a memoir? A mere scribbler. . . . My memoirs, which are always private, and at their best only about proposals of marriage, seductions by half-brothers, encounters with Ottoline and so on, must soon run dry. . . . I can speak a kind of dog French and mongrel Italian; but so ignorant am I, so badly educated, that if you ask me the simplest question—for instance, where is Guatemala?—I am forced to turn the conversation. . . ."

—from "Am I a Snob?" read to the Memoir Club, "close friends of long standing," in 1936 *(Moments of Being,* 1976). The chaffing tone is instructive.

Restricted personal-social only. The savage (and to me great) essay, *Three Guineas* (as *A Room of One's Own*), comes partly out of genius brooding on that exclusion (restriction).*

> The public and the private worlds are inseparably connected; the tyrannies and servilities of the one are the tyrannies and servilities of the other

she observed in *Three Guineas*. She gave us inexhaustible fiction on the private, the restricted personal; but all her hard-won genius, to little avail in imaginatively creating for us the inseparable connection; the public worlds; the full beings of the men as they affected history;—the circumference.

> I should have liked a closer and thicker knowledge of life. I should have liked to deal with real things sometimes.
>
> —Virginia Woolf

Think: If Tolstoy had been born a woman.

Restriction, Deprivation, Exclusion

*Emily Dickinson's Testimony: Some Beginning Lines of Some Poems**

> I breathed enough to take the Trick—
> And now, removed from Air—
> I simulate the Breath . . .
>
> ———————
>
> Why—do they shut Me out of Heaven?
> Did I sing—too loud?
>
> ———————
>
> Before I got my eye put out
> I liked as well to see—
> As other Creatures, that have Eyes
> And know no other way—

---

*The impairment of all women resulting from exclusion, and the denial of full circumference for her own work, are recurrent threads throughout Woolf's essays, letters, diaries—and fiction.

**From *The Complete Poems of Emily Dickinson;* the entire poems could not be quoted, but it is hoped they will be read in entirety.

It knew no Medicine—
It was not Sickness— then—

———————————

It would have starved a Gnat—
To live so small as I—
And yet I was a living Child—
With Food's necessity

Upon me—like a Claw—

———————————

I had been hungry, all the Years—
My Noon had Come—to dine—
I trembling drew the Table near—
And touched the Curious Wine—

———————————

They shut me up in Prose—
As when a little Girl
They put me in the Closet—
Because they liked me "still"—

———————————

I never hear the word "escape"
Without a quicker blood,

———————————

Victory comes late—
And is held low to freezing lips—
Too rapt with frost
To take it—

———————————

'Tis true—They shut me in the Cold—
But then—Themselves were warm

———————————

Deprived of other Banquet,
I entertained Myself—

———————————

Had I not seen the Sun
I could have borne the shade
But Light a newer Wilderness
My Wilderness has made—

———————————

I was the slightest in the House—
I took the smallest Room—

———————————

A loss of something ever felt I—
The first that I could recollect
Bereft I was—of what I knew not

Not with a Club, the Heart is broken
Nor with a Stone—
A Whip so small you could not see it

"I want"—it pleaded—All its life—

Hope is a subtle Glutton—
He feeds upon the Fair—
And yet—inspected closely
What Abstinence is there—

"My business is circumference."

But even Emily Dickinson could not free herself to consummate her business. Trespass vision cannot make circumference. Nor can the most ascendant imagination. Vision must have a place from which (as well as territory) to observe. Imagination must have freedom, velocity—and ground from which to soar.

(And time, confidence, concentration, means.)

Many a woman writer seeking circumference—of whom I am one *(Circumference, thou Bride of Awe)*—has had to abide by, solace herself with trespass vision; the "being one on whom nothing is lost." They do not suffice.

> O! dreadful is the check—intense the agony—
> When the ear begins to hear, and the eye begins to see;
> When the pulse begins to throb, the brain to think again;
> The soul to feel the flesh, and the flesh to feel the chain.
> —Emily Brontë

SOME EFFECTS OF HAVING TO COUNTER AND ENCOUNTER HARMFUL TREATMENT AND CIRCUMSTANCES AS A WRITER WHO IS FEMALE. DENIAL OF CIRCUMFERENCE.

These pressures toward censorship, self-censorship; toward accepting, abiding by entrenched attitudes, thus falsifying one's own reality, range, vision, truth, voice . . .

Constriction to One Dimension—I: "Writing Like a Man"*

When Charlotte Brontë, still publishing as Currer Bell, wrote to George Lewes in 1849

---

*Akin to "passing": the attempt to escape inferior status, penalties, injustices, by concealing one's color, class, origin. Identifying oneself as of the dominant.

"Several men have through the years said to me: You write like a man. They consider this a compliment. I want to ask: Which man? I never have. Without the answer, I do not feel complimented."—Harriette Arnow, 1973.

Arnow's "*which* man?" is of course the right question-answer. It is significant that, until recently, this affront was considered unquestionable accolade, for all its inherent assumption of distinctively male and female characteristics and orders of writing—the male, naturally superior.

> I wish you did not think me a woman. I wish all reviewers believed
> "Currer Bell" to be a man: they would be more just to him

she had no intention of or desire to write like a man. She wished
to have the privileges of one, that is, have her work accorded
serious, just treatment; and to have equality of circumstance in
writing, that is, be able to write *"as author only,"* unsex-con-
sciously, freely.

It was in that hope that she, her sisters, and other women
writers before and since—from George Sand, George Eliot, Ralph
Irons (Olive Schreiner), Henry Handel Richardson, I. Compton-
Burnett, to A.G. Motjabai—camouflaged themselves under male
pen names or neutral initials. Innocent, evident strategem—and
ineffective.

The "as author only" situation yet to be achieved, it is inevitable
that distortions of work will result—most often in writers of highest aim, to whom the overt/covert woman's place ("women writers, woman experience, and literature written by women are by
definition . . . minor") damnation (humiliation!) is intolerable.

The coercion to "write like a man" takes vari-forms:

Denying profound (woman) life comprehensions and experi-
ences expression* (sometimes not even bringing them to consciousness)—as not legitimate or important or interesting enough material for literature. Overt, covert effect of their major absence from
the dominant "male-stream" ("the great tradition"), and of the
attitude that "women's subjects" are minor, trivial.

*Casting (embodying) deepest comprehensions and truths in the
character or voice of a male,* as of greater import, impact, significance. (Rebecca Davis, a Hugh instead of a Deb, a *Life in the Iron
Mills* instead of *Life in the Textile Mills;* Willa Cather, a male
narrator in "Wagner Matinee," *My Antonia, Lost Lady;* Jo Sin-
clair, a male hero in her autobiographical *Wasteland.*)

In writing of women, characterizations, material, understand-

---

*Among these: a different existential sense of life; a different placing of what is
important; an opposing vision. Motherhood in the voice of mothers themselves;
children. "The sense of wrong." Fear. Feeling for other women. Sexuality. Truth
of one's body.

ings, identical to that of most male writers. In the extreme: repeating male stereotypings, indictments, diminishings of women. Nurse Ratchetts. Portnoy mothers. Francis MacComber bitches. Parasites, bores, gabs, dummies, nags, whiners. Not asking the writer's question: is this true? is this all? if indeed gargoyled, then what misshapen? (Mary McCarthy's *The Group.* How more perceptively—and as tragedy—would these women's lives be written today.)

Refusing "woman's sphere" subjects altogether. (A form, as are these all, of acceding to the patriarchal injunction: if you are going to practice literature—a man's domain, profession—divest yourself of what might identify you as woman.)

Writing in dominant male forms, style, although what seeks to be expressed might ask otherwise. In its extreme, consciously seeking (stereotypically) male-identified characteristics, bluntness, thrust, force (the phallacy of biological analogy); abstraction, detachment, "the large canvas," etc. Far deeper, more pervasive, is the unexamined acceptance of forms (subjects, vision) as one's own.*

Proclaiming that one's sex has nothing to do with one's writing: In its understandable, but unadmirable form, what Margaret Atwood analyzes as:

> the often observed phenomenon of the member of a despised social group who manages to transcend the limitation imposed on the group, at least enough to become "successful," disassociating him/ herself from the group. . . . Thus the [successful] women who say: "I've never had any problems. I don't know what they're talking about." . . . Why carry with you the stigma attached to that dismal category you've escaped from?

In its traditional form: accepting or seeming to accept that the circumstances for and the practice of literature are above gender. "Every artist is either a man or a woman, and the struggle is pretty much the same for both," proclaims Elizabeth Hardwick (quoted earlier).

---

*Jane Cooper's account in *Maps and Windows* of the process is searching and complex; especially illuminating the pull toward these forms—so great in our cultural heritage.

... The term "woman writer" ... has no meaning, not intellectually, not morally, not historically. A writer is a writer.

declares Cynthia Ozick at a symposium on *Literary Women*
(1976).*

As a writer-woman wrote to another one century and a half
ago:

> Thou large brained woman and large hearted man,
> Self called George Sand whose soul amid the lions
> Of thy tumultuous senses, moans defiance
> And answers roar for roar . . .
>
> True genius, but true woman! Dost deny
> Thy woman's nature with a manly scorn
> And break away the gauds and armlets worn
> By weaker women in captivity? . . .
>
> Ah, vain denial! That revolted cry
> Is sobbed in by a woman's voice forlorn!
> Thy woman's hair, my sister, all unshorn
> Floats back—dishevelled strength in agony . . .**

Dishevelled strength in agony

*Surely it is evident that heretofore, and in what follows, I am writing
of (and against) pressures, impediments, to what should rightfully
be the writer's fullest freedom to write of anything—in any sex,
voice, style—in accordance with the best need of whatever seeks
expression.*

---

*"Feminism, as I continue to understand it, demands that sex be regarded as
irrelevant to merit and ambition," Ozick explained later that evening, disclosing
that she mistook a consummation devoutly to be worked for, for past and present
reality.

**Elizabeth Barrett Browning.

Constriction to One Dimension—II: Writing Like a Woman

Woman's Place. "Obliged to shut off three-fourths of one's being"

The obverse twin, Siamese, to "writing like a man"—enforced, created, by the same causes (although there is no complementary (complimentary) "you write like a woman" expression*) compounded by the great crippler, lack of confidence in one's own experiences, one's own authenticity, one's own potential powers.

Among the vari-forms, overlapping:

*"The mirror to magnify man."** "A sensibility that will not threaten man."*

Being charming, entertaining, "small," *feminine,* when full development of material would require a serious or larger tone and treatment. Pulling away from depths and complexity. Irony, wit, the arch, instead of directness; diffuse emotion or detachment instead of tragedy. Avoiding seriousness altogether. Concealing intellect, analytical ability, objectivity; or refusing to credit that one is capable of them. Abdicating "male" realms: "the large," the social, the political.

Accepting that one's writing is only within the (reductively defined) feminine. The personal, the intuitive, the sensuous, the inner, the narcissistic: "swathed in self." "Love is a woman's whole existence." Centrality of the male. Centrality of sexuality. Confinement to biological (sex-partner) woman. The trap of biological analogy: glorifying womb, female form imagery; or softness, the inner.† Earth mother, serving vessel, sex goddess, irre-

---

*There is an analogous common expression: the "you're a real woman" (or "a real man's woman").

**Virginia Woolf, of course. The angel in the house of literature: "My dear, be sympathetic, be tender, flatter, deceive; use all the arts and wiles of our sex. Never let anybody guess that you have a mind of your own. . . ."

†To be clearly distinguished from the only-beginning-to-be-won right of women to "tell the truth about one's body."

sistible romantic heroine; victim; "do with me as you will" stereotype.

Not being ambitious in accordance with one's capacities. Using writing as "a means of self-expression instead of an art" when, with seriousness and ambition, the art might be achieved as well (applicable only to women writers of favored background and circumstances for whom the attainment might have been possible).

"Leaving out what most men writers leave out": woman's most basic experiences once they get up out of bed and childbed; other common female realities.* "Sparing him, and so on."

Deferring to, accepting, writing from dominant male attitudes, assumptions, interpretations of human behavior and motivation (even regarding oneself). ** Repeating male stereotypings, indictments, diminishings of women, in woman form. As was said a few pages ago. Not asking the writer's question: is this true? is this true in my own experience and life-knowledge?

Incorporating prevailing male (and class) values—ignoring or contempt for the work and services most women do in and out of the home—contrary to one's lived knowledge of their essentiality, substance, challenge, worth, yes—for some aspects of our being, self-development, fulfillment of potentials. (In rarer form, exalting

---

*See footnote page 43. "Ways in which innate human drives and capacities . . . denied development and scope, nevertheless struggle to express themselves and function."

**Especially, given prevalent practice, theory, can this be formidable for the analyzed writer-woman; deflecting, blinding, robbing of sources of one's own authority (that is: basic woman-experience comprehensions, and "motherhood truths" not yet incorporated into literature and other disciplines, let alone into psychiatric theory and practice). Among the too often deferred to: reductive formulas: sex as primary; once suicidal, always suicidal; assignment of certain characteristics, behavior, as innately female; masochism, passivity, "every woman loves a Nazi," you (women) want to fail, be seduced, raped, punished. Oedipus, Electra. Mother blaming. Guilt where it is not guilt at all but the workings of an intolerable situation. The springs of achievement. Mind-body relationship.

In addition, there is the danger of fixing to the past; to self-involvement; the distortion of memory; the focus on the personal (most the psycho-sexual); the ignoring of societal roots, causes, effects. All of which diminish, make shallow, falsify one's writing.

or romanticizing aspects of these services, ignoring the criminality of their consuming most of women's lives.)

Constriction to One Dimension—III: Confinement to Biological (Sex-Partner) Woman▲

"Killing the angel in the house, I think I solved," Virginia Woolf wrote in her already-quoted discussion of problems before women writers, "but the second [problem], telling the truth about my own experiences as a body, I do not think I solved."*

Fifty years after, still to be solved.

With motherhood (and in this instance, in spite of thousands of books by men and hundreds by women on "love" and, now, on sexuality) the least understood, the most tormentingly complex experience to wrest to truth.

Telling the truth about one's experiences as a body, forbidden, not possible, for centuries.

Rights of one's own body denied to woman for centuries. Men owned us. Babies inhabited our bodies year after year.

Knowledge of one's body that comes only through free use of it, even free exercise of it, denied. (Thoreau's birthday wish for himself one year: "to inhabit his body with inexpressible satisfaction." Never possible for his sister Sophia. He could swim—and naked, walk to exhaustion, "dithyrambic leap" about; all physical activity was open to him. Never for Sophia—or any woman—that inexpressible satisfaction.)

The way-making to do.

The obvious coercions: to "write like a man" (of one's experiences as most men write, have written, of us—Miller, Lawrence, Chaucer's Wife of Bath); to "write like a woman" (flatter, conciliate, please; lie; the mirror to magnify man). The problem of finding one's own truth through the primacy accorded sexual-

---

*"The obstacles are still immensely powerful," Woolf goes on to say, "and yet they are very difficult to define."

▲ ONE OUT OF TWELVE, P. 42

ity* by our times. The pornographic, the Freudian, times. Our freer—that is, voluntary about reproduction—times. Our still restrictive, defining sexuality as heterosexual, times.

The confusion of "sexual liberation" (genitally defined) with the genuine liberation of woman: "the exercise of vital powers along lines of excellence in a society affording them scope." The unworked through, unassessed relationship between body difference and the actual power relationship permeating associations between the sexes. The question of the place, proportion, *actual* importance of sexuality in our (now) longer-lived, more various, woman lives.

Telling the truth about one's body: a necessary, freeing subject for the woman writer.

---

*Carolyn Heilbrun might add: "the exploration of experience *only* through sexuality, which is exactly where men have always told them that such an exploration should take place."

OTHER OBSTACLES, BALKS, ENCUMBRANCES IN COMING TO ONE'S OWN VOICE, VISION, CIRCUMFERENCE

Do not forget:
   The overwhelmingness of the dominant.
   The daily saturation.
   Isolations.
   The knife of the perfectionist attitude.
   The insoluble.
   Economic imperatives.

How much it takes to become a writer. Bent (far more common than we assume), circumstances, time, development of craft—but beyond that: how much conviction as to the importance of what one has to say, one's right to say it. And the will, the measureless store of belief in oneself to be able to come to, cleave to, find the form for one's own life comprehensions. Difficult for any male not born into a class that breeds such confidence. Almost impossible for a girl, a woman.

These pressures toward censorship, self-censorship; toward accepting, abiding by entrenched attitudes, thus falsifying one's own reality, range, vision, truth, voice, are extreme for women writers . . . remain a complex problem for women writing in our time.

To discuss and define them is, I think, of great value and importance, for thus only can the labour be shared, the difficulties solved.
                                                                    —Virginia Woolf

Fear

Fear is a powerful reason; those who are economically dependent have strong reasons for fear. . . . But [even with economic independence] some fear, some ancestral memory prophesying war, still remains, it seems. . . .

What then can be the nature of the fear that still makes concealment necessary . . . and reduces our boasted freedom to a farce? . . . Again there are three dots; again they represent a gulf—of silence this time, of silence inspired by fear. And since we lack both the courage to explain it and the skill . . .

—from Woolf's great Three Guineas

"And here I must step warily, for already I feel the lash upon my shoulder."

—Virginia Woolf

Fear. How could it be otherwise, as one is also a woman.

The centuries past. The other determining difference—not biology—for woman. Constrictions, coercions, penalties for being female. Enforced. Sometimes physically enforced.

Reprisals, coercions, penalties for not remaining in what was, is, deemed suitable in her sex.

The writer-woman is not excepted, because she writes.

Fear—the need to please, to be safe—in the literary realm too. Founded fear. Power is still in the hands of men. Power of validation, publication, approval, reputation, coercions, penalties.

"The womanhood emotion." Fear to hurt.*

"Liberty is the right not to lie."
"What are rights without means?"

---

*"Whenever a man [appeals to the womanhood emotion] he rouses in her, it is safe to say, a conflict of emotions of a very deep and primitive kind which it is extremely difficult for her to analyze or to reconcile."

—Woolf, Three Guineas

Love

Of course it is not fear alone.

Fear—in itself—is assailable. As every revolt against oppressive power throughout the human past testifies.

There is also—love. The need to love and be loved.

It has never yet been a world right for love, for those we love, for ourselves, for flowered human life.

The oppression of women* is like no other form of oppression (class, color—though these have parallels). It is an oppression entangled through with human love, human need, genuine (core) human satisfactions, identifications, fulfillments.

How to separate out the chains from the bonds, the harms from the value, the truth from the lies.**

What compounds the personal agony for us, is that portion of the harm which comes to us from the beings we are close to, who are close to us. Their daily part in the balks, lessenings, denials. Which we must daily encounter.

And counter?

"The times are not ripe for us," the times are "not yet." Except for a privileged few who escape, who benefit from its effects, it remains a maiming sex-class-race world for ourselves, for those we love. The changes that will enable us to live together without harm ("no one's fullness of being at the cost of another's") are as yet only in the making (and we are not only beings seeking to change; changing; we are also that which our past has made us). In such circumstances, taking for one's best achievement means almost inevitably at the cost of others' needs.

(And where there are children. . . . And where there are children. . . .)

Leechings, balks, encumbrances.
Harms.

AND YET THE TREE DID—DOES—BEAR FRUIT.

---

*—which, among all else, results in our being one out of twelve in recognized achievement—

**Writer, as well as human, task.

Creativity; Potentiality
First Generation

CREATIVITY; POTENTIALITY.
FIRST GENERATION

"Silences"—the original talk given in 1962 under the name "Death of the Creative Process"—began:

"Though I address myself only to silences in literature and the ways in which writing ceases to be, this dying and death of capacity encompasses more than literature, the arts, or even Wordsworth's 'widening of the sphere of human sensibility,' or Thoreau's 'to affect the quality of the day: that is the highest art.'

"At a national conference on Creativity, yes there really was such a gathering, at the University of Michigan several years ago (1959 I believe), they considered (their words) 'the emerging discovery of the tremendous, unsuspected potentialities in the creativity of man in the meaning of respect for the individual,' and concluded:

Creativity was in each one of us as a small child. In children it is universal. Among adults it is almost nonexistent. The great question is: what has happened to this enormous and universal human capacity? That is the question of the age.

"Not many would accede to creativity as an enormous and *universal* human capacity (let alone recognize its extinction as the question of the age). I am one of those who, in almost unbearable, based conviction, believe that it is so.

"To establish its truth incontrovertibly would require an ending to the age-old denial of enabling circumstances—because of one's class, color, sex—which has stunted (not extinguished) most of humanity's creativity. Few of us have been permitted 'the exercise of vital powers along lines of excellence in a life affording them scope.' "*

"Silences" was an attempt, as later were "One Out of Twelve," "Rebecca Harding Davis," and now the rest of this book, to expand the too sparse evidence on the relationship between circumstances and creation. (All limited to only one area of recognized human achievement: written literature.)

There is another undeniable evidence.

We ourselves (writers, others in the arts, the professions) who are the first in generations of our families and/or sex to become so.

Our different emergences into literature as circumstances permit. Remember women's silence of centuries; the silences of most of the rest of humanity. Not until several centuries ago do women writers appear. Sons of working people, a little more than a century ago. Then black writers (1950 was the watershed year). The last decades, more and more writer-mothers. Last of all, women writers, including women of color, of working class origin, perhaps one generation removed; rarest of all, the worker-mother-writer.

And all, although in increasingly significant numbers, still exceptional: statistically rare.**

Born a generation earlier, in the circumstances for their class, and/or race, and/or sex, no Chekhov, Brontë sisters, Emily Dickinson, Thomas Hardy, Maxim Gorky, no D. H. Lawrence, Virginia Woolf, Sean O'Casey, no Franz Kafka, Albert Camus—the list comes long now: say, for a sampling, no A. E. Coppard, Charles Olson, Richard Wright, Philip Roth, Cynthia Ozick, Joyce Carol Oates, Toni Morrison, Alice Walker, etc. etc. etc. etc.

---

*From the tape transcription.

**The "only," the occasional, the tiny handful of exceptions writing before, do not alter these datings.

> *What they came into by virtue of their birth,*
> *we have had to earn at the cost of years and*
> *our youth.*
>
> —Anton Chekhov

> *However, it was my poverty and not my will*
> *that consented to be beaten. It takes two or*
> *three generations to do what I tried to do in*
> *one.*
>
> —Hardy's *Jude the Obscure*

Of the first generation . . .

A phenomenon of our time, the increasingly significant number of first (or second) generation of our people to aspire to the kinds of uses of capacity possible through the centuries only for few human beings of privilege—among these, to write.

Marginal. Against complex odds. ▲ Exhausting (though exhilarating) achievement.

This the barest of indications as to vulnerabilities, balks, blights; reasons for lessenings and silencings:*

The education, most often gotten part-time, over years and with difficulty; seldom full-time for absorption in it. Often inferiority of it. Intimidations.**

Anxieties, shamings. "Hidden injuries of class." Prevailing attitudes toward our people as "lower class," "losers," (they just didn't have it); contempt for their lives and the work they do ("the manure theory of social organization" is what W. E. B. Du Bois called it).

The blood struggle for means: one's own development so often

---

*Some of what has been written here of the writer-woman is parallel; clues (and many writer-women are first generation of their families, women or men, to write).

**Little teaching of writing as process to fortify against measuring one's earlier work against that of established writers. (No anthology of the work that admired writers were doing *their* earlier years.) Little reinforcement to the V. Woolf conception that if writing "explains much and tells much" it is valid. Little to rouse confident sense of one's own source material—the importance of what one has to bring into literature that is not there now, and one's right to say it.

at the cost of others giving themselves up for us or of our own inability to help our kin. "Love, tenderness, responsibility, would only have meant pain, suffering, defeat, the repetition of my mother's life for another generation" (Agnes Smedley).

Likelihood of part-time, part-self writing. Having to support self by means other than writing. Problems of getting to writing at all. Problems of roots; ties; separation.

Camus's "loving with despair"; sense of possibilities not come to; knowledge of the latent, the unfulfilled, the gargoyled, in our kin.

Coercions to "pass"; to write with the attitude of, and/or in the manner of, the dominant. Little to validate our different sense of reality, to help raise one's own truths, voice, against the prevalent.

Problems of what Chekhov (a first generation) called "squeezing the serf out of one's soul."

Meagerest of indications only.

Class—economic circumstance; problems of being in the first generation of one's family to come to writing—its relationship to works of literature: the great unexamined.

> Literature is no one's private ground; literature is common ground. Let us trespass freely and fearlessly and find our own way for ourselves. It is thus that English literature will survive if commoners and outsiders like ourselves make that country our own country, if we teach ourselves how to read and how to write, how to preserve, and how to create.
>
> —Virginia Woolf

Excerpts from
LIFE IN THE IRON MILLS;
or,
THE KORL WOMAN
by Rebecca Harding Davis

The Atlantic Monthly, April 1861

A cloudy day: do you know what that is in a town of iron-works? The sky sank down before dawn, muddy, flat, immovable. The air is thick, clammy with the breath of crowded human beings. It stifles me. I open the window, and, looking out, can scarcely see through the rain the grocer's shop opposite, where a crowd of drunken Irishmen are puffing Lynchburg tobacco in their pipes. I can detect the scent through all the foul smells ranging loose in the air.

The idiosyncrasy of this town is smoke. It rolls sullenly in slow folds from the great chimneys of the iron-foundries, and settles down in black, slimy pools on the muddy streets. Smoke on the wharves, smoke on the dingy boats, on the yellow river,—clinging in a coating of greasy soot to the house-front, the two faded poplars, the faces of the passers-by. The long train of mules, dragging masses of pig-iron through the narrow street, have a foul vapor hanging to their reeking sides. Here, inside, is a little broken figure of an angel pointing upward from the mantel-shelf; but even its wings are covered with smoke, clotted and black. Smoke everywhere! A dirty canary chirps desolately in a cage beside me. Its dream of green fields and sunshine is a very old dream,—almost worn out, I think.

From the back-window I can see a narrow brick-yard sloping down to the river-side, strewed with rain-butts and tubs. The river, dull and tawny-colored, *(la belle rivière!)* drags itself sluggishly along, tired of the heavy weight of boats and coal-barges. What wonder? When I was a child, I used to fancy a look of weary, dumb appeal upon the face of the negro-like river slavishly bearing its burden day after day. Something of the same idle notion comes to me to-day, when from the street-window I look on the slow stream of human life creeping past, night and morning, to the great mills. Masses of men, with dull, besotted faces bent to the ground, sharpened here and there by pain or cunning; skin and muscle and flesh begrimed with smoke and ashes; stooping all night over boiling caldrons of metal, laired by day in dens of drunkenness and infamy; breathing from infancy to death an air saturated with fog and grease and soot, vileness for soul and body. . . .

. . . I want you to hide your disgust, take no heed to your clean clothes, and come right down with me,—here, into the thickest of the fog and mud and foul effluvia. I want you to hear this story. There is a secret down here, in this nightmare fog, that has lain dumb for centuries: I want to make it a real thing to you. You, Egoist, or Pantheist, or Arminian, busy in making straight paths for your feet on the hills, do not see it clearly,—this terrible question which men here have gone mad and died trying to answer. I dare not put this secret into words. I told you it was dumb. These men, going by with drunken faces and brains full of unawakened power, do not ask it of Society or of God. Their lives ask it; their deaths ask it. There is no reply. I will tell you plainly that I have a great hope; and I bring it to you to be tested. It is this: that this terrible dumb question is its own reply; that it is not the sentence of death we think it, but, from the very extremity of its darkness, the most solemn prophecy which the world has known of the Hope to come. . . .

. . . This house is the one where the Wolfes lived. There were the father and son,—both hands, as I said, in one of Kirby & John's mills for making railroad-iron,—and Deborah, their cousin, a picker in some of the cotton-mills. The house was rented then to half a dozen families. The Wolfes had two of the cellar-rooms. The old man, like many of the puddlers and feeders of the mills, was Welsh,—had spent half of his life in the Cornish tin-mines. You may pick the Welsh emigrants, Cornish miners, out of the throng passing the windows, any day. They are a trifle more filthy; their muscles are not so brawny; they stoop more. When they are drunk, they neither yell, nor shout, nor stagger, but skulk along like beaten hounds. . . . Their lives . . . incessant labor, sleeping in kennel-like rooms, eating rank pork and molasses, drinking—God and the distillers only know what; with an occasional night in jail, to atone for some drunken excess. Is that all of their lives?—of the portion given to them and these their duplicates swarming the streets to-day?—nothing beneath?—all? So many a political reformer will tell you,—and many a private reformer, too, who has gone among them with a heart tender with Christ's charity, and come out outraged, hardened. . . .

A heap of ragged coats was heaved up, and the face of a young girl emerged, staring sleepily at the woman.

"Deborah," she said, at last, "I'm here the night."

"Yes, child. Hur's welcome," she said, quietly eating on.

The girl's face was haggard and sickly; her eyes were heavy with sleep and hunger: real Milesian eyes they were, dark, delicate blue, glooming out from black shadows with a pitiful fright.

"I was alone," she said, timidly.

"Where's the father?" asked Deborah, holding out a potato, which the girl greedily seized.

"He's beyant,—wid Haley,—in the stone house." (Did you ever hear the word *jail* from an Irish mouth?) "I came here. Hugh told me never to stay me-lone."

"Hugh?"

"Yes."

A vexed frown crossed her face. The girl saw it, and added quickly,—

"I have not seen Hugh the day, Deb. The old man says his watch lasts till the mornin'."

The woman sprang up, and hastily began to arrange some bread and flitch* in a tin pail, and to pour her own measure of ale into a bottle. Tying on her bonnet, she blew out the candle.

"Lay ye down, Janey dear," she said, gently, covering her with the old rags. "Hur can eat the potatoes, if hur's hungry."

"Where are ye goin', Deb? The rain's sharp."

"To the mill, with Hugh's supper."

"Let him bide till th' morn. Sit ye down."

"No, no,"—sharply pushing her off. "The boy'll starve."

She hurried from the cellar, while the child wearily coiled herself up for sleep. The rain was falling heavily, as the woman, pail in hand, emerged from the mouth of the alley, and turned down the narrow street, that stretched out, long and black, miles before her. Here and there a flicker of gas lighted an uncertain space of muddy footwalk and gutter; the long rows of houses, except an occasional lager-bier shop, were closed; now and then she met a band of mill-hands skulking to or from their work. . . .

As Deborah hurried down through the heavy rain, the noise of these thousand engines sounded through the sleep and shadow of the city like far-off thunder. The mill to which she was going lay on the river, a mile below the city-limits. It was far, and she was

---

*Rank salt pork.

weak, aching from standing twelve hours at the spools.* Yet it was her almost nightly walk to take this man his supper, though at every square she sat down to rest, and she knew she should receive small word of thanks.

Perhaps, if she had possessed an artist's eye, the picturesque oddity of the scene might have made her step stagger less, and the path seem shorter; but to her the mills were only "summat deilish to look at by night."

The road leading to the mills had been quarried from the solid rock, which rose abrupt and bare on one side of the cinder-covered road, while the river, sluggish and black, crept past on the other. The mills for rolling iron are simply immense tent-like roofs, covering acres of ground, open on every side. Beneath these roofs Deborah looked in on a city of fires, that burned hot and fiercely in the night. Fire in every horrible form: pits of flame waving in the wind; liquid metal-flames writhing in tortuous streams through the sand; wide caldrons filled with boiling fire, over which bent ghastly wretches stirring the strange brewing; and through all, crowds of half-clad men, looking like revengeful ghosts in the red light, hurried, throwing masses of glittering fire. It was like a street in Hell. Even Deborah muttered, as she crept through, "'T looks like t' Devil's place!" It did,—in more ways than one.

She found the man she was looking for, at last, heaping coal on a furnace. He had not time to eat his supper; so she went behind the furnace, and waited. . . .

If you could go into this mill where Deborah lay, and drag out from the hearts of these men the terrible tragedy of their lives, taking it as a symptom of the disease of their class, no ghost Horror would terrify you more. A reality of soul-starvation, of living death, that meets you every day under the besotted faces on the street,—I can paint nothing of this, only give you the outside outlines of a night, a crisis in the life of one man: whatever muddy depth of soul-history lies beneath you can read according to the eyes God has given you.

Wolfe, while Deborah watched him as a spaniel its master, bent

---

*Without lunch or stop for it.

over the furnace with his iron pole, unconscious of her scrutiny, only stopping to receive orders. Physically, Nature had promised the man but little. He had already lost the strength and instinct vigor of a man, his muscles were thin, his nerves weak, his face (a meek, woman's face) haggard, yellow with consumption. In the mill he was known as one of the girl-men: "Molly Wolfe" was his *sobriquet.* He was never seen in the cockpit, did not own a terrier, drank but seldom; when he did, desperately. He fought sometimes, but was always thrashed, pommelled to a jelly. The man was game enough, when his blood was up: but he was no favorite in the mill; he had the taint of school-learning on him,—not to a dangerous extent, only a quarter or so in the free-school in fact,* but enough to ruin him as a good hand in a fight.

For other reasons, too, he was not popular; . . . silent, with foreign thoughts and longings breaking out through his quietness in innumerable curious ways: this one, for instance. In the neighboring furnace-buildings lay great heaps of the refuse from the ore after the pig-metal is run. *Korl* we call it here: a light, porous substance, of a delicate, waxen, flesh-colored tinge. Out of the blocks of this korl, Wolfe, in his off-hours from the furnace, had a habit of chipping and moulding figures,—hideous, fantastic enough, but sometimes strangely beautiful: even the mill-men saw that, while they jeered at him. It was a curious fancy in the man, almost a passion. The few hours for rest he spent hewing and hacking with his blunt knife, never speaking, until his watch came again,—working at one figure for months, and, when it was finished, breaking it to pieces perhaps, in a fit of disappointment. A morbid, gloomy man, untaught, unled, left to feed his soul in grossness and crime, and hard, grinding labor.

I want you to come down and look at this Wolfe, standing there among the lowest of his kind, and see him just as he is, that you may judge him justly when you hear the story of this night. I want you to look back, as he does every day, at his birth in vice, his starved infancy; to remember the heavy years he has groped through as boy and man,—the slow, heavy years of constant, hot

---

*Even a quarter year in the free-school was exceptional. Most mill workers were illiterate.

work. So long ago he began, that he thinks sometimes he has worked there for ages. There is no hope that it will ever end. Think that God put into this man's soul a fierce thirst for beauty,—to know it, to create it; to *be*—something, he knows not what,—other than he is. There are moments when a passing cloud, the sun glinting on the purple thistles, a kindly smile, a child's face, will rouse him to a passion of pain,—when his nature starts up with a mad cry of rage against God, man, whoever it is that has forced this vile, slimy life upon him. With all this groping, this mad desire, a great blind intellect stumbling through wrong, a loving poet's heart, the man was by habit only a coarse, vulgar laborer, familiar with sights and words you would blush to name. Be just: when I tell you about this night, see him as he is. Be just,—not like man's law, which seizes on one isolated act, but like God's judging angel, whose clear, sad eye saw all the countless cankering days of this man's life, all the countless nights, when, sick with starving, his soul fainted in him, before it judged him for this night, the saddest of all. . . .

"Here, some of you men!" said Kirby, "bring up those boards. We may as well sit down, gentlemen, until the rain is over. It cannot last much longer at this rate."

"Pig-metal,"—mumbled the reporter,—"um!—coal facilities, —um!—hands employed, twelve hundred,—bitumen,—um!—all right, I believe, Mr. Clarke;—sinking-fund,—what did you say was your sinking-fund?"

"Twelve hundred hands?" said the stranger, the young man who had first spoken. "Do you control their votes, Kirby?"

"Control? No." The young man smiled complacently. "But my father brought seven hundred votes to the polls for his candidate last November. No force-work, you understand,—only a speech or two, a hint to form themselves into a society, and a bit of red and blue bunting to make them a flag. The Invincible Roughs,—I believe that is their name. I forget the motto: 'Our country's hope,' I think." . . .

The men began to withdraw the metal from the caldrons. The mills were deserted on Sundays, except by the hands who fed the fires, and those who had no lodgings and slept usually on the ash-heaps. The three strangers sat still during the next hour, watching the men cover the furnaces, laughing now and then at some jest of Kirby's.

"Do you know," said Mitchell, "I like this view of the works better than when the glare was fiercest? These heavy shadows and the amphitheatre of smothered fires are ghostly, unreal. One could fancy these red smouldering lights to be the half-shut eyes of wild beasts, and the spectral figures their victims in the den."

Kirby laughed. "You are fanciful. Come, let us get out of the den. The spectral figures, as you call them, are a little too real for me to fancy a close proximity in the darkness,—unarmed, too."

The others rose, buttoning their over-coats, and lighting cigars.

"Raining, still," said Doctor May, "and hard. Where did we leave the coach, Mitchell?"

"At the other side of the works.—Kirby, what's that?"

Mitchell started back, half-frightened, as, suddenly turning a corner, the white figure of a woman faced him in the darkness,— a woman, white, of giant proportions, crouching on the ground, her arms flung out in some wild gesture of warning.

"Stop! Make that fire burn there!" cried Kirby, stopping short.

The flame burst out, flashing the gaunt figure into bold relief. Mitchell drew a long breath.

"I thought it was alive," he said, going up curiously.

The others followed.

"Not marble, eh?" asked Kirby, touching it.

One of the lower overseers stopped.

"Korl, Sir."

"Who did it?"

"Can't say. Some of the hands; chipped it out in off-hours."

"Chipped to some purpose, I should say. What a flesh-tint the stuff has! Do you see, Mitchell?"

"I see."

He had stepped aside where the light fell boldest on the figure, looking at it in silence. There was not one line of beauty or grace in it: a nude woman's form, muscular, grown coarse with labor, the powerful limbs instinct with some one poignant longing. One idea: there it was in the tense, rigid muscles, the clutching hands, the wild, eager face, like that of a starving wolf's. Kirby and Doctor May walked around it, critical, curious. Mitchell stood aloof, silent. The figure touched him strangely.

"Not badly done," said Doctor May. "Where did the fellow learn that sweep of the muscles in the arm and hand? Look at them! They are groping,—do you see?—clutching: the peculiar action of a man dying of thirst."

"They have ample facilities for studying anatomy," sneered Kirby, glancing at the half-naked figures.

"Look," continued the Doctor, "at this bony wrist, and the strained sinews of the instep! A working-woman,—the very type of her class."

"God forbid!" muttered Mitchell.

"Why?" demanded May. "What does the fellow intend by the figure? I cannot catch the meaning."

"Ask him," said the other, dryly. "There he stands,"—pointing to Wolfe, who stood with a group of men, leaning on his ash-rake.

The Doctor beckoned him with the affable smile which kind-hearted men put on, when talking with these people.

"Mr. Mitchell has picked you out as the man who did this,—I'm sure I don't know why. But what did you mean by it?"

"She be hungry."

Wolfe's eyes answered Mitchell, not the Doctor.

"Oh-h! But what a mistake you have made, my fine fellow! You have given no sign of starvation to the body. It is strong,—terribly strong. It has the mad, half-despairing gesture of drowning."

Wolfe stammered, glanced appealingly at Mitchell, who saw the soul of the thing, he knew. But the cool, probing eyes were turned on himself now,—mocking, cruel, relentless.

"Not hungry for meat," the furnace-tender said at last.

"What then? Whiskey?" jeered Kirby, with a coarse laugh.

Wolfe was silent a moment, thinking.

"I dunno," he said, with a bewildered look. "It mebbe. Summat to make her live, I think,—like you. Whiskey ull do it, in a way."

The young man laughed again. Mitchell flashed a look of disgust somewhere,—not at Wolfe.

"May," he broke out impatiently, "are you blind? Look at that woman's face! It asks questions of God, and says, 'I have a right to know.' Good God, how hungry it is!"

They looked a moment; then May turned to the mill-owner:—

"Have you many such hands as this? What are you going to do with them? Keep them at puddling iron?"

Kirby shrugged his shoulders. Mitchell's look had irritated him.

"*Ce n'est pas mon affaire.* I have no fancy for nursing infant geniuses. I suppose there are some stray gleams of mind and soul among these wretches. The Lord will take care of his own; or else they can work out their own salvation. I have heard you call our American system a ladder which any man can scale. Do you doubt it? Or perhaps you want to banish all social ladders, and put us all on a flat table-land,—eh, May?"

The Doctor looked vexed, puzzled. Some terrible problem lay hid in this woman's face, and troubled these men. Kirby waited for an answer, and, receiving none, went on, warming with his subject.

"I tell you, there's something wrong that no talk of '*Liberté*' or '*Égalité*' will do away. If I had the making of men, these men who do the lowest part of the world's work should be machines,— nothing more,—hands. It would be kindness. God help them! What are taste, reason, to creatures who must live such lives as that?" He pointed to Deborah, sleeping on the ash-heap. "So many nerves to sting them to pain. What if God had put your brain, with all its agony of touch, into your fingers, and bid you work and strike with that?"

"You think you could govern the world better?" laughed the Doctor.

"I do not think at all."

"That is true philosophy. Drift with the stream, because you cannot dive deep enough to find bottom, eh?"

"Exactly," rejoined Kirby. "I do not think. I wash my hands of all social problems,—slavery, caste, white or black. My duty to my operatives has a narrow limit,—the pay-hour on Saturday night. Outside of that, if they cut korl, or cut each other's throats, (the more popular amusement of the two,) I am not responsible."

The Doctor sighed,—a good honest sigh, from the depths of his stomach.

"God help us! Who is responsible?"

"Not I, I tell you," said Kirby, testily. "What has the man who pays them money to do with their souls' concerns, more than the grocer or butcher who takes it?"

"And yet," said Mitchell's cynical voice, "look at her! How hungry she is!" . . .

"Money has spoken!" [Mitchell] said, seating himself lightly on a stone with the air of an amused spectator at a play. "Are you answered?"—turning to Wolfe his clear, magnetic face. . . . He looked at the furnace-tender as he had looked at a rare mosaic in the morning; only the man was the more amusing study of the two.

"Are you answered? Why, May, look at him! *'De profundis clamavi.'* Or, to quote in English, 'Hungry and thirsty, his soul faints in him.' And so Money sends back its answer into the depths through you, Kirby! Very clear the answer, too!— . . . Now, Doctor, the pocket of the world having uttered its voice, what has the heart to say? You are a philanthropist, in a small way,—*n'est-ce pas?* Here, boy, this gentleman can show you how to cut korl better,—or your destiny. Go on, May!" . . .

He went to Wolfe and put his hand kindly on his arm. Something of a vague idea possessed the Doctor's brain that much good was to be done here by a friendly word or two: a latent genius to be warmed into life by a waited-for sun-beam. Here it was: he had brought it. So he went on complacently:—

"Do you know, boy, you have it in you to be a great sculptor, a great man?—do you understand?" (talking down to the capacity of his hearer: it is a way people have with children, and men like Wolfe,)—"to live a better, stronger life than I, or Mr. Kirby here? A man may make himself anything he chooses. God has given you stronger powers than many men, —me, for instance."

May stopped, heated, glowing with his own magnanimity. And it was magnanimous. The puddler had drunk in every word, looking through the Doctor's flurry, and generous heat, and self-approval, into his will, with those slow, absorbing eyes of his.

"Make yourself what you will. It is your right."

"I know," quietly. "Will you help me?"

Mitchell laughed again. The Doctor turned now, in a passion,—

"You know, Mitchell, I have not the means. You know, if I had, it is in my heart to take this boy and educate him for"—

"The glory of God, and the glory of John May."

May did not speak for a moment; then, controlled, he said,—

"Why should one be raised, when myriads are left?—I have not the money, boy," to Wolfe, shortly.

"Money?" He said it over slowly, as one repeats the guessed answer to a riddle, doubtfully. "That is it? Money?"

"Yes, money,—that is it," said Mitchell, rising, and drawing his furred coat about him. "You've found the cure for all the world's diseases.—Come, May, find your good-humor, and come home. This damp wind chills my very bones. Come and preach your Saint-Simonian doctrines to-morrow to Kirby's hands. Let them have a clear idea of the rights of the soul, and I'll venture next week they'll strike for higher wages. That will be the end of it. . . .

"Besides," [he] added, "it would be of no use. I am not one of them. . . . Reform is born of need, not pity. No vital movement of the people's has worked down, for good or evil; fermented, instead, carried up the heaving, cloggy mass. Think back through history, and you will know it. What will this lowest deep—thieves, Magdalens, negroes—do with the light filtered through ponderous Church creeds, Baconian theories, Goethe schemes? Some day, out of their bitter need will be thrown up their own light-bringer, —their Jean Paul, their Cromwell, their Messiah." . . .

[It is "his right" to keep the money she has stolen from Mitchell, Deb tells Hugh.]

His right! The word struck him. Doctor May had used the same. He washed himself, and went out to find this man Mitchell. His right! Why did the chance word cling to him so obstinately? . . .

He did not deceive himself. Theft! That was it. At first the word sickened him, then he grappled with it. Sitting there on a broken cart-wheel, the fading day, the noisy groups, the church-bells' tolling passed before him like a panorama, while the sharp struggle went on within. This money! He took it out, and looked at it. If he gave it back, what then? He was going to be cool about it.

People going by to church saw only a sickly mill-boy watching them quietly at the alley's mouth. They did not know that he was mad, or they would not have gone by so quietly: mad with hunger; stretching out his hands to the world, that had given so much to them, for leave to live the life God meant him to live. His soul within him was smothering to death; he wanted so much, thought so much, and *knew*—nothing. There was nothing of which he was

certain, except the mill and things there. Of God and heaven he
had heard so little, that they were to him what fairy-land is to a
child: something real, but not here; very far off. His brain, greedy,
dwarfed, full of thwarted energy and unused powers, questioned
these men and women going by, coldly, bitterly. . . . Was it not
his right to live as they,—a pure life, a good, true-hearted life, full
of beauty and kind words? He only wanted to know how to use
the strength within him. His heart warmed, as he thought of it.
He suffered himself to think of it longer. If he took the money?

Then he saw himself as he might be, strong, helpful, kindly. The
night crept on, as this one image slowly evolved itself from the
crowd of other thoughts and stood triumphant. He looked at it.
As he might be! What wonder, if it blinded him to delirium,—the
madness that underlies all revolution, all progress, and all fall?

You laugh at the shallow temptation? You see the error under-
lying its argument so clearly,—that to him a true life was one of
full development rather than self-restraint? that he was deaf to the
higher tone in a cry of voluntary suffering for truth's sake than in
the fullest flow of spontaneous harmony? I do not plead his cause.
I only want to show you the mote in my brother's eye: then you
can see clearly to take it out. . . .

. . . Do you want to hear the end of it? You wish me to make
a tragic story out of it? Why, in the police-reports of the morning
paper you can find a dozen such tragedies: hints of shipwrecks
unlike any that ever befell on the high seas; hints that here a power
was lost to heaven,—that there a soul went down where no tide
can ebb or flow. Commonplace enough the hints are. . . .

Doctor May, a month after the night I have told you of, was
reading to his wife at breakfast from this fourth column of the
morning-paper: an unusual thing,—these police-reports not being,
in general, choice reading for ladies; but it was only one item he
read.

"Oh, my dear! You remember that man I told you of, that we
saw at Kirby's mill?—that was arrested for robbing Mitchell?
Here he is; just listen:—'Circuit Court. Judge Day. Hugh Wolfe,
operative in Kirby & John's Loudon Mills. Charge, grand larceny.
Sentence, nineteen years hard labor in penitentiary.'—Scoundrel!
Serves him right! After all our kindness that night! Picking Mitchell's pocket at the very time!"

His wife said something about the ingratitude of that kind of people, and then they began to talk of something else.

Nineteen years! How easy that was to read! What a simple word for Judge Day to utter! Nineteen years! Half a lifetime!*

Hugh Wolfe sat on the window-ledge of his cell, looking out. His ankles were ironed. Not usual in such cases; but he had made two desperate efforts to escape. "Well," as Haley, the jailer, said, "small blame to him! Nineteen years' imprisonment was not a pleasant thing to look forward to." Haley was very good-natured about it, though Wolfe had fought him savagely.

"When he was first caught," the jailer said afterwards, in telling the story, "before the trial, the fellow was cut down at once,—laid there on that pallet like a dead man, with his hands over his eyes. Never saw a man so cut down in my life. Time of the trial, too, came the queerest dodge of any customer I ever had. Would choose no lawyer. Judge gave him one, of course. Gibson it was. He tried to prove the fellow crazy; but it wouldn't go. Thing was plain as day-light: money found on him. 'Twas a hard sentence, —all the law allows; but it was for 'xample's sake. These mill-hands are gettin' onbearable. When the sentence was read, he just looked up, and said the money was his by rights, and that all the world had gone wrong. That night, after the trial, a gentleman came to see him here, name of Mitchell,—him as he stole from. Talked to him for an hour. Thought he came for curiosity, like. After he was gone, thought Wolfe was remarkable quiet, and went into his cell. Found him very low; bed all bloody. Doctor said he had been bleeding at the lungs. He was as weak as a cat; yet, if ye'll b'lieve me, he tried to get a-past me and get out. I just carried him like a baby, and threw him on the pallet. Three days after, he tried it again: that time reached the wall. Lord help you! he fought like a tiger,—giv' some terrible blows. Fightin' for life, you see; for he can't live long, shut up in the stone crib down yonder. Got a death-cough now. 'T took two of us to bring him down that day; so I just put the irons on his feet. There he sits, in there. Goin'

---

*Nineteen years was literally half a lifetime. Life expectancy for a white male in the 1850s was thirty-seven years. Hugh Wolfe is nineteen years old, for all his "lifetime" in the mills, the "slow heavy years of constant hot work." As was common at the time, he had probably been in the mills since he was nine or ten.

to-morrow, with a batch more of 'em. That woman, hunchback, tried with him,—you remember?—she's only got three years. 'Complice. But *she's* a woman, you know. He's been quiet ever since I put on irons: giv' up, I suppose. Looks white, sick-lookin'. It acts different on 'em, bein' sentenced. Most of 'em gets reckless, devilish-like. Some prays awful, and sings them vile songs of the mills, all in a breath. That woman, now, she's desper't'. Been beggin' to see Hugh, as she calls him, for three days. I'm a-goin' to let her in. She don't go with him. Here she is in this next cell. I'm a-goin' now to let her in.". . .

It was market day. The narrow windows of the jail looked down directly on the carts and wagons drawn up in a long line, where they had unloaded. He could see, too, and hear distinctly the clink of money as it changed hands, the busy crowd of whites and blacks shoving, pushing one another, and the chaffering and swearing at the stalls. Somehow, the sound, more than anything else had done, wakened him up,—made the whole real to him. He was done with the world and the business of it. He let the tin fall, and looked out, pressing his face close to the rusty bars. How they crowded and pushed! And he,—he should never walk that pavement again! There came Neff Sanders, one of the feeders at the mill, with a basket on his arm. Sure enough, Neff was married the other week. He whistled, hoping he would look up; but he did not. He wondered if Neff remembered he was there,—if any of the boys thought of him up there, and thought that he never was to go down that old cinder-road again. Never again! He had not quite understood it before; but now he did. Not for days or years, but never!—that was it.

How clear the light fell on that stall in front of the market! and how like a picture it was, the dark-green heaps of corn, and the crimson beets, and golden melons! There was another with game: how the light flickered on that pheasant's breast, with the purplish blood dripping over the brown feathers! He could see the red shining of the drops, it was so near. In one minute he could be down there. It was just a step. So easy, as it seemed, so natural to go! Yet it could never be—not in all the thousands of years to come—that he should put his foot on that street again! He thought of himself with a sorrowful pity, as of some one else. There was a dog down in the market, walking after his master with such a stately, grave look!—only a dog, yet he could go backwards and forwards just as he pleased: he had good luck! Why, the very vilest cur, yelping there in the gutter, had not lived his life, had been free to act out whatever thought God had put into his brain; while he —No, he would not think of that! He tried to put the thought away, and to listen to a dispute between a countryman and a woman about some meat; but it would come back. He, what had he done to bear this?

Then came the sudden picture of what might have been, and now. He knew what it was to be in the penitentiary,—how it went with men there. He knew how in these long years he should slowly die, but not until soul and body had become corrupt and rotten, —how, when he came out, if he lived to come, even the lowest of the mill-hands would jeer him,—how his hands would be weak, and his brain senseless and stupid. He believed he was almost that now. He put his hand to his head, with a puzzled, weary look. It ached, his head, with thinking. He tried to quiet himself. It was only right, perhaps; he had done wrong. But was there right or wrong for such as he? What was right? And who had ever taught him? He thrust the whole matter away. A dark, cold quiet crept through his brain. It was all wrong; but let it be! It was nothing to him more than the others. Let it be! . . .

"It is best, Deb. I cannot bear to be hurted any more."

"Hur knows," she said, humbly.

"Tell my father good-bye; and—and kiss little Janey."

She nodded, saying nothing, looked in his face again, and went out of the door. As she went, she staggered.

"Drinkin' to-day?" broke out Haley, pushing her before him. "Where the Devil did you get it? Here, in with ye!" and he shoved her into her cell, next to Wolfe's, and shut the door.

Along the wall of her cell there was a crack low down by the floor, through which she could see the light from Wolfe's. She had discovered it days before. She hurried in now, and, kneeling down by it, listened, hoping to hear some sound. Nothing but the rasping of the tin on the bars. He was at his old amusement again. Something in the noise jarred on her ear, for she shivered as she heard it. Hugh rasped away at the bars. A dull old bit of tin, not fit to cut korl with.

He looked out of the window again. People were leaving the market now. A tall mulatto girl, following her mistress, her basket on her head, crossed the street just below, and looked up. She was laughing; but, when she caught sight of the haggard face peering out through the bars, suddenly grew grave, and hurried by. A free, firm step, a clear-cut olive face, with a scarlet turban tied on one side, dark, shining eyes, and on the head the basket poised, filled with fruit and flowers, under which the scarlet turban and bright eyes looked out half-shadowed. The picture caught his eye. It was good to see a face like that. He would try to-morrow, and cut one like it. *To-morrow!* He threw down the tin, trembling, and covered his face with his hands. When he looked up again, the daylight was gone.

Deborah, crouching near by on the other side of the wall, heard no noise. He sat on the side of the low pallet, thinking. Whatever was the mystery which the woman had seen on his face, it came out now slowly, in the dark there, and became fixed,—a something never seen on his face before. The evening was darkening fast. The market had been over for an hour; the rumbling of the carts over the pavement grew more infrequent: he listened to each, as it passed, because he thought it was to be for the last time. For the same reason, it was, I suppose, that he strained his eyes to catch a glimpse of each passer-by, wondering who they were, what kind of homes they were going to, if they had children,—listening eagerly to every chance word in the street, as if—. . .—as if he never should hear human voices again.

It was quite dark at last. The street was a lonely one. The last passenger, he thought, was gone. No,—there was a quick step: Joe Hill, lighting the lamps. Joe was a good old chap; never passed a fellow without some joke or other. He remembered once seeing the place where he lived with his wife. "Granny Hill" the boys called her. Bedridden she was; but so kind as Joe was to her! kept the room so clean!—and the old woman, when he was there, was laughing at "some of t' lad's foolishness." The step was far down the street; but he could see him place the ladder, run up, and light the gas. A longing seized him to be spoken to once more.

"Joe!" he called, out of the grating. "Good-bye, Joe!"

The old man stopped a moment, listening uncertainly; then hurried on. The prisoner thrust his hand out of the window, and

called again, louder; but Joe was too far down the street. It was
a little thing; but it hurt him,—this disappointment.

"Good-bye, Joe!" he called, sorrowfully enough.

"Be quiet!" said one of the jailers, passing the door, striking on
it with his club.

Oh, that was the last, was it?

There was an inexpressible bitterness on his face, as he lay down
on the bed, taking the bit of tin, which he had rasped to a tolerable
degree of sharpness, in his hand. . . .

. . . I think in that one hour that came then he lived back over
all the years that had gone before. I think that all the low, vile life,
all his wrongs, all his starved hopes, came then, and stung him
with a farewell poison that made him sick unto death. . . .

The hour was over at last. The moon, passing over her nightly
path, slowly came nearer, and threw the light across his bed on
his feet. He watched it steadily, as it crept up, inch by inch, slowly.
It seemed to him to carry with it a great silence. He had been so
hot and tired there always in the mills! The years had been so fierce
and cruel! There was coming now quiet and coolness and sleep.
His tense limbs relaxed, and settled in a calm languor. The blood
ran fainter and slow from his heart. He did not think now with
a savage anger of what might be and was not; he was conscious
only of deep stillness creeping over him. At first he saw a sea of
faces: the mill-men,—women he had known, drunken and
bloated,—Janeys timid and pitiful,—poor old Debs: then they
floated together like a mist, and faded away, leaving only the clear,
pearly moonlight. . . .

Nothing remains to tell that the poor Welsh puddler once lived,
but this figure of the mill-woman cut in korl. I have it here in a
corner of my library. I keep it hid behind a curtain,—it is such a
rough, ungainly thing. Yet there are about it touches, grand
sweeps of outline, that show a master's hand. Sometimes,—to-
night, for instance,—the curtain is accidentally drawn back, and
I see a bare arm stretched out imploringly in the darkness, and an
eager, wolfish face watching mine: a wan, woful face, through
which the spirit of the dead korl-cutter looks out, with its
thwarted life, its mighty hunger, its unfinished work. Its pale,
vague lips seem to tremble with a terrible question. "Is this the

End?" they say,—"nothing beyond?—no more?" Why, you tell me you have seen that look in the eyes of dumb brutes,—horses dying under the lash. I know.

The deep of the night is passing while I write. The gas-light wakens from the shadows here and there the objects which lie scattered through the room: only faintly, though; for they belong to the open sunlight. As I glance at them, they each recall some task or pleasure of the coming day. A half-moulded child's head; Aphrodite; a bough of forest-leaves; music; work; homely fragments, in which lie the secrets of all eternal truth and beauty. Prophetic all! Only this dumb, woful face seems to belong to and end with the night. I turn to look at it. Has the power of its desperate need commanded the darkness away? While the room is yet steeped in heavy shadow, a cool, gray light suddenly touches its head like a blessing hand, and its groping arm points through the broken cloud to the far East, where, in the flickering, nebulous crimson, God has set the promise of the Dawn.

SUBJECT INDEX

NAME INDEX

Aaron, Daniel, 98*n*
Abernathy, Ralph, 39*n*
Alcott, Bronson, 78–79
Alcott, Louisa May, 16, 30*n*, 77
Alta, 32*n*, 209
Altick, Richard, 24*n*
Alvarez, A., 241
Anderson, Margaret, 219
Anderson, Sherwood, 10, 153, 165
Anthony, Susan B., 108
Appleton, Sarah, 195*n*
Arata, 146
Arnold, June, 32*n*
Arnold, Matthew, 27*n*
Arnow, Harriette, 32*n*, 35*n*, 36*n*, 40, 42, 44, 249*n*
Artaud, Antonin, 149
Ashton-Warner, Sylvia, 32*n*, 42
Atwood, Margaret, 230–231, 250
Auden, W. H., 238–239
Austen, Jane, 8, 16, 23, 30*n*, 140, 227; *Persuasion,* 181–182, 235
Austin, Mary, 40, 227
Aveling, Edward, 112

Babel, Isaac, 9, 165
Baker, Ida, 215
Balzac, Honoré de, 12, 18, 33*n*, 143, 154
Barnes, Djuna, 31
Barriault, Gina, 32*n*

Baudelaire, Charles Pierre, 149; *My Heart Laid Bare,* 150
Baum, Charlotte, 183
Beach, Sylvia, 219
Beecher, Henry Ward, 81
Behn, Aphra, 23, 42
Bell, Currer. *See* Brontë, Charlotte
Bellow, Saul, 147
Berryman, John, 31*n*, 149
Betts, Doris, 32*n*
Bingham, Sallie, 32*n*, 210
Biology, 25–26, 42–43
Birstein, Ann, 219
Blake, William, 8, 29*n*, 38, 139, 168–169, 177, 181*n*
Bogan, Louise, 145, 153, 221, 227
Bone, Robert, 9*n*, 146
Booth, Edwin, 108
Borges, Jorge Luis, 219*n*, 220
Borghese, Elizabeth Mann, 31
Borowski, Tadeusz, 155
Bowen, Elizabeth, 16, 31, 40, 227
Bowles, Jane, 219
Bowles, Paul, 219*n*
Boyle, Kay, 16, 32*n*, 40, 227
Bridges, Robert, 128–133
Brontë, Charlotte, 16, 30*n*, 41, 56*n*, 227, 228; appearance, 233–234; *Jane Eyre,* 60–61, 234
Brontë, Emily, 16, 30*n*, 227, 247
Brooks, Van Wyck, 80
Brown, Rosellen, 32*n*, 232
Browne, Sir Thomas, 231

The following authors and titles referred to by Tillie Olsen in this book are published by Virago:

For more information write to Virago Press, 5 Wardour Street, London W1V 3HE

SYLVIA ASHTON-WARNER
I Passed This Way

Spinster
New Introduction by Fleur Adcock

Teacher
New Introduction by Dora Russell

MARGARET ATWOOD
Life Before Man

Surfacing
New Introduction by Francine du Plessix Gray

The Edible Woman
New Introduction by the author

JANE BOWLES
Two Serious Ladies
New Introduction by Francine du Plessix Gray

KAY BOYLE
Plagued by the Nightingale
New Introduction by the author

WILLA CATHER
A Lost Lady
New Introduction by A. S. Byatt

My Antonia
New Introduction by A. S. Byatt

MARY ELLMANN
Thinking About Women

HENRY HANDEL RICHARDSON
The Getting of Wisdom
New Introduction by Germaine Greer

ELIZABETH HARDWICK
Sleepless Nights

JANE LAZARRE
On Loving Men

YVONNE KAPP
Eleanor Marx
Volume I: *Family Life 1855–83*
Volume II: *The Crowded Years 1884–98*

KATE MILLETT
Sexual Politics

GRACE PALEY
Enormous Changes at the Last Minute
New Introduction by A. S. Byatt

The Little Disturbances of Man
New Introduction by A. S. Byatt

ADRIENNE RICH
Of Woman Born: *Motherhood as Experience and Institution*

On Lies, Secrets and Silence: *Selected Prose 1966–78*

Virago

If you would like to know more about Virago books, write to us at 5 Wardour Street, London W1V 3HE for a full catalogue.

Please send a stamped addressed envelope

Give them
the pleasure of choosing
Book Tokens can be bought
and exchanged at most
bookshops

Please renew or return items by the date
shown on your receipt

www.hertfordshire.gov.uk/libraries

Renewals and enquiries: **0300 123 4049**
Textphone for hearing or   **01992 555506**
speech impaired users:

L32b/12.19

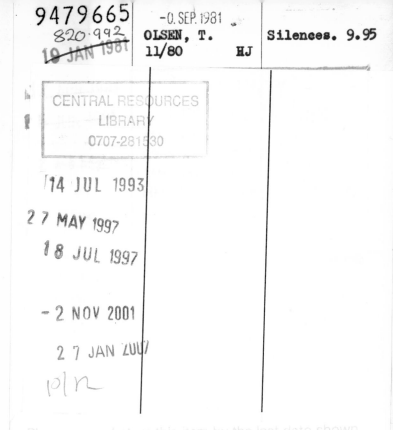

Hertfordshire